SEVEN SEAS ENTERTAINMENT PRESENTS

PENGUINDRUM

by ISUZU SHIBATA LILY HOSHINO VOL. 2

TRANSLATION
Beni Axia Conrad

ADAPTATION
Lora Gray

LETTERING
Jennifer Skarupa

COVER DESIGN
KC Fabellon

PROOFREADER
Danielle King

EDITOR
Jenn Grunigen

PREPRESS TECHNICIAN
iannon Rasmussen-Silverstein

PRODUCTION MANAGER
Lissa Pattillo

MANAGING EDITOR
Julie Davis

ASSOCIATE PUBLISHER
Adam Arnold

PUBLISHER
Jason DeAngelis

Original Japanese edition published in 2014 by GENTOSHA COMICS Inc.
English translation rights arranged worldwide with GENTOSHA COMICS Inc.
through Digital Catapult Inc., Tokyo.

Seven Seas press and purchase enquiries can be sent to Marketing Manager Lianne Sentar at press@gomanga.com. Information regarding the distribution and purchase of digital editions is available from Digital Manager CK Russell at digital@gomanga.com.

ISBN: 978-1-64505-222-7

Printed in Canada

First Printing: March 2020

10 9 8 7 6 5 4 3 2 1

LOW US ONLINE: *www.sevenseasentertainment.com*

READING DIRECTIONS

s book
his is
ding f
e it fr
nbere
t, but you'll get the hang of it! Have fun!!

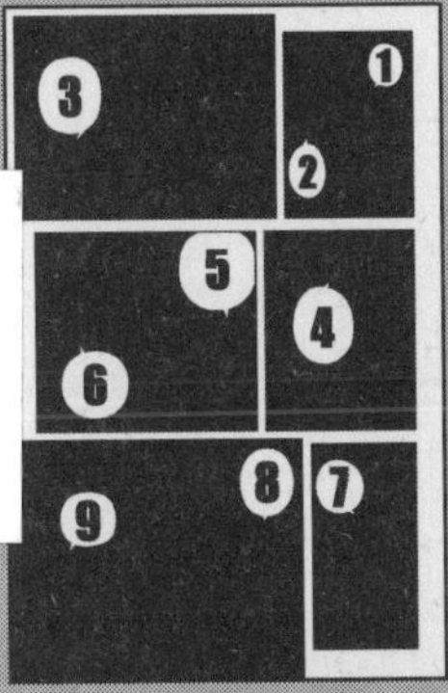
1
2
3
4
5
6
7
8
9

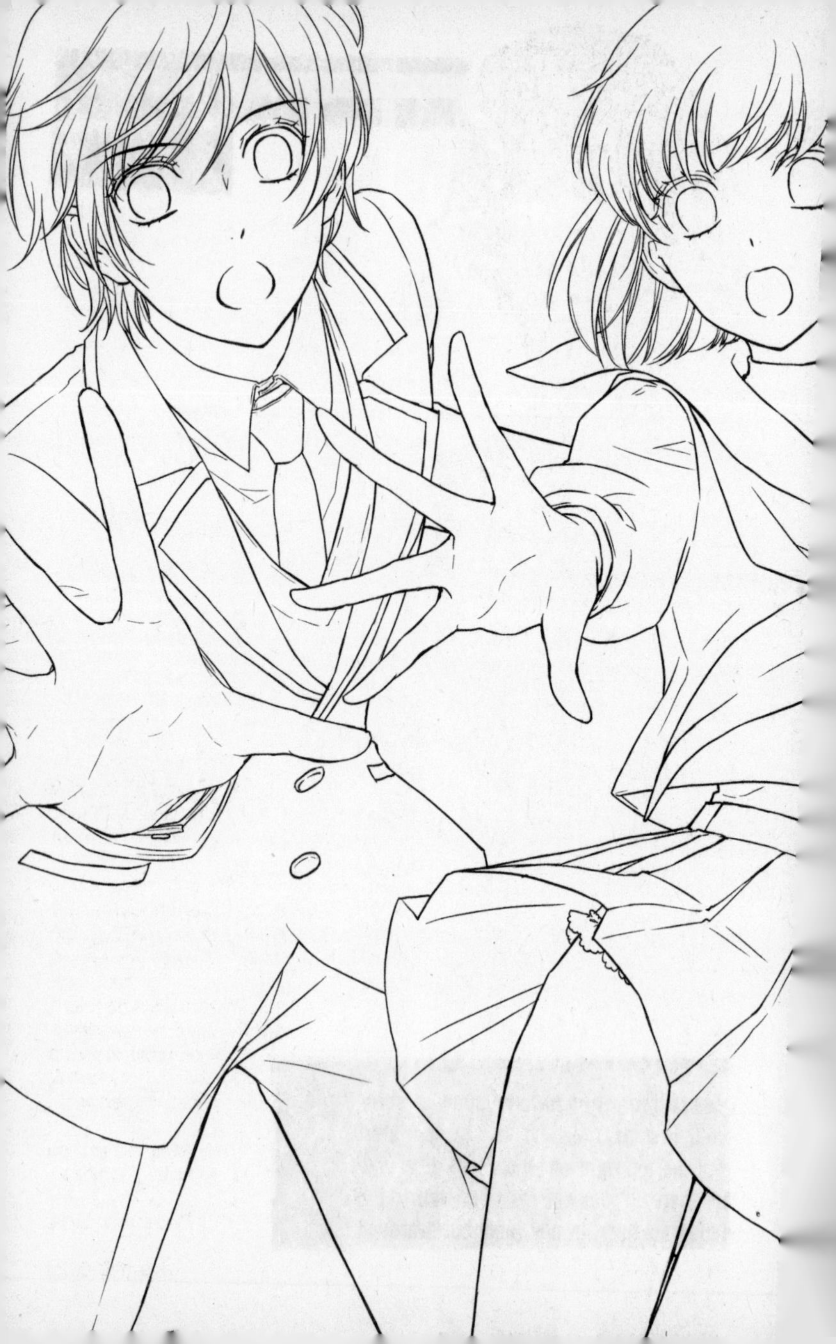

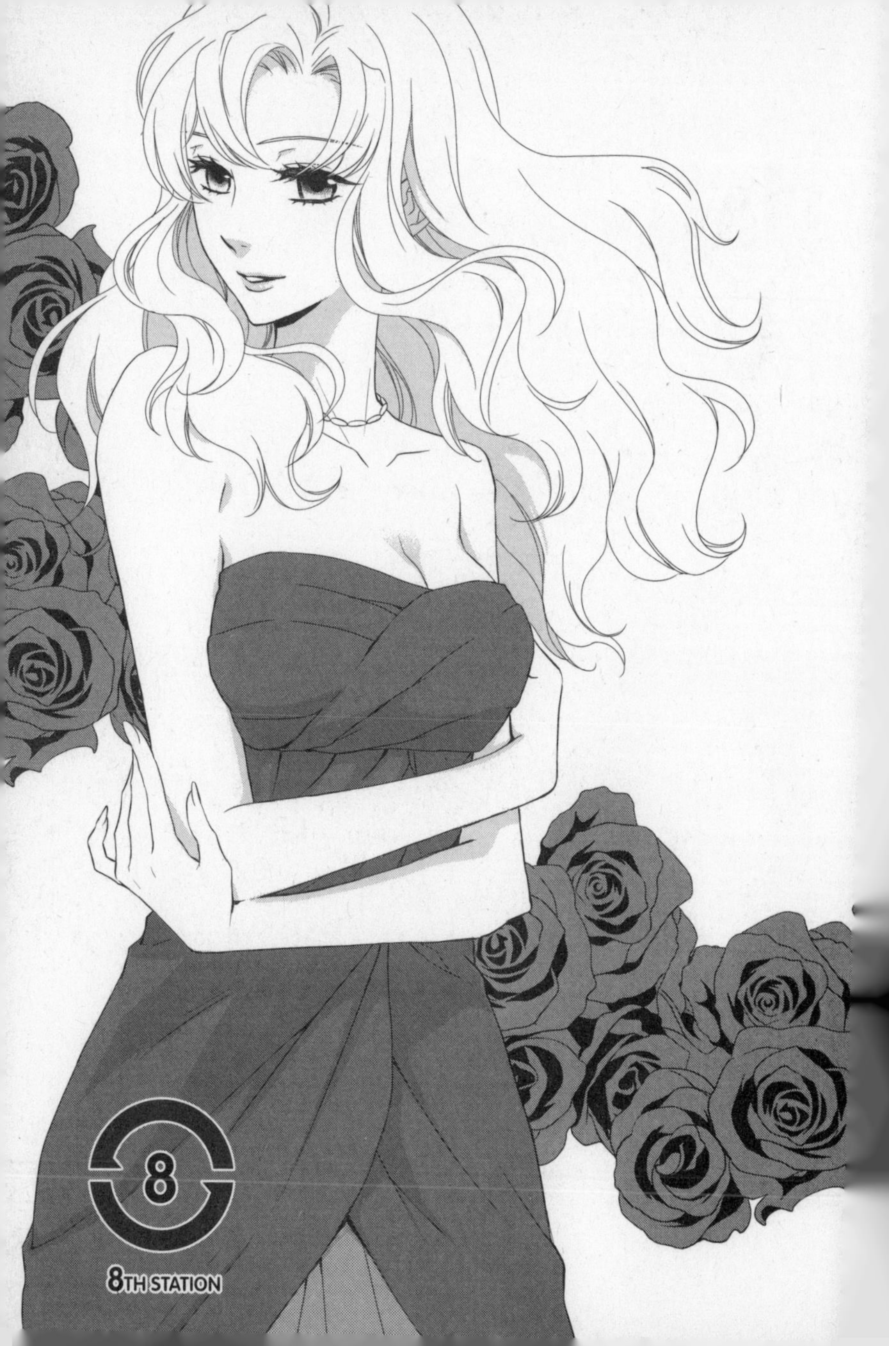
8
8TH STATION

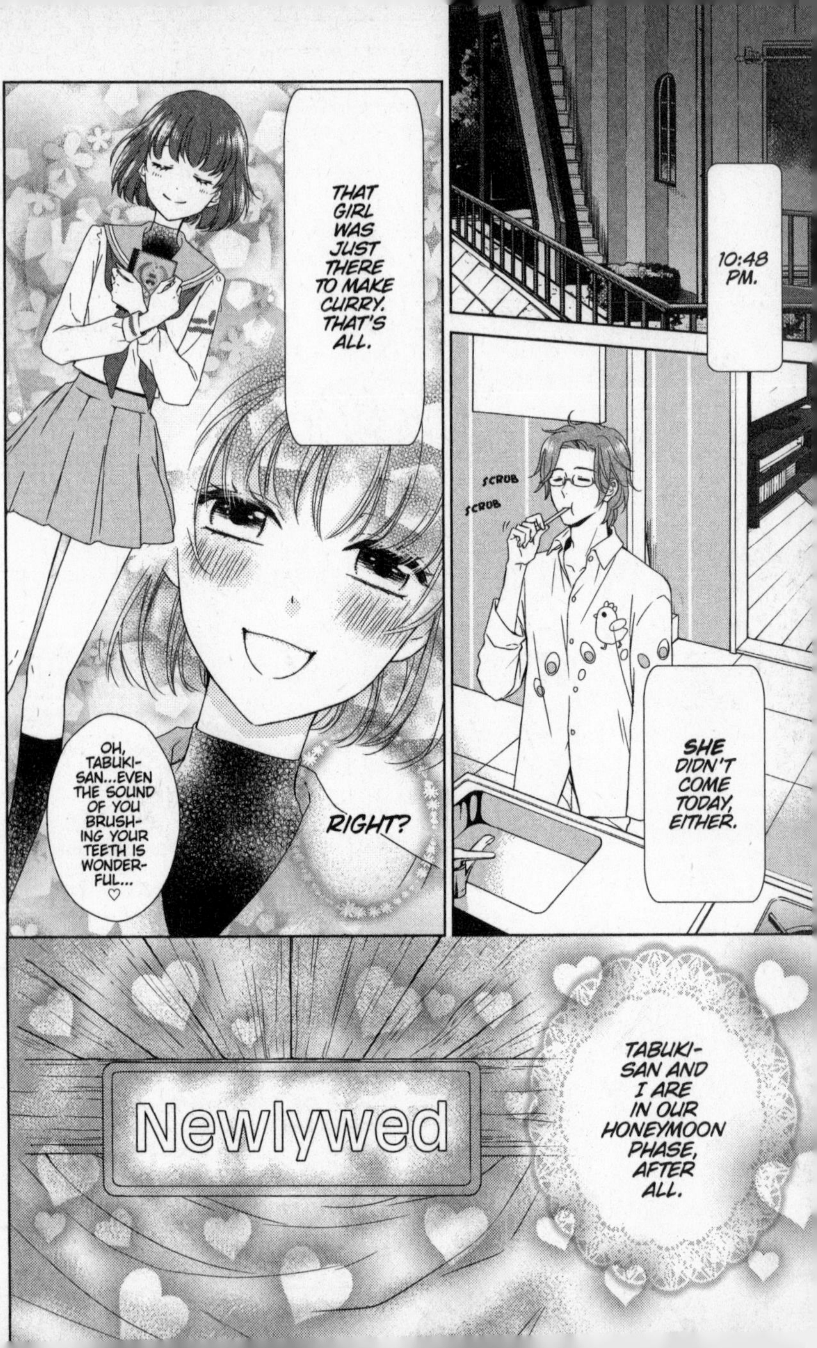
10:48 PM.
SCRUB
SCRUB
SHE DIDN'T COME TODAY, EITHER.
THAT GIRL WAS JUST THERE TO MAKE CURRY. THAT'S ALL.
RIGHT?
OH, TABUKI-SAN...EVEN THE SOUND OF YOU BRUSHING YOUR TEETH IS WONDERFUL... ♡
TABUKI-SAN AND I ARE IN OUR HONEYMOON PHASE, AFTER ALL.
Newlywed

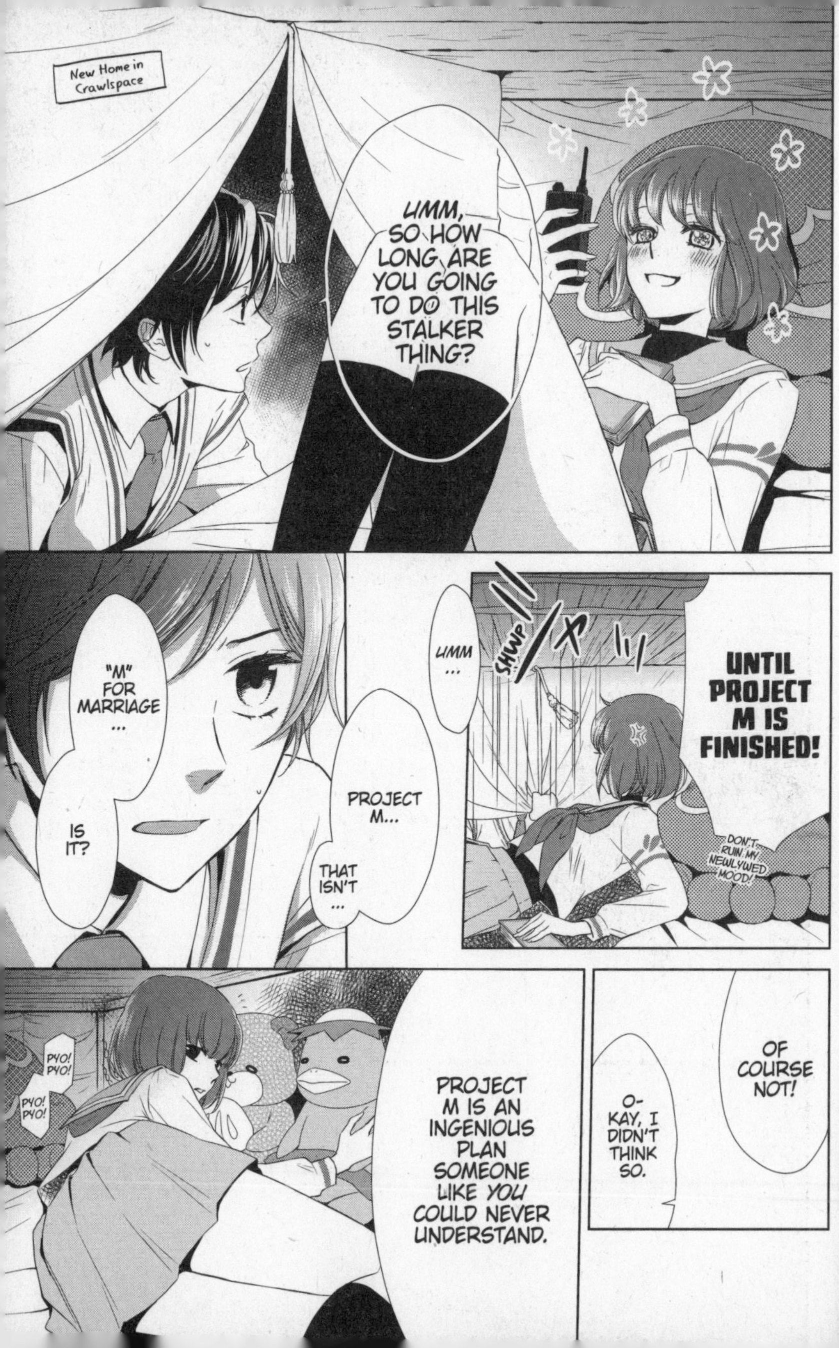
New Home in Crawlspace
UMM, SO HOW LONG ARE YOU GOING TO DO THIS STALKER THING?
SHWP
UNTIL PROJECT M IS FINISHED!
DON'T RUIN MY NEWLYWED MOOD!
UMM ...
PROJECT M...
THAT ISN'T ...
"M" FOR MARRIAGE ...
IS IT?
OF COURSE NOT!
O-KAY, I DIDN'T THINK SO.
PROJECT M IS AN INGENIOUS PLAN SOMEONE LIKE *YOU* COULD NEVER UNDERSTAND.
PYO! PYO!
PYO! PYO!

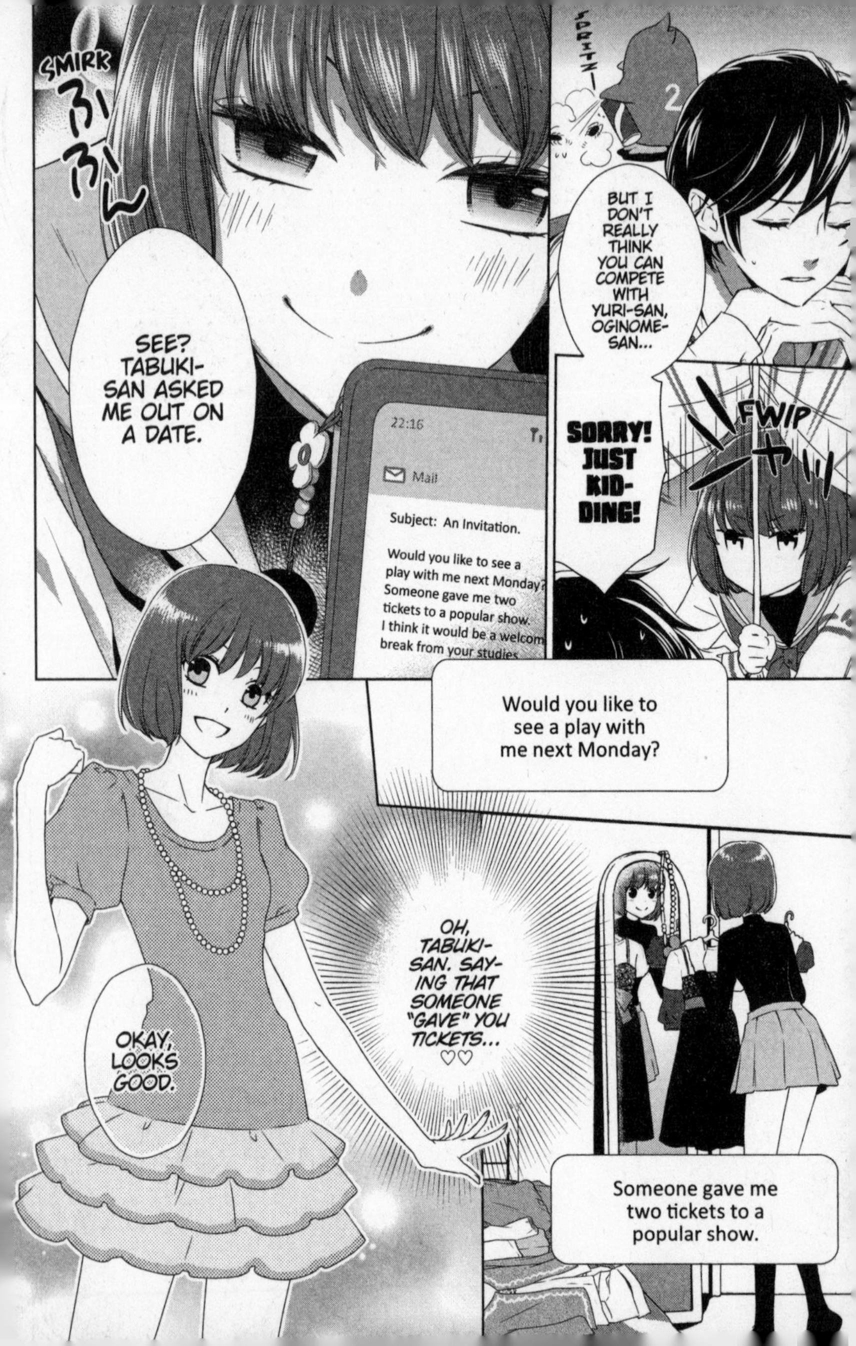
SPRITZ
BUT I DON'T REALLY THINK YOU CAN COMPETE WITH YURI-SAN, OGINOME-SAN...
SORRY! JUST KIDDING!
FWIP
SMIRK
ふふん
SEE? TABUKI-SAN ASKED ME OUT ON A DATE.
22:16
Mail
Subject: An Invitation.
Would you like to see a play with me next Monday? Someone gave me two tickets to a popular show. I think it would be a welcom
break from your studies
Would you like to see a play with me next Monday?
Someone gave me two tickets to a popular show.
OH, TABUKI-SAN. SAYING THAT SOMEONE "GAVE" YOU TICKETS... ♡♡
OKAY, LOOKS GOOD.

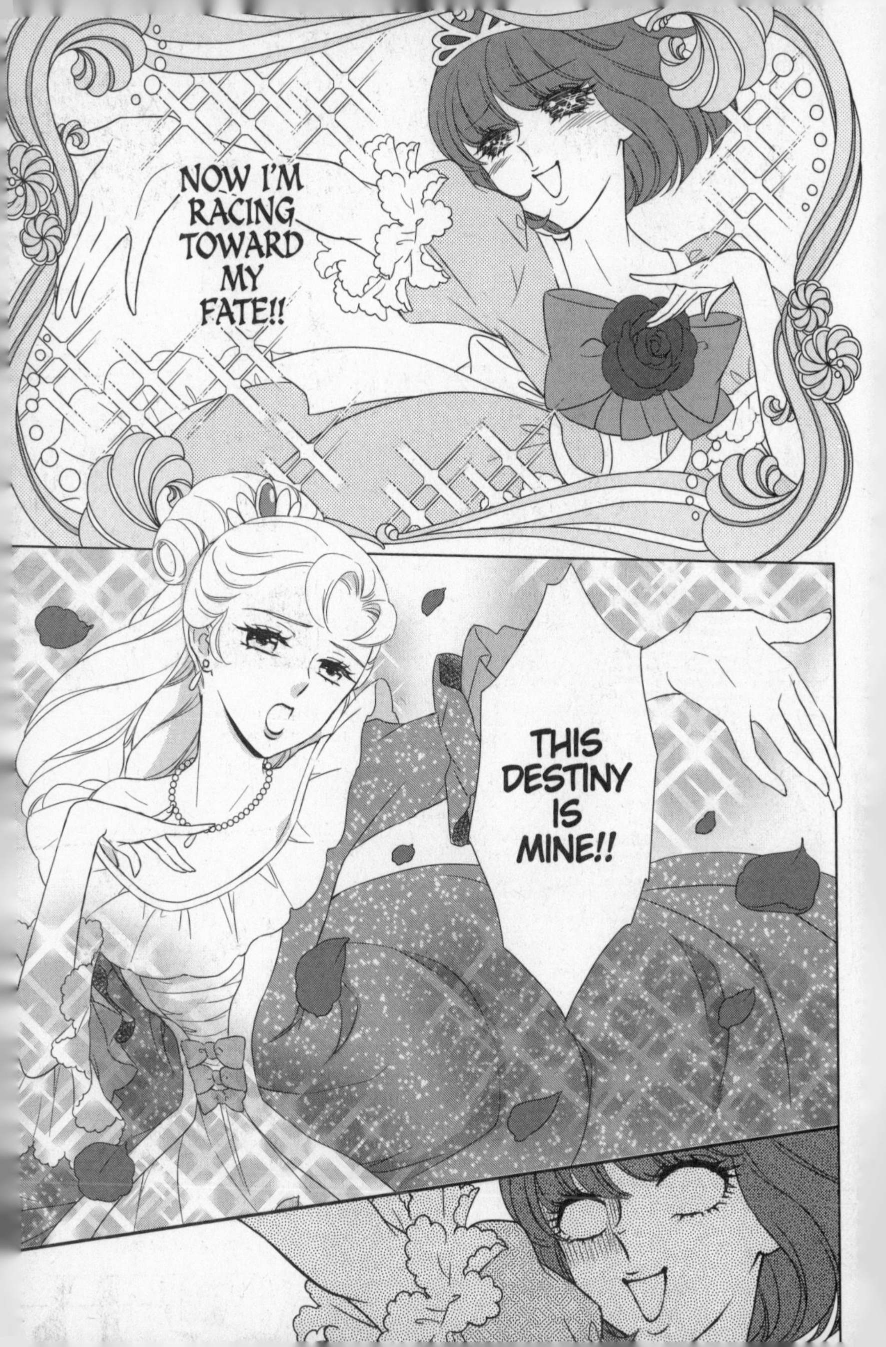
NOW I'M RACING TOWARD MY FATE!!
THIS DESTINY IS MINE!!

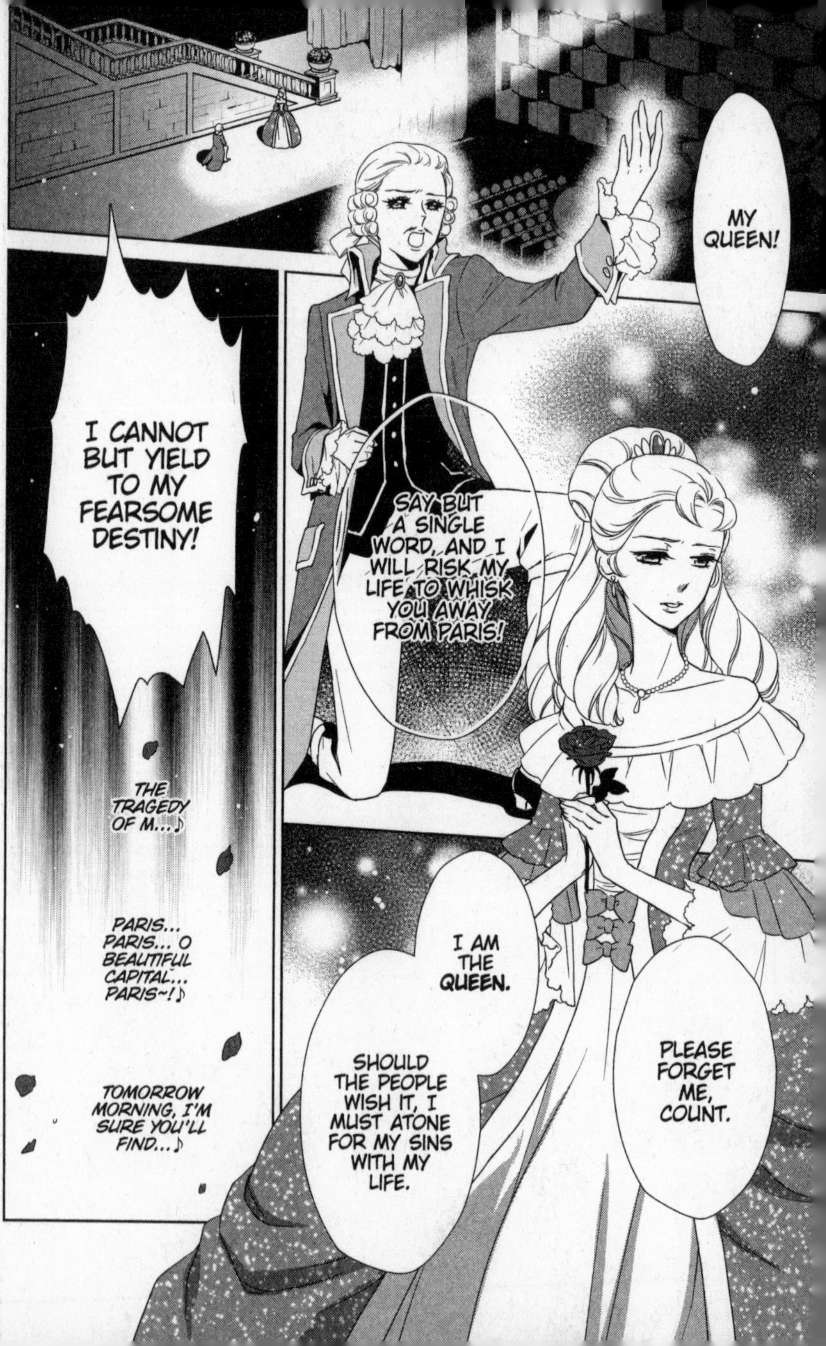
MY QUEEN!
SAY BUT A SINGLE WORD, AND I WILL RISK MY LIFE TO WHISK YOU AWAY FROM PARIS!
I AM THE QUEEN.
SHOULD THE PEOPLE WISH IT, I MUST ATONE FOR MY SINS WITH MY LIFE.
PLEASE FORGET ME, COUNT.
I CANNOT BUT YIELD TO MY FEARSOME DESTINY!
THE TRAGEDY OF M...♪
PARIS... PARIS... O BEAUTIFUL CAPITAL... PARIS~!♪
TOMORROW MORNING, I'M SURE YOU'LL FIND...♪

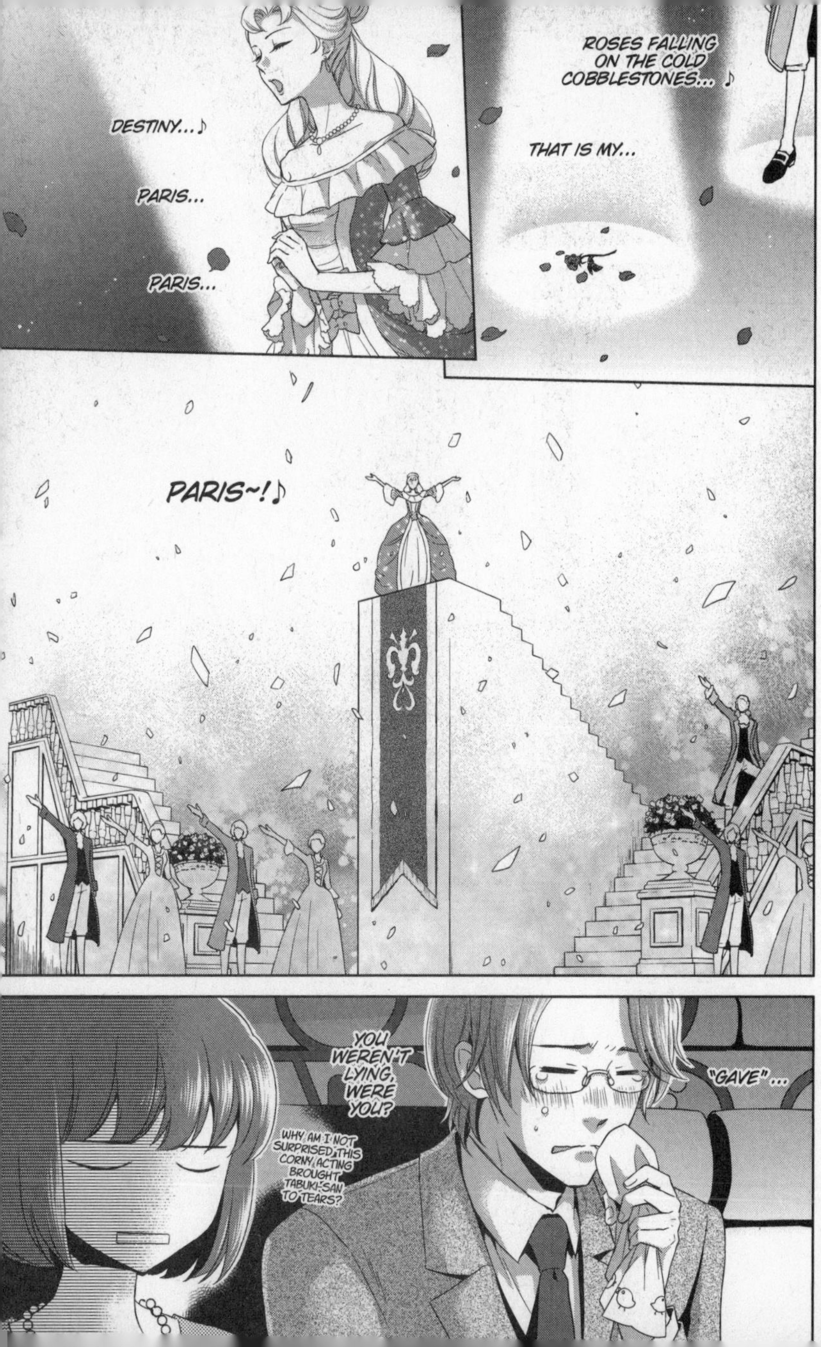
ROSES FALLING ON THE COLD COBBLESTONES... ♪
THAT IS MY...
DESTINY... ♪
PARIS...
PARIS...
PARIS~! ♪
"GAVE"...
YOU WEREN'T LYING, WERE YOU?
WHY AM I NOT SURPRISED THIS CORNY ACTING BROUGHT TABUKI-SAN TO TEARS?

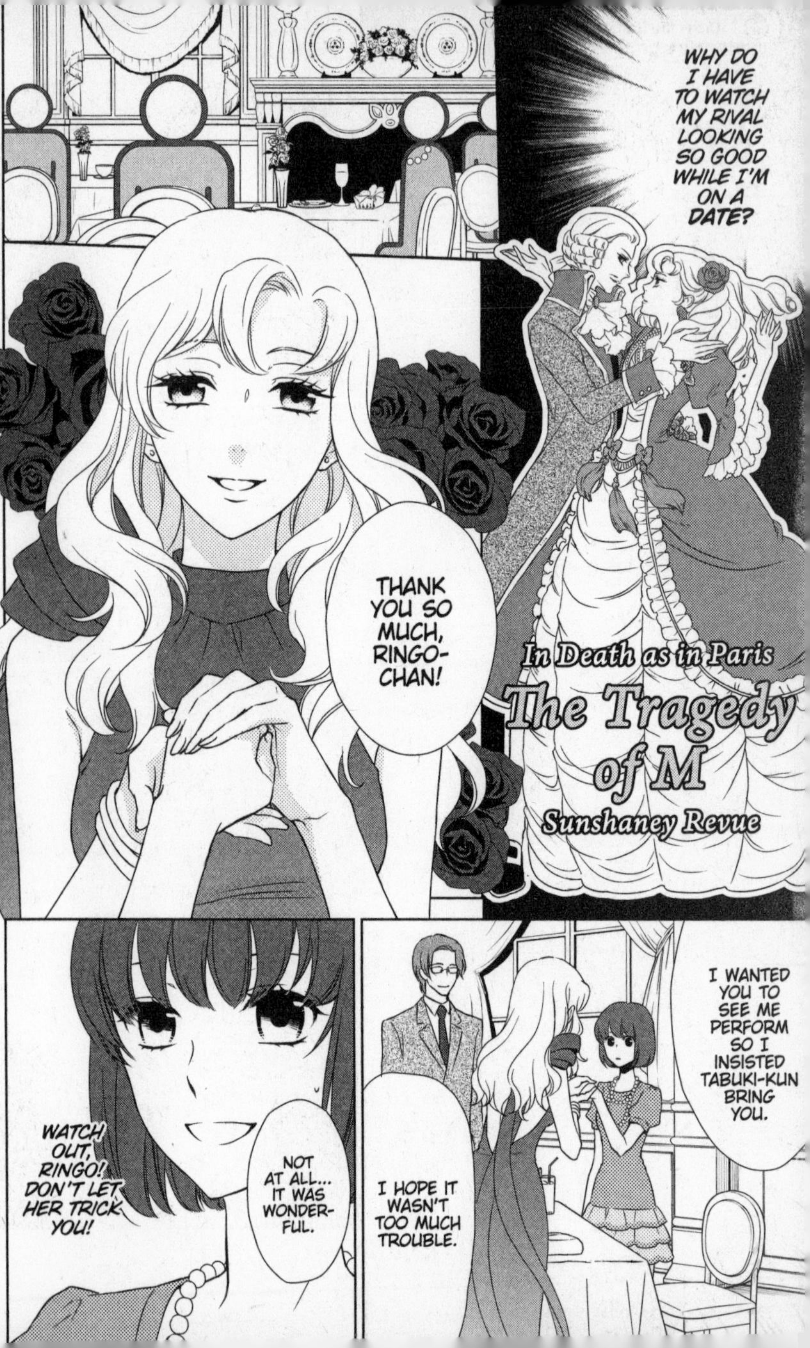
WHY DO I HAVE TO WATCH MY RIVAL LOOKING SO GOOD WHILE I'M ON A DATE?
In Death as in Paris
The Tragedy of M
Sunshaney Revue
THANK YOU SO MUCH, RINGO-CHAN!
I WANTED YOU TO SEE ME PERFORM SO I INSISTED TABUKI-KUN BRING YOU.
I HOPE IT WASN'T TOO MUCH TROUBLE.
NOT AT ALL... IT WAS WONDERFUL.
WATCH OUT, RINGO! DON'T LET HER TRICK YOU!

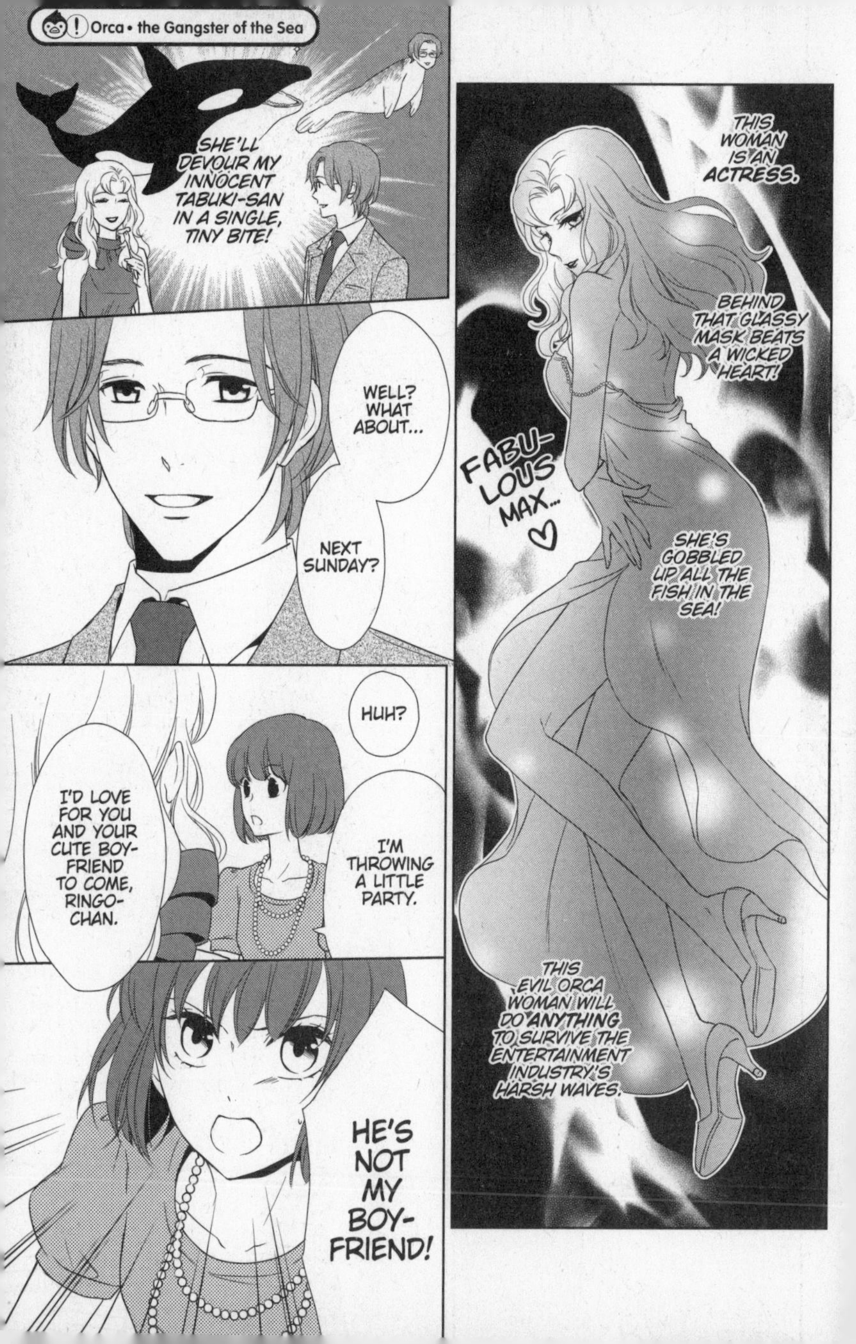
THIS WOMAN IS AN ACTRESS.
BEHIND THAT GLASSY MASK BEATS A WICKED HEART!
SHE'S GOBBLED UP ALL THE FISH IN THE SEA!
FABU-LOUS MAX... ♡
THIS EVIL ORCA WOMAN WILL DO ANYTHING TO SURVIVE THE ENTERTAINMENT INDUSTRY'S HARSH WAVES.
Orca • the Gangster of the Sea
SHE'LL DEVOUR MY INNOCENT TABUKI-SAN IN A SINGLE, TINY BITE!
WELL? WHAT ABOUT...
NEXT SUNDAY?
HUH?
I'M THROWING A LITTLE PARTY.
I'D LOVE FOR YOU AND YOUR CUTE BOY-FRIEND TO COME, RINGO-CHAN.
HE'S NOT MY BOY-FRIEND!

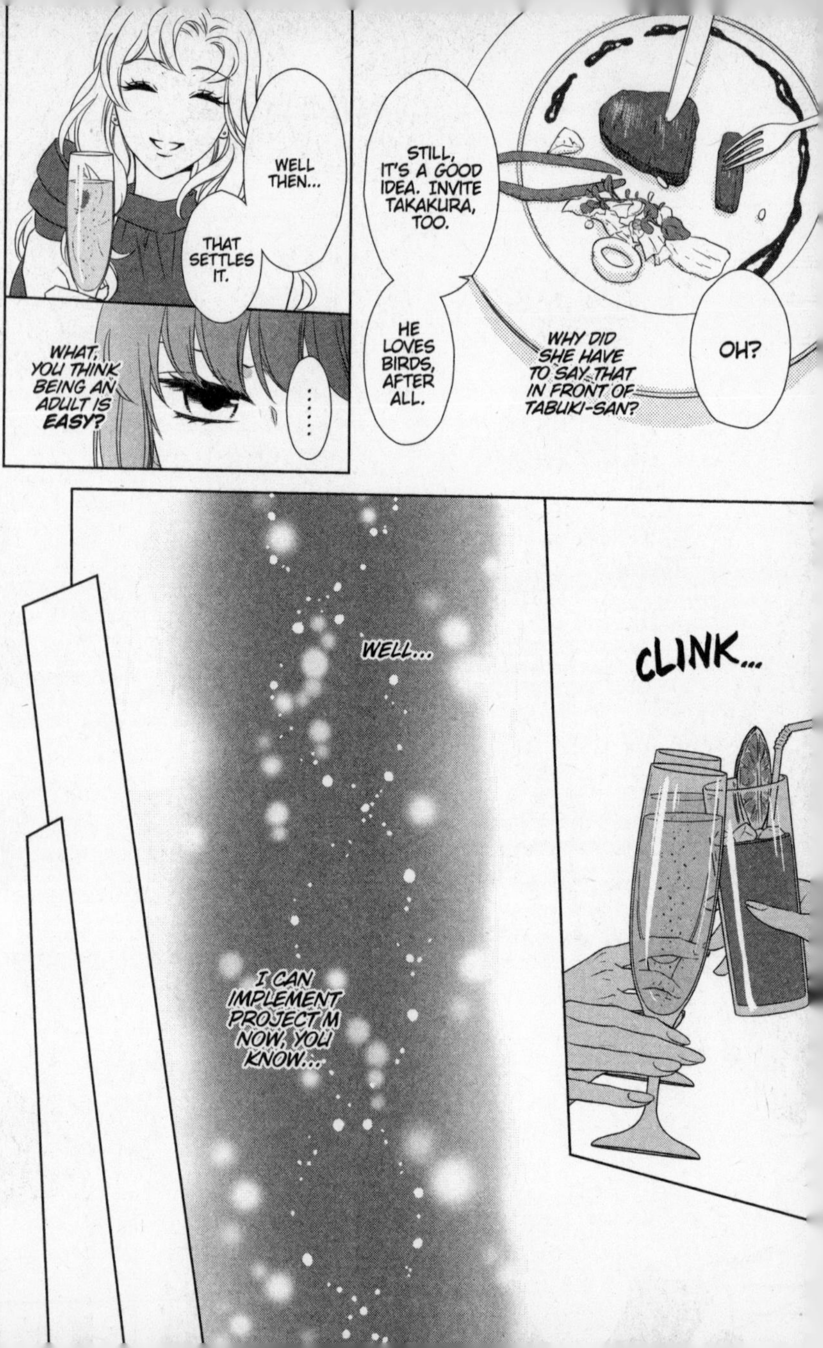
STILL, IT'S A GOOD IDEA. INVITE TAKAKURA, TOO.
HE LOVES BIRDS, AFTER ALL.
OH?
WHY DID SHE HAVE TO SAY THAT IN FRONT OF TABUKI-SAN?
WELL THEN...
THAT SETTLES IT.
......
WHAT, YOU THINK BEING AN ADULT IS EASY?
CLINK...
WELL...
I CAN IMPLEMENT PROJECT M NOW, YOU KNOW...

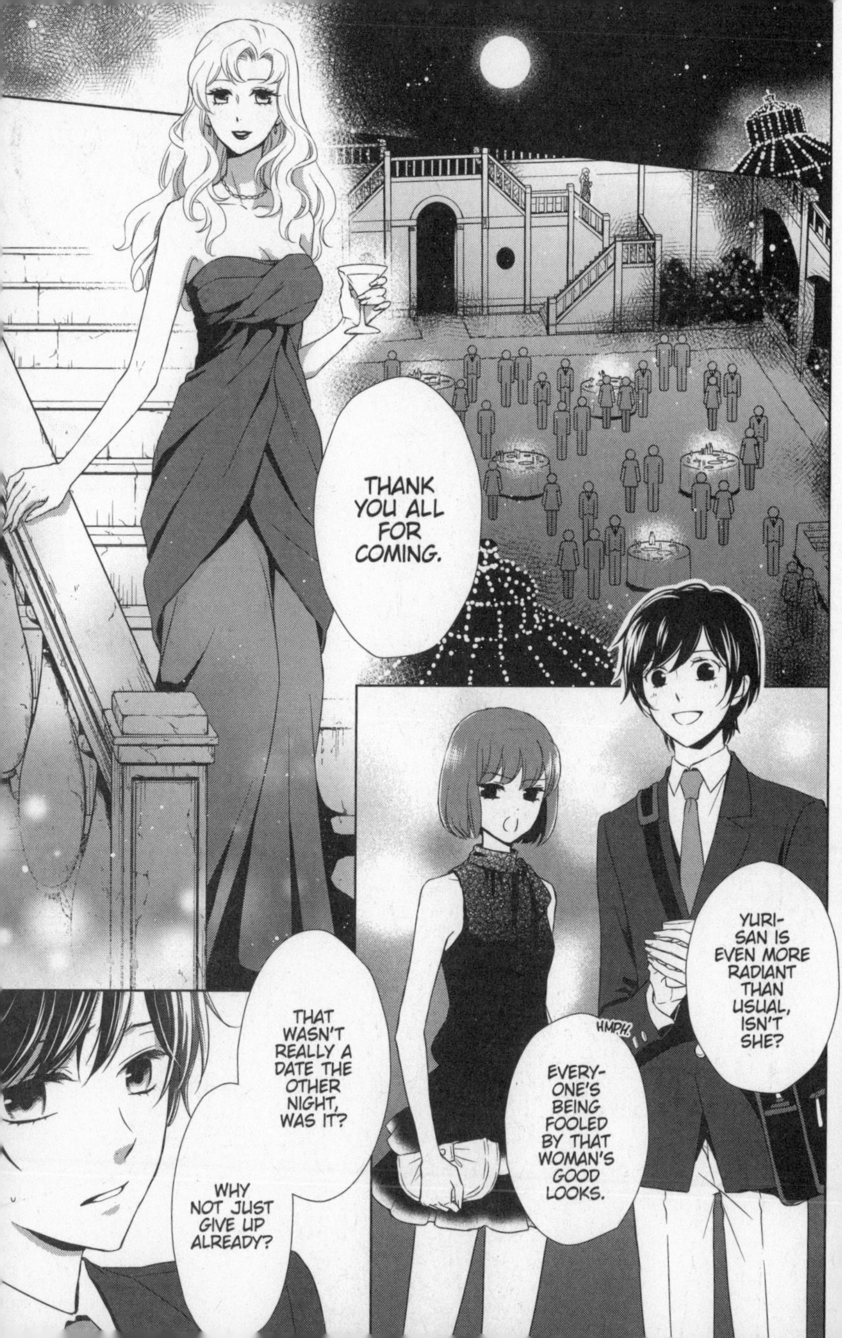
THANK YOU ALL FOR COMING.
YURI-SAN IS EVEN MORE RADIANT THAN USUAL, ISN'T SHE?
HMPH.
EVERY-ONE'S BEING FOOLED BY THAT WOMAN'S GOOD LOOKS.
THAT WASN'T REALLY A DATE THE OTHER NIGHT, WAS IT?
WHY NOT JUST GIVE UP ALREADY?

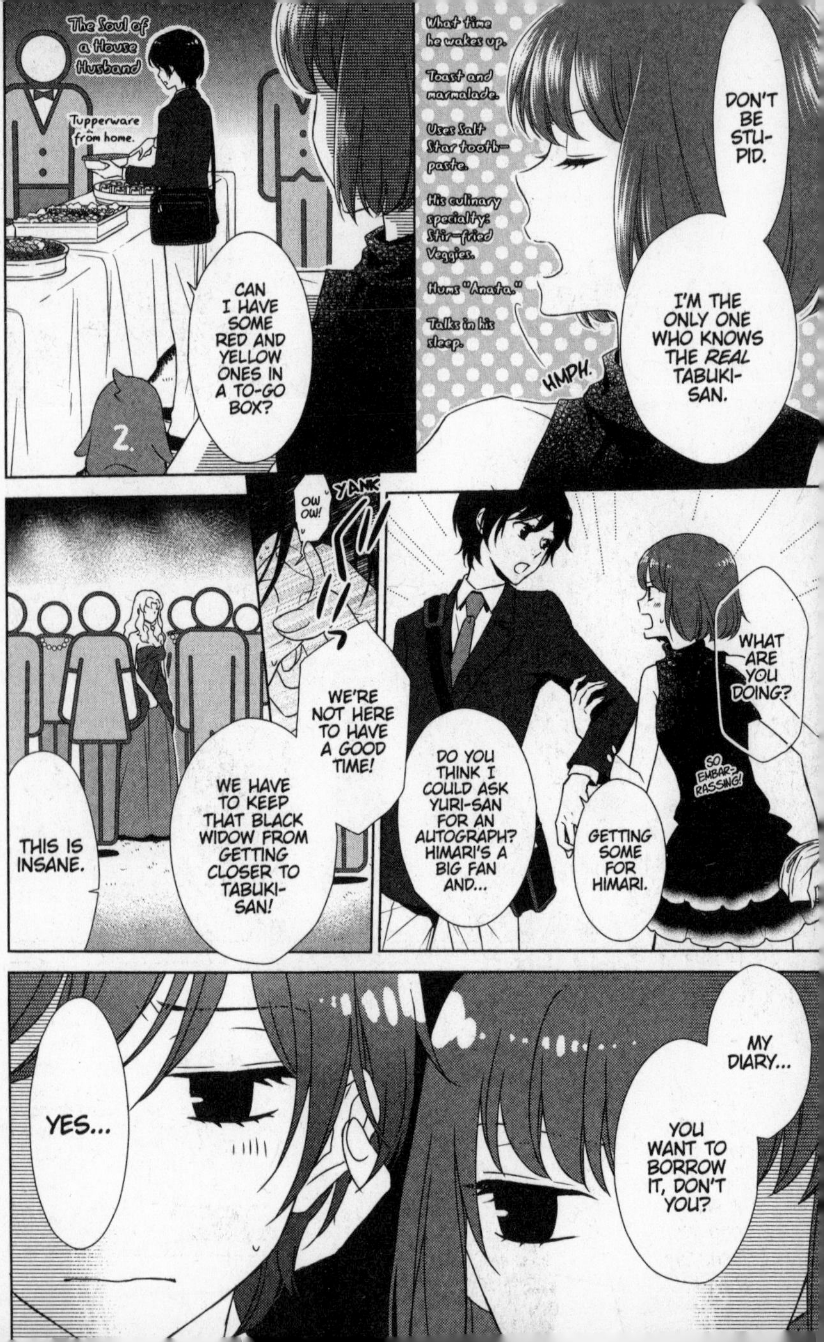
DON'T BE STUPID.
What time he wakes up.
Toast and marmalade.
Uses Salt Star toothpaste.
His culinary specialty: Stir-fried Veggies.
Hums "Anata."
Talks in his sleep.
I'M THE ONLY ONE WHO KNOWS THE REAL TABUKI-SAN.
HMPH.
The Soul of a House Husband
Tupperware from home.
CAN I HAVE SOME RED AND YELLOW ONES IN A TO-GO BOX?
WHAT ARE YOU DOING?
SO EMBARRASSING!
GETTING SOME FOR HIMARI.
DO YOU THINK I COULD ASK YURI-SAN FOR AN AUTOGRAPH? HIMARI'S A BIG FAN AND...
YANK
OW OW!
WE'RE NOT HERE TO HAVE A GOOD TIME!
WE HAVE TO KEEP THAT BLACK WIDOW FROM GETTING CLOSER TO TABUKI-SAN!
THIS IS INSANE.
MY DIARY...
YOU WANT TO BORROW IT, DON'T YOU?
YES...

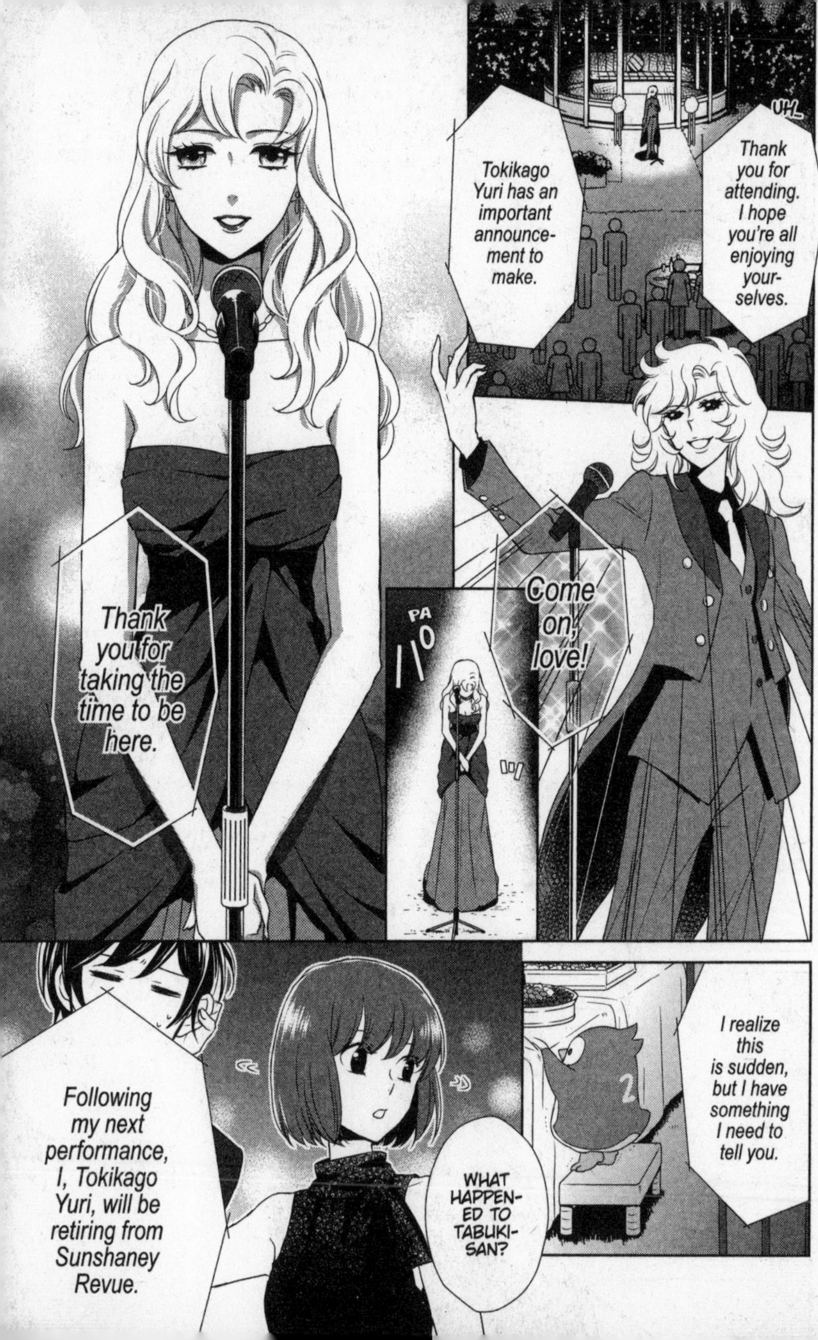

Thank you for attending. I hope you're all enjoying yourselves.
Tokikago Yuri has an important announcement to make.
Come on, love!
PA
Thank you for taking the time to be here.
I realize this is sudden, but I have something I need to tell you.
WHAT HAPPENED TO TABUKI-SAN?
Following my next performance, I, Tokikago Yuri, will be retiring from Sunshaney Revue.

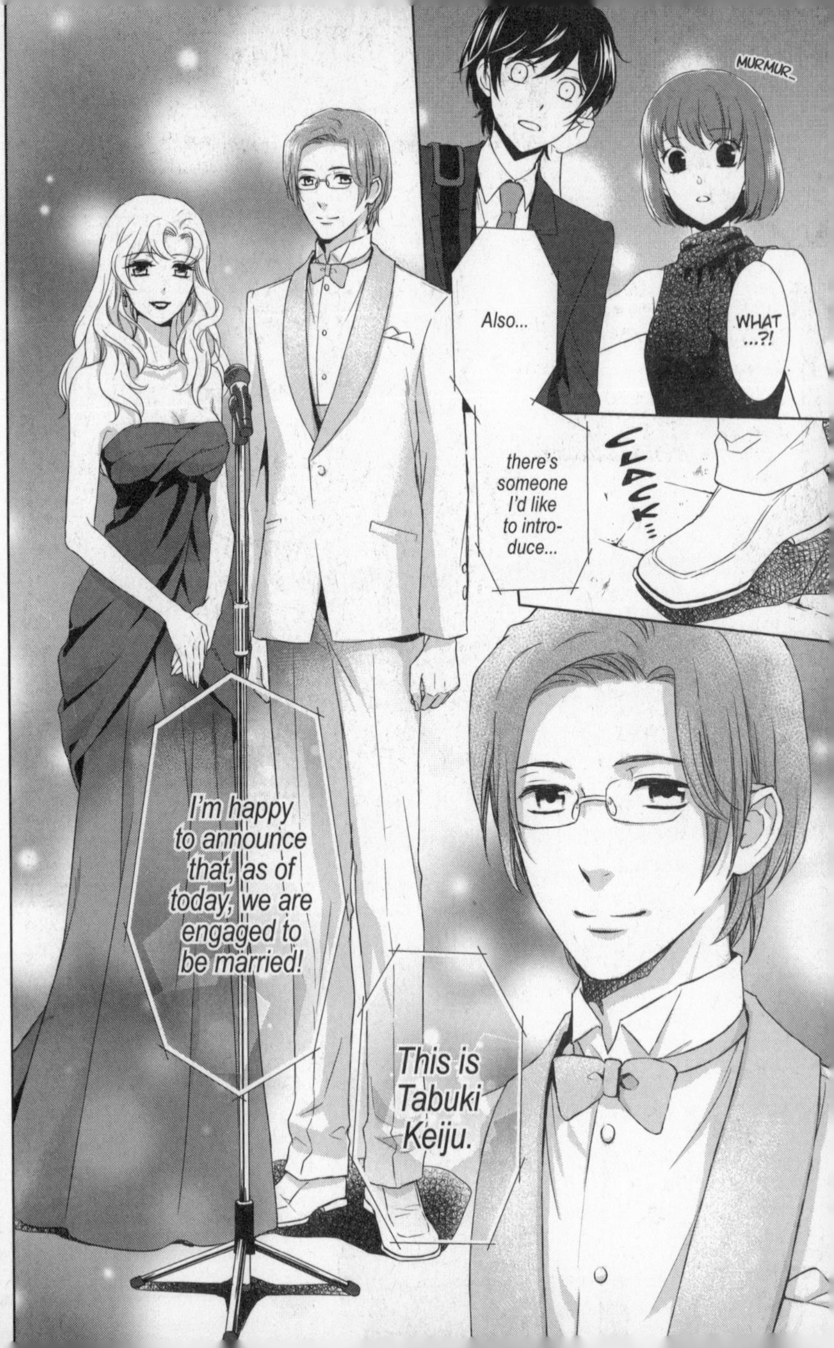
MURMUR...
WHAT ...?!
Also...
CLACK...
there's someone I'd like to introduce...
This is Tabuki Keiju.
I'm happy to announce that, as of today, we are engaged to be married!

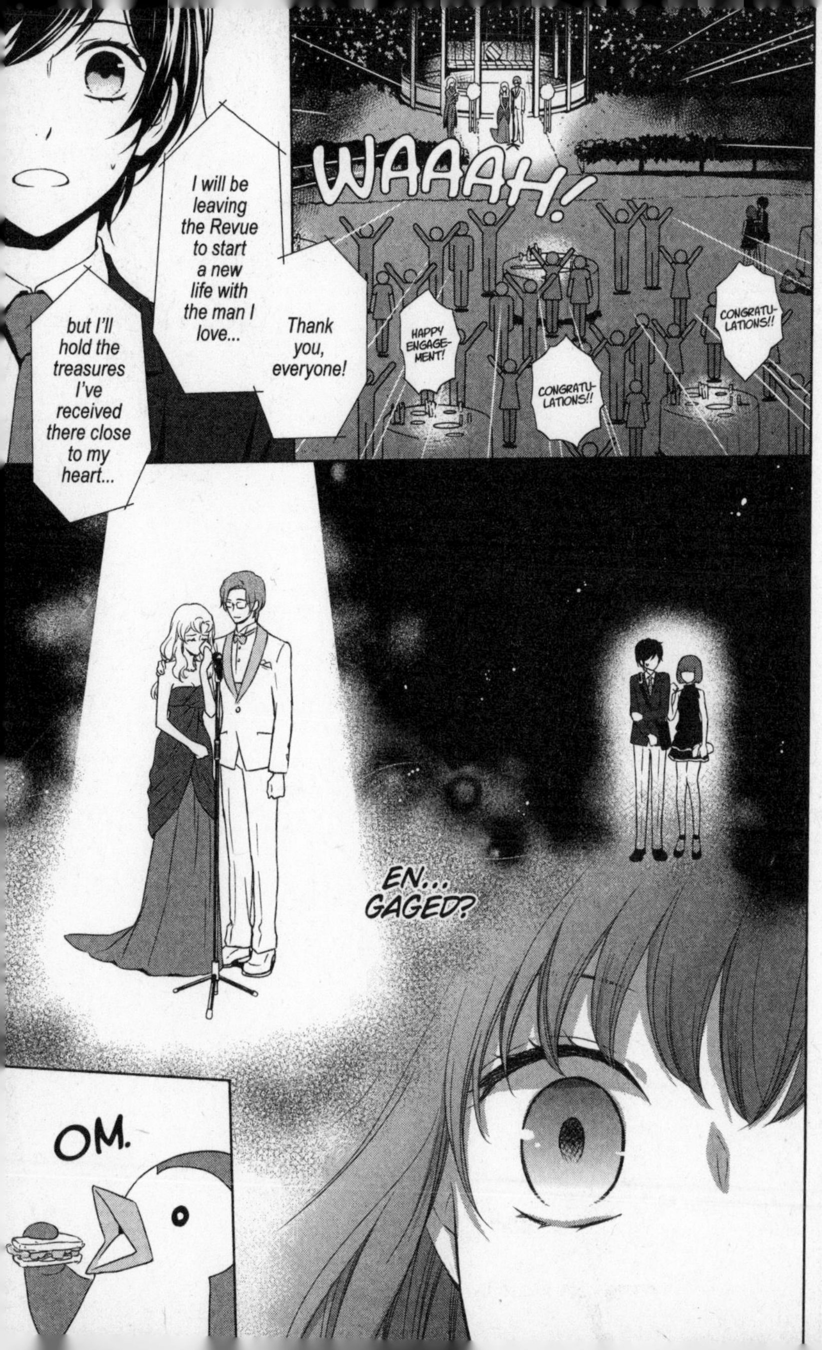
WAAAH!
CONGRATU-LATIONS!!
CONGRATU-LATIONS!!
HAPPY ENGAGE-MENT!
Thank you, everyone!
I will be leaving the Revue to start a new life with the man I love...
but I'll hold the treasures I've received there close to my heart...
EN... GAGED?
OM.

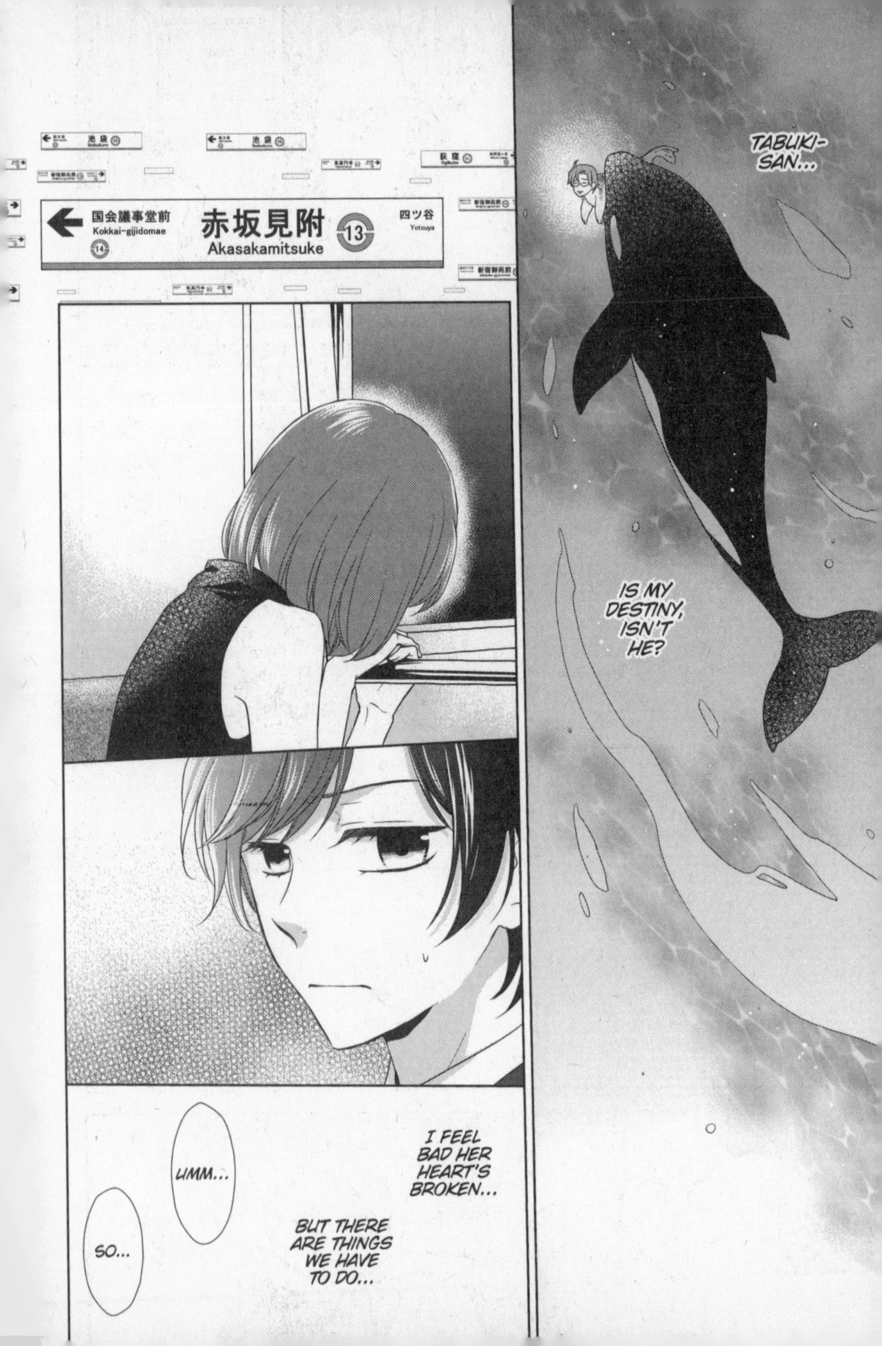
TABUKI-SAN...
IS MY DESTINY, ISN'T HE?
国会議事堂前
Kokkai-gijidomae
14
赤坂見附
Akasakamitsuke
13
四ツ谷
Yotsuya
池袋
池袋
荻窪
I FEEL BAD HER HEART'S BROKEN...
BUT THERE ARE THINGS WE HAVE TO DO...
UMM...
SO...

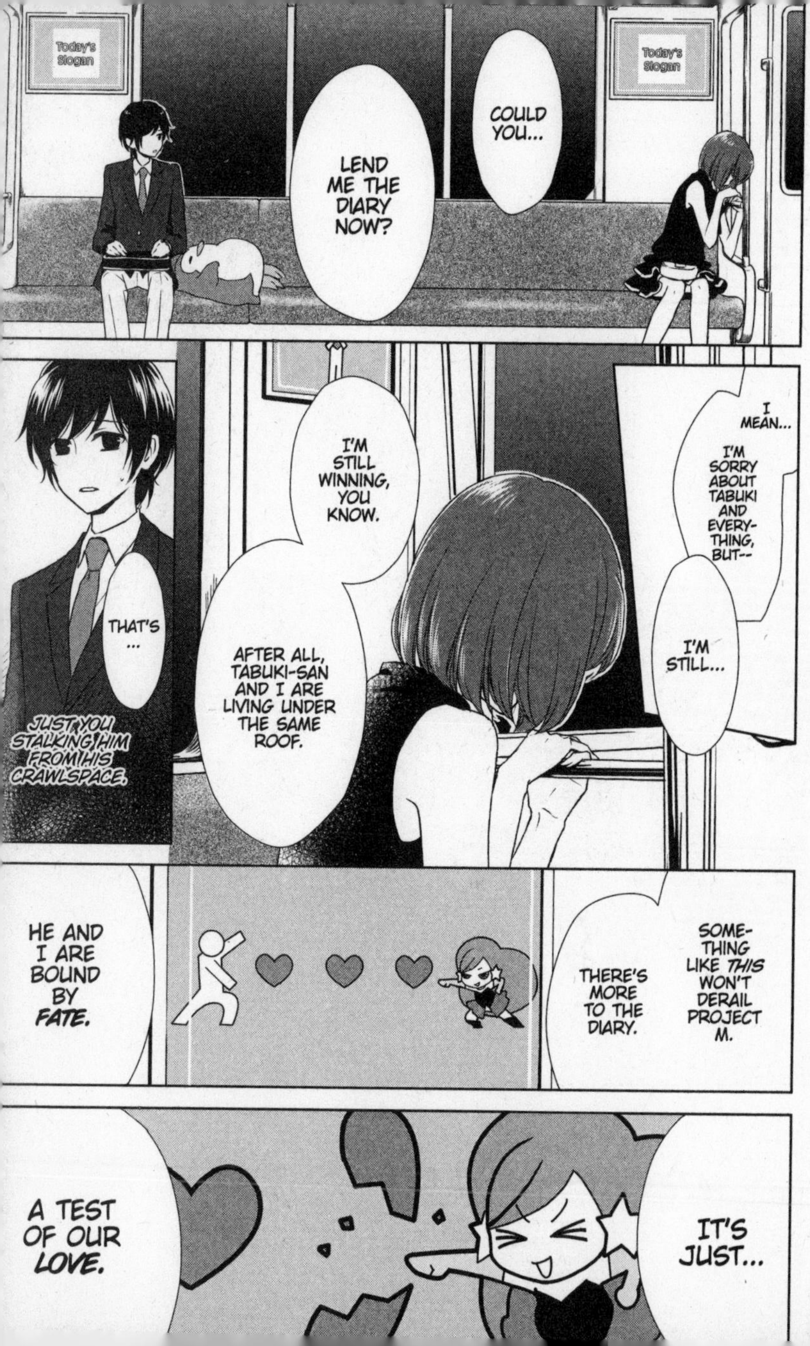

Today's Slogan
COULD YOU...
LEND ME THE DIARY NOW?
Today's Slogan
I MEAN... I'M SORRY ABOUT TABUKI AND EVERY-THING, BUT--
I'M STILL...
I'M STILL WINNING, YOU KNOW.
AFTER ALL, TABUKI-SAN AND I ARE LIVING UNDER THE SAME ROOF.
THAT'S ...
JUST YOU STALKING HIM FROM HIS CRAWLSPACE.
SOME-THING LIKE *THIS* WON'T DERAIL PROJECT M.
THERE'S MORE TO THE DIARY.
HE AND I ARE BOUND BY ***FATE.***
IT'S JUST...
A TEST OF OUR ***LOVE.***

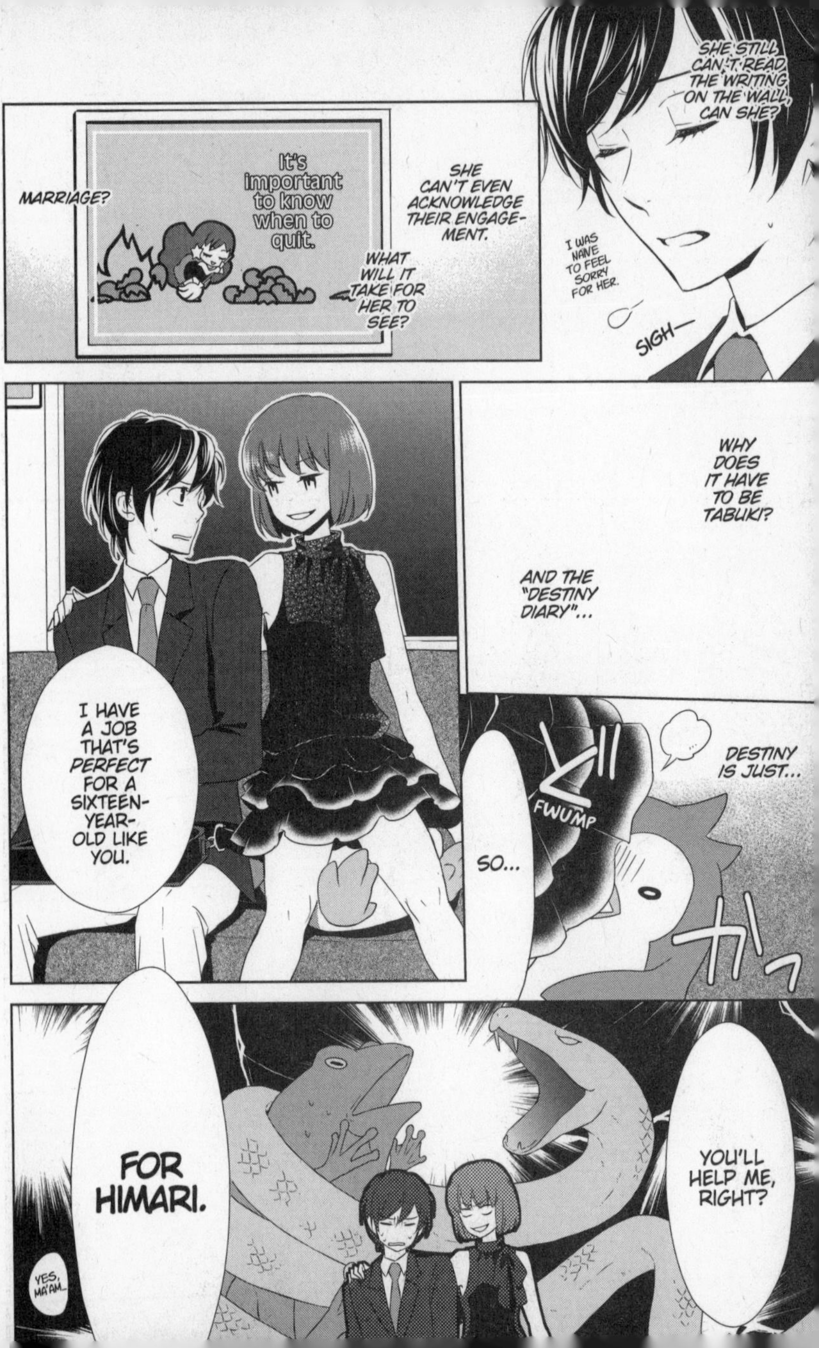
SHE STILL CAN'T READ THE WRITING ON THE WALL, CAN SHE?
I WAS NAIVE TO FEEL SORRY FOR HER.
SIGH—
SHE CAN'T EVEN ACKNOWLEDGE THEIR ENGAGE-MENT.
It's important to know when to quit.
MARRIAGE?
WHAT WILL IT TAKE FOR HER TO SEE?
WHY DOES IT HAVE TO BE TABUKI?
AND THE "DESTINY DIARY"...
DESTINY IS JUST...
FWUMP
SO...
カッ
I HAVE A JOB THAT'S PERFECT FOR A SIXTEEN-YEAR-OLD LIKE YOU.
YOU'LL HELP ME, RIGHT?
FOR HIMARI.
YES, MA'AM...

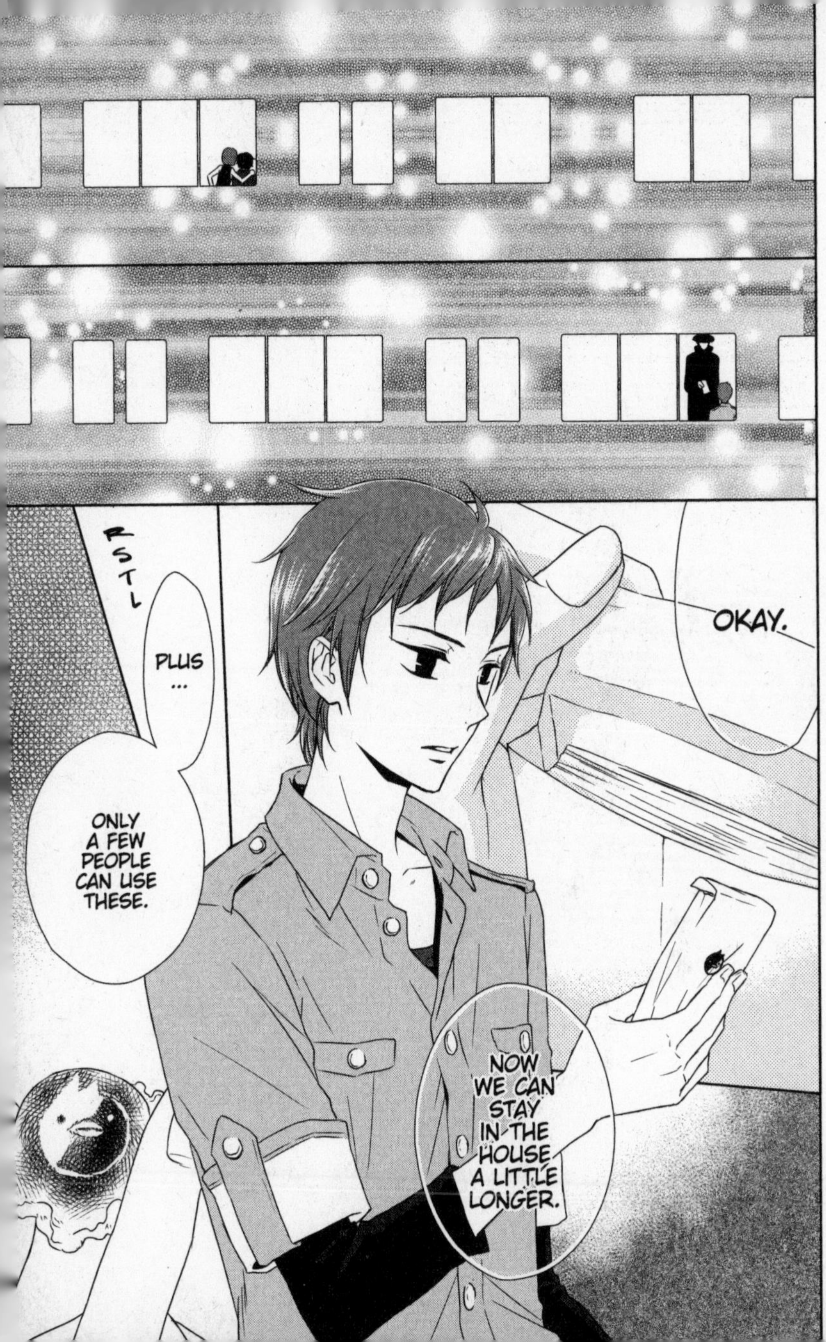
OKAY.
RSTL
PLUS ...
ONLY A FEW PEOPLE CAN USE THESE.
NOW WE CAN STAY IN THE HOUSE A LITTLE LONGER.

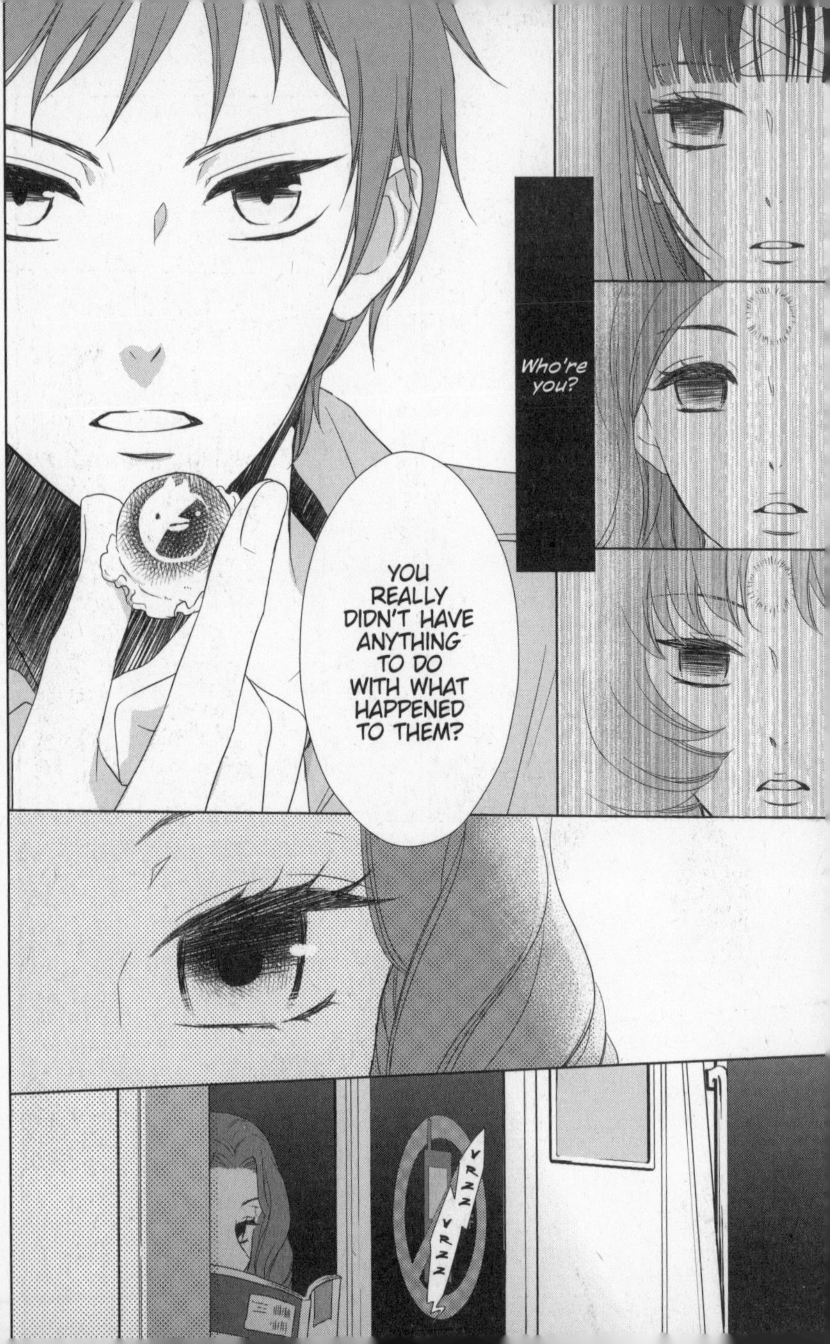
Who're you?
YOU REALLY DIDN'T HAVE ANYTHING TO DO WITH WHAT HAPPENED TO THEM?
VRZZ VRZZ VRZZ

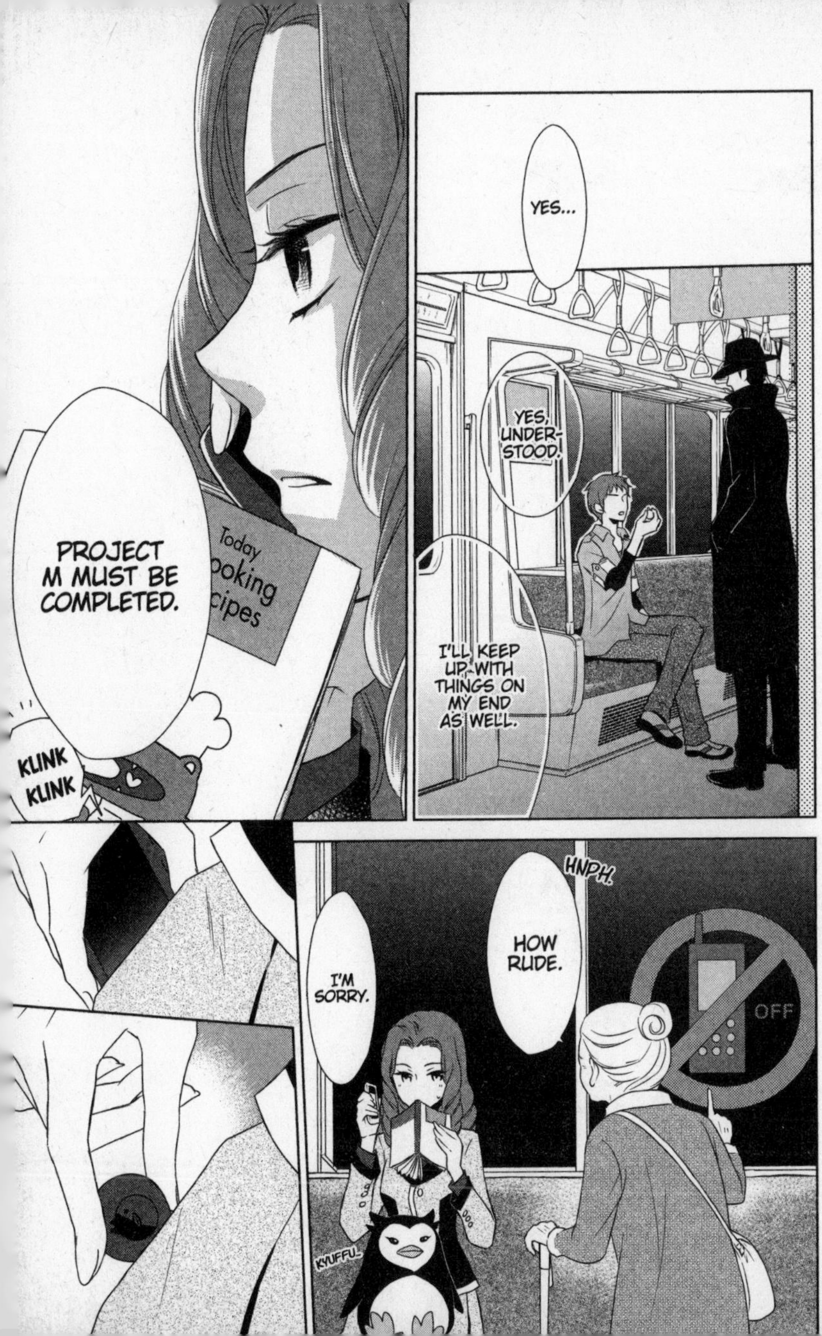
YES...
YES, UNDERSTOOD.
I'LL KEEP UP WITH THINGS ON MY END AS WELL.
PROJECT M MUST BE COMPLETED.
Today
KLINK KLINK
HNPH.
HOW RUDE.
OFF
I'M SORRY.
KYUFFU

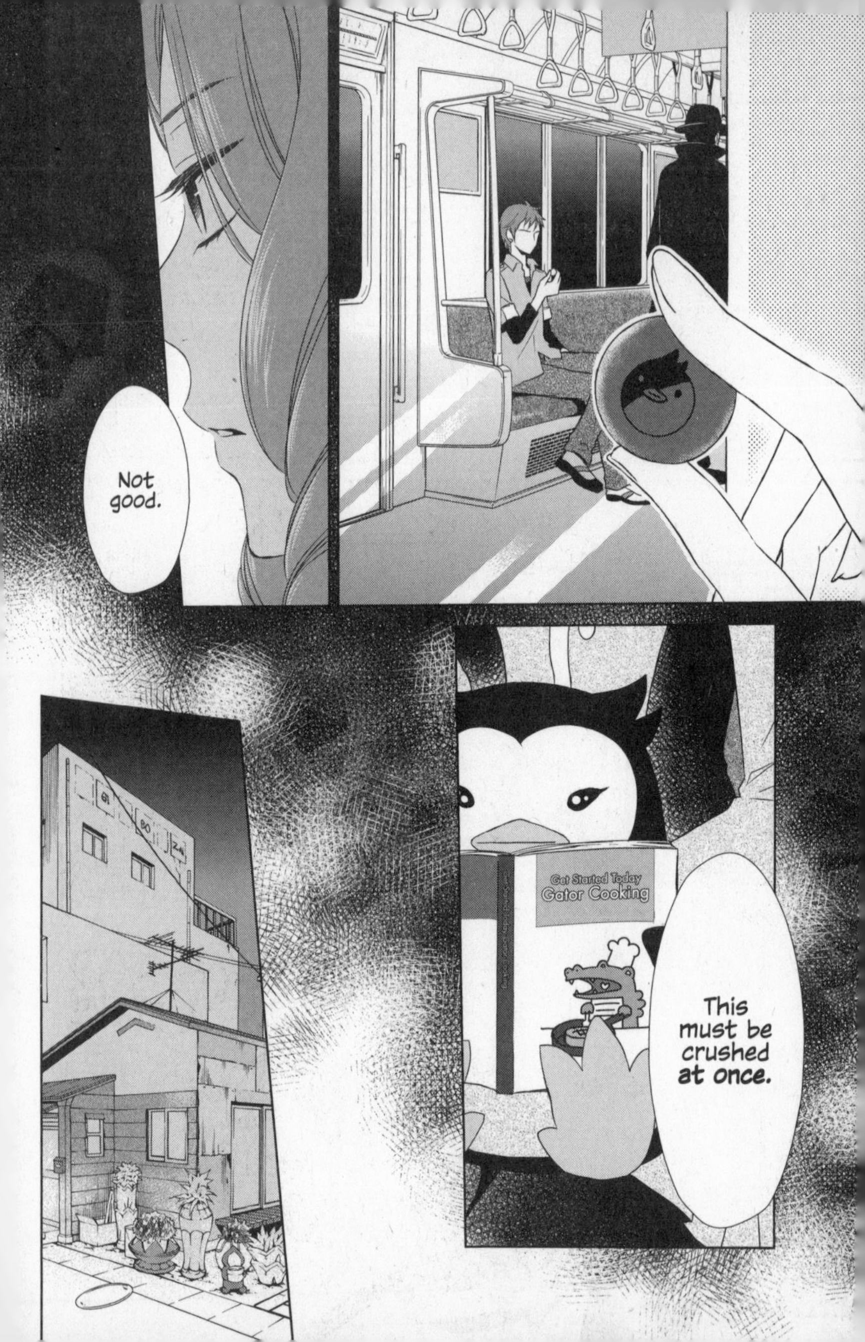
Not good.
Get Started Today
Gator Cooking
This must be crushed at once.

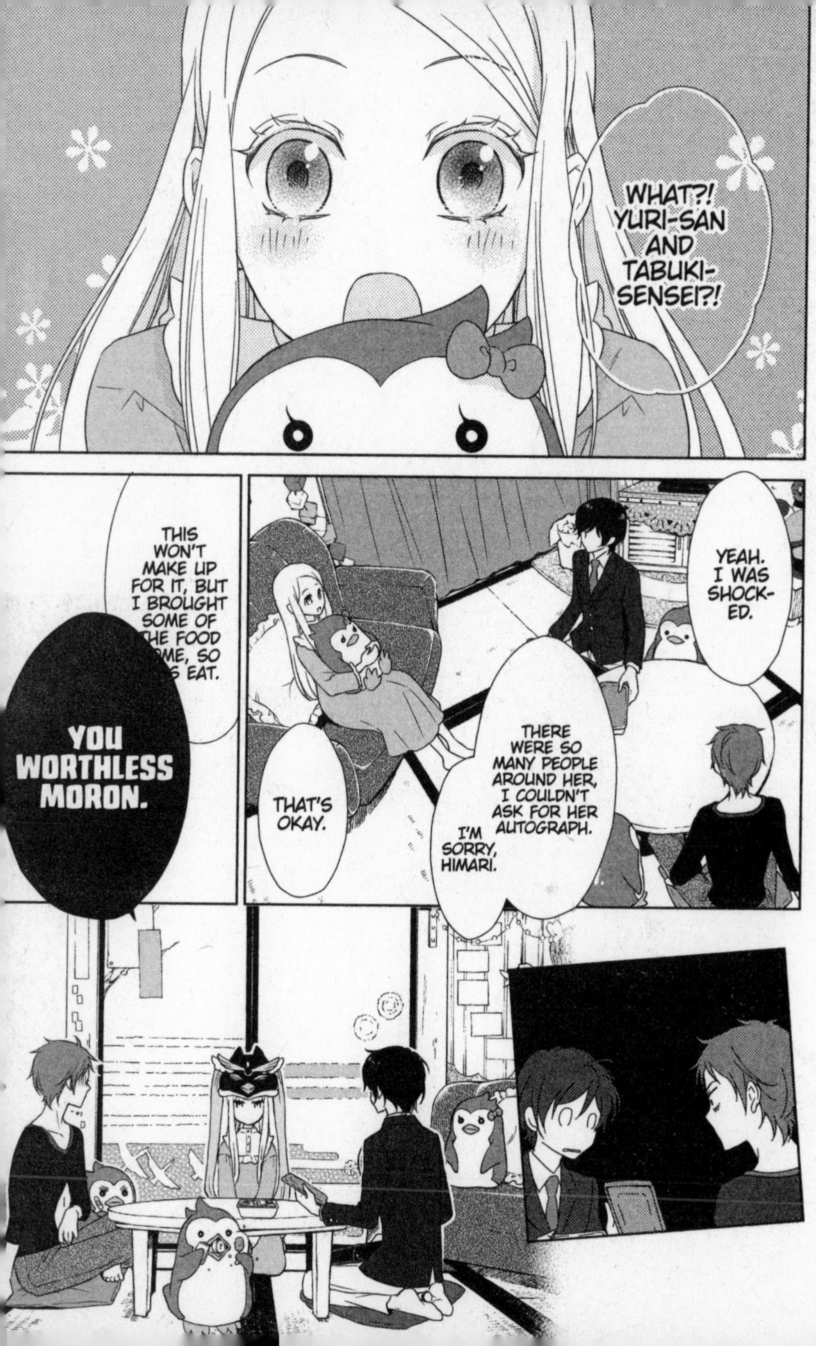
WHAT?! YURI-SAN AND TABUKI-SENSEI?!
YEAH. I WAS SHOCK-ED.
THERE WERE SO MANY PEOPLE AROUND HER, I COULDN'T ASK FOR HER AUTOGRAPH.
I'M SORRY, HIMARI.
THAT'S OKAY.
THIS WON'T MAKE UP FOR IT, BUT I BROUGHT SOME OF THE FOOD
YOU WORTHLESS MORON.

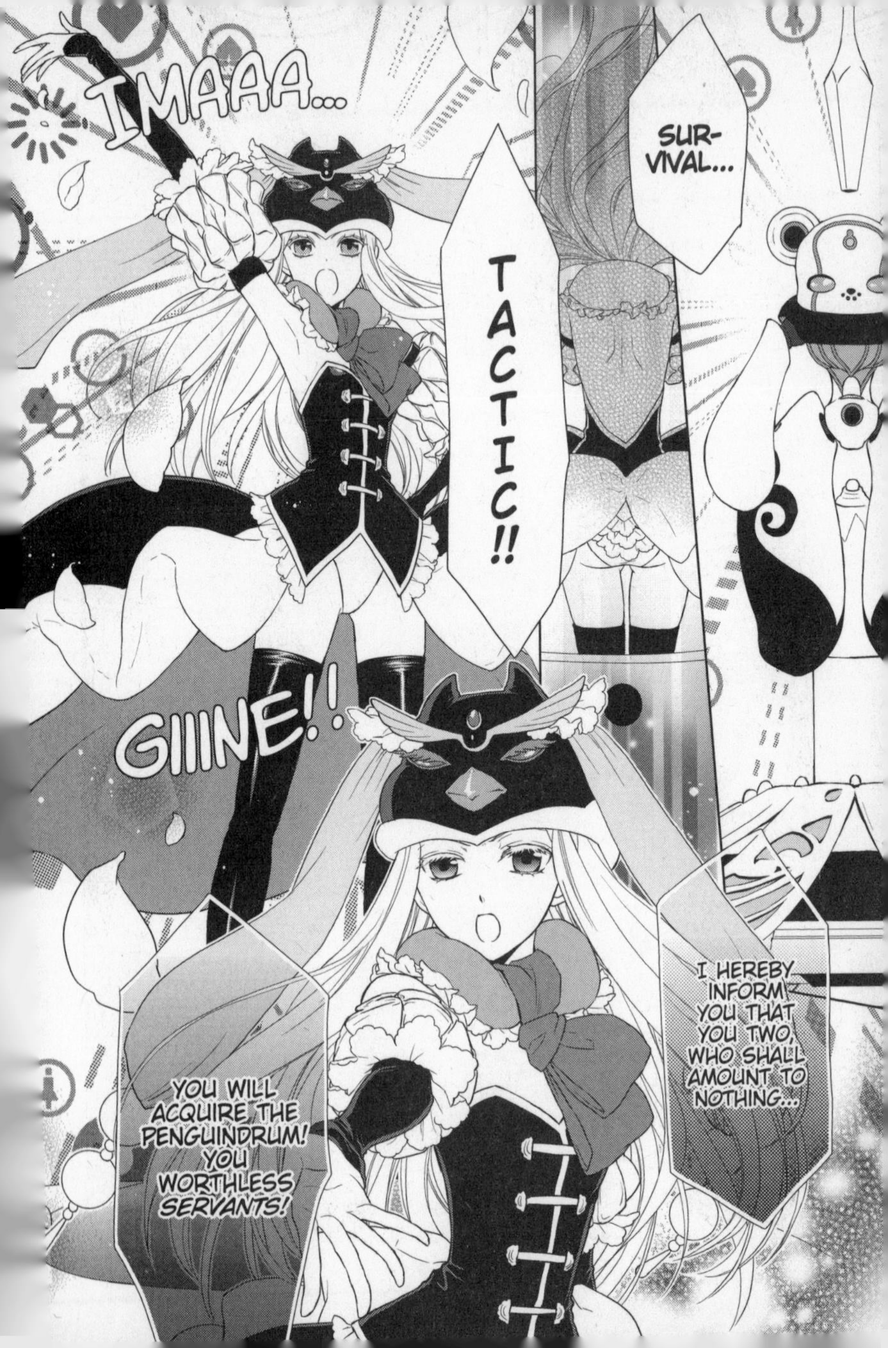
SUR-VIVAL...
TACTIC!!
IMAAAA...
GIIINE!!
I HEREBY INFORM YOU THAT YOU TWO, WHO SHALL AMOUNT TO NOTHING...
YOU WILL ACQUIRE THE PENGUINDRUM! YOU WORTHLESS SERVANTS!

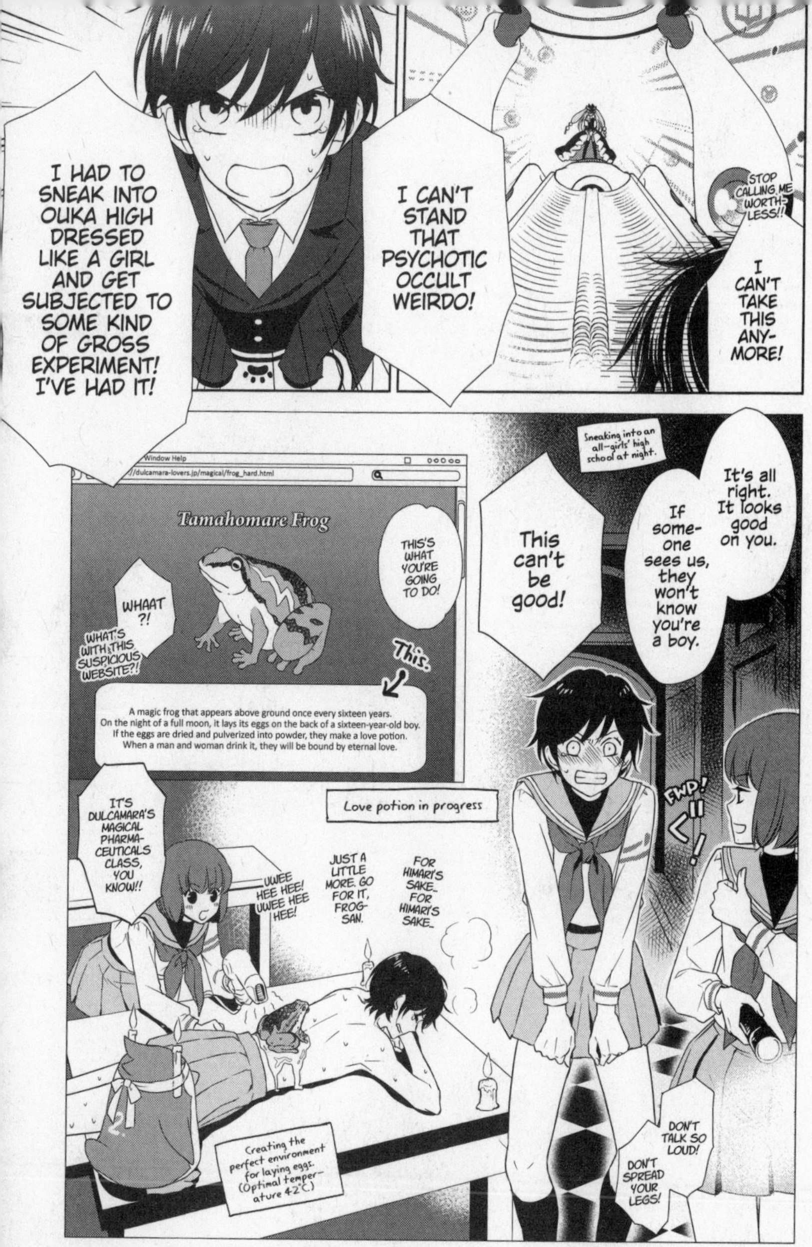
STOP CALLING ME WORTHLESS!!
I CAN'T TAKE THIS ANYMORE!
I CAN'T STAND THAT PSYCHOTIC OCCULT WEIRDO!
I HAD TO SNEAK INTO OUKA HIGH DRESSED LIKE A GIRL AND GET SUBJECTED TO SOME KIND OF GROSS EXPERIMENT! I'VE HAD IT!
Sneaking into an all-girls' high school at night.
It's all right. It looks good on you.
If someone sees us, they won't know you're a boy.
This can't be good!
FWP!
DON'T TALK SO LOUD!
DON'T SPREAD YOUR LEGS!
Window Help
://dulcamara-lovers.jp/magical/frog_hard.html
Tamahomare Frog
THIS'S WHAT YOU'RE GOING TO DO!
WHAAT?!
WHAT'S WITH THIS SUSPICIOUS WEBSITE?!
This.
A magic frog that appears above ground once every sixteen years.
On the night of a full moon, it lays its eggs on the back of a sixteen-year-old boy.
If the eggs are dried and pulverized into powder, they make a love potion.
When a man and woman drink it, they will be bound by eternal love.
Love potion in progress
IT'S DULCAMARA'S MAGICAL PHARMACEUTICALS CLASS, YOU KNOW!!
FOR HIMARI'S SAKE... FOR HIMARI'S SAKE...
JUST A LITTLE MORE. GO FOR IT, FROG-SAN.
UWEE HEE HEE! UWEE HEE HEE!
Creating the perfect environment for laying eggs. (Optimal temperature 42°C.)

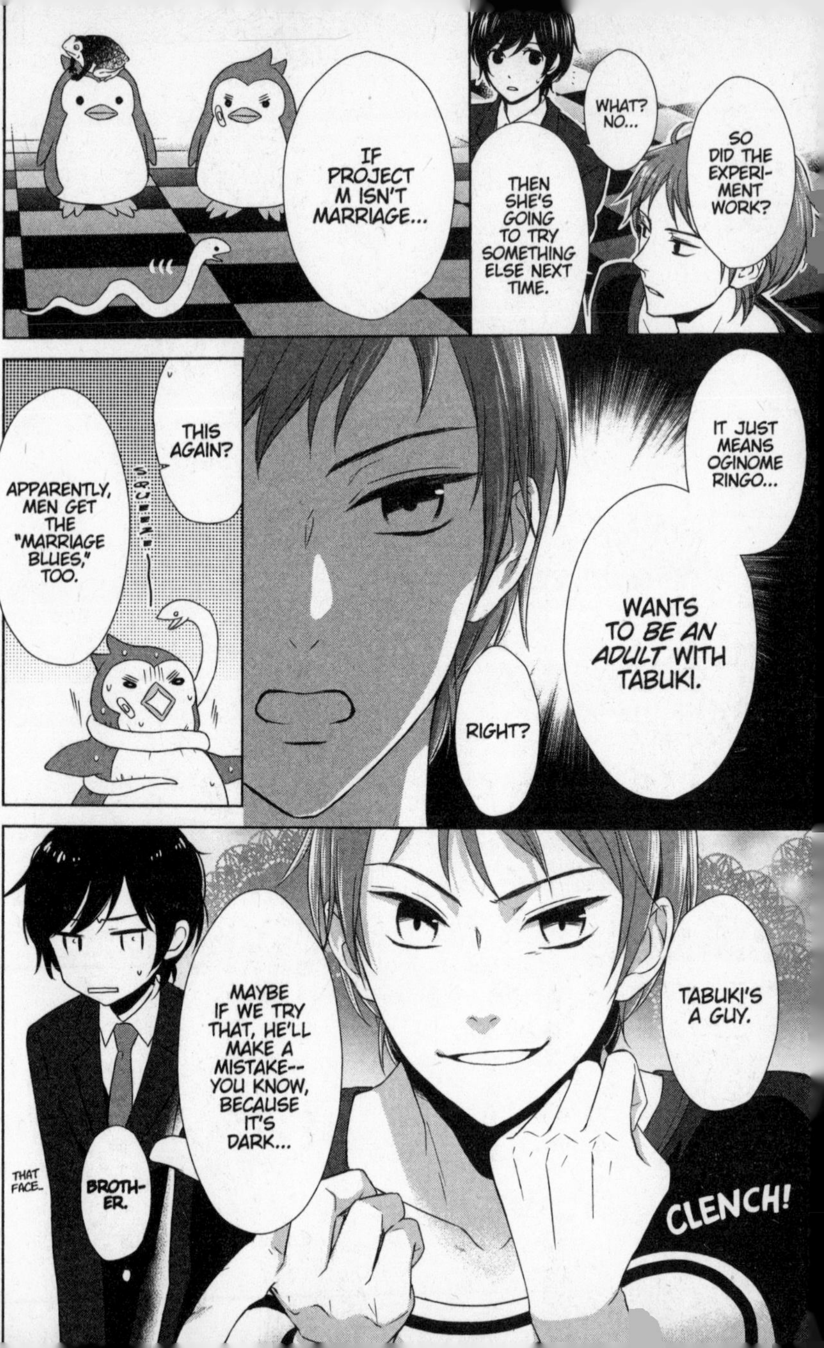
SO DID THE EXPERIMENT WORK?
WHAT? NO...
THEN SHE'S GOING TO TRY SOMETHING ELSE NEXT TIME.
IF PROJECT M ISN'T MARRIAGE...
IT JUST MEANS OGINOME RINGO...
WANTS TO BE AN ADULT WITH TABUKI.
RIGHT?
THIS AGAIN?
APPARENTLY, MEN GET THE "MARRIAGE BLUES," TOO.
TABUKI'S A GUY.
MAYBE IF WE TRY THAT, HE'LL MAKE A MISTAKE--YOU KNOW, BECAUSE IT'S DARK...
CLENCH!
BROTHER.
THAT FACE...

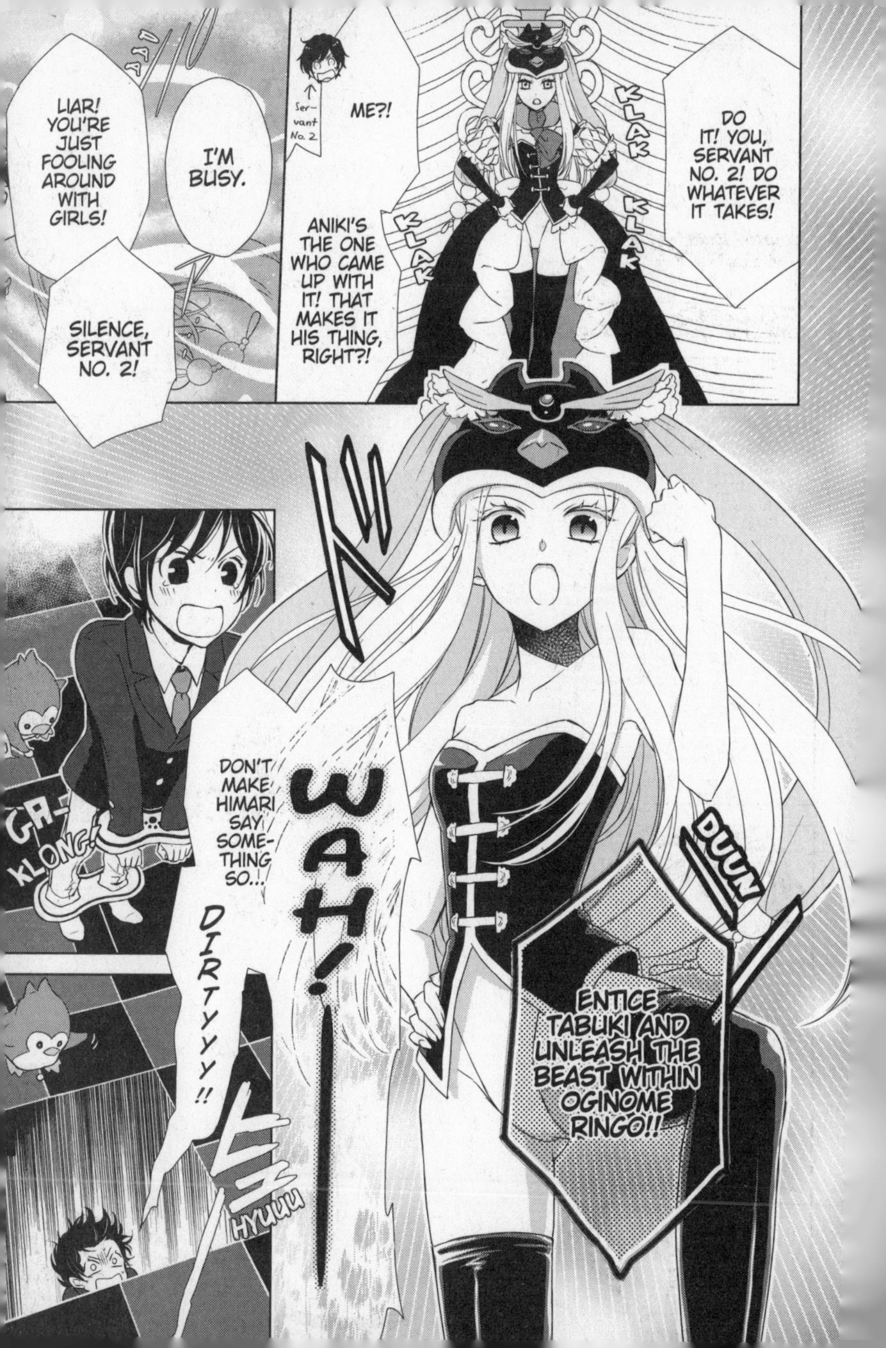
DO IT! YOU, SERVANT NO. 2! DO WHATEVER IT TAKES!
KLAK KLAK
KLAK
ME?!
Servant No. 2
ANIKI'S THE ONE WHO CAME UP WITH IT! THAT MAKES IT HIS THING, RIGHT?!
I'M BUSY.
LIAR! YOU'RE JUST FOOLING AROUND WITH GIRLS!
SILENCE, SERVANT NO. 2!
DUUN
ENTICE TABUKI AND UNLEASH THE BEAST WITHIN OGINOME RINGO!!
WAH!
DON'T MAKE HIMARI SAY SOMETHING SO..!
GA-KLONG!
DIRTYYY!!
HYUUU

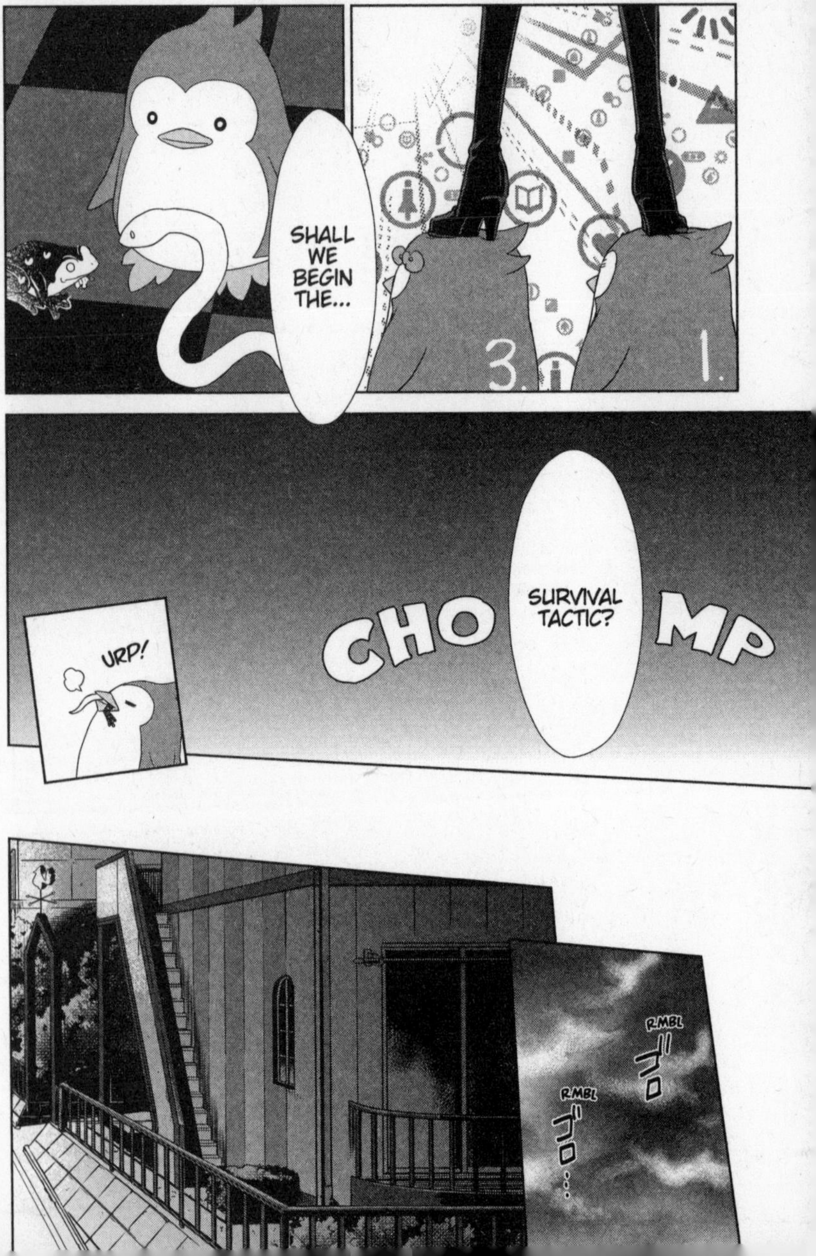
1.
3.
SHALL WE BEGIN THE...
SURVIVAL TACTIC?
CHOMP
URP!
RMBL
ゴロ
RMBL
ゴロ…

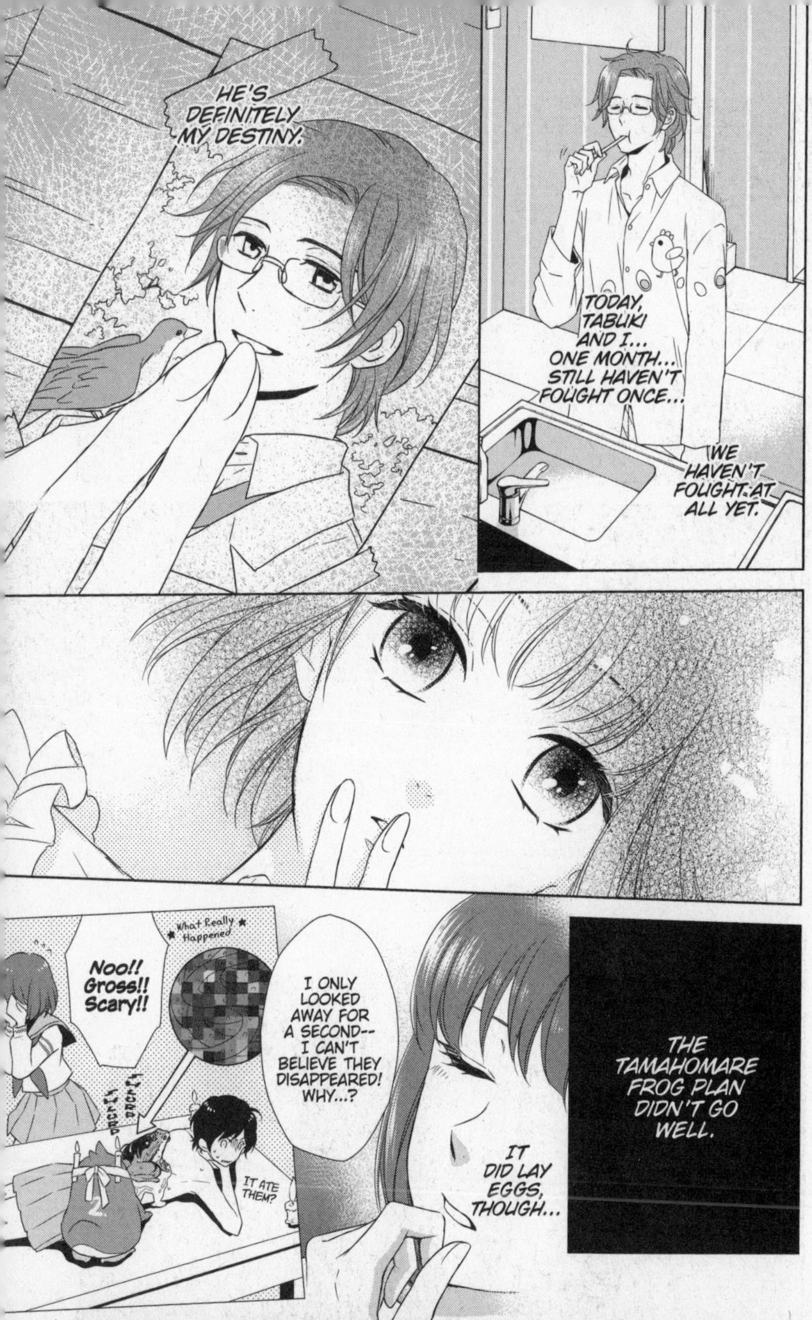
TODAY, TABUKI AND I... ONE MONTH... STILL HAVEN'T FOUGHT ONCE...
WE HAVEN'T FOUGHT AT ALL YET.
HE'S DEFINITELY MY DESTINY.
THE TAMAHOMARE FROG PLAN DIDN'T GO WELL.
IT DID LAY EGGS, THOUGH...
I ONLY LOOKED AWAY FOR A SECOND-- I CAN'T BELIEVE THEY DISAPPEARED! WHY...?
What Really Happened
Noo!! Gross!! Scary!!
IT ATE THEM?

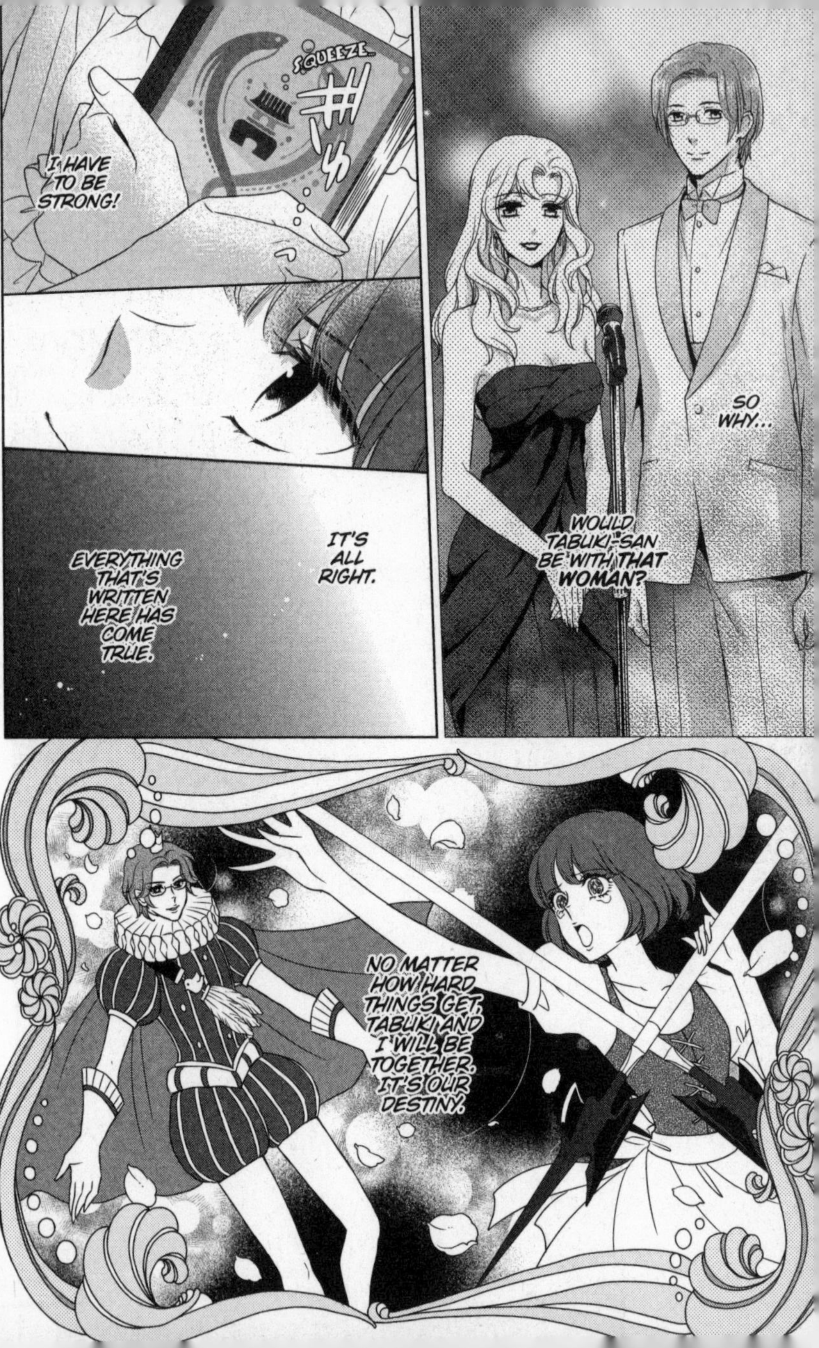
SO WHY...
WOULD TABUKI-SAN BE WITH THAT WOMAN?
SQUEEZE...
I HAVE TO BE STRONG!
IT'S ALL RIGHT.
EVERYTHING THAT'S WRITTEN HERE HAS COME TRUE.
NO MATTER HOW HARD THINGS GET, TABUKI AND I WILL BE TOGETHER. IT'S OUR DESTINY.

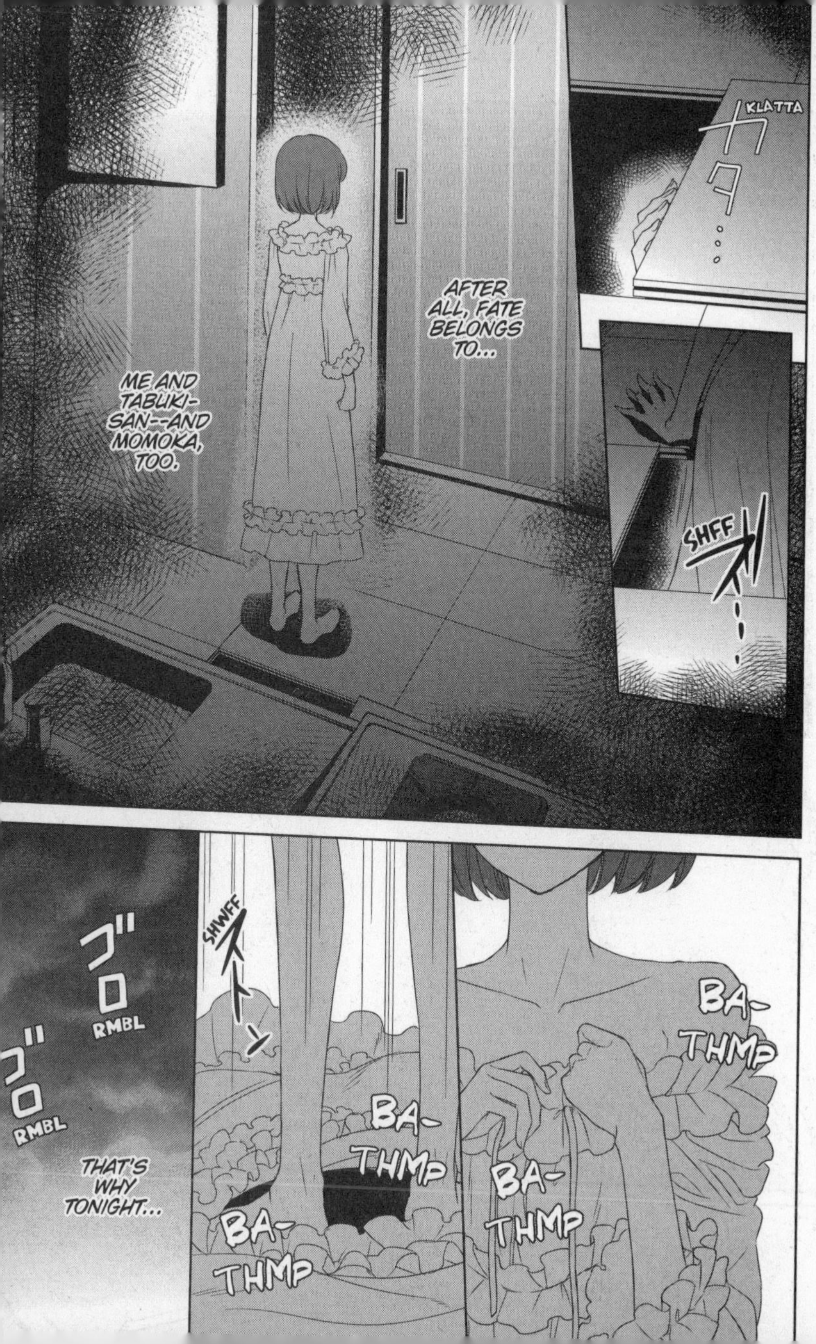
KLATTA
カタ…
SHFF
AFTER ALL, FATE BELONGS TO...
ME AND TABUKI-SAN--AND MOMOKA, TOO.
BA-THMP
SHWFF
ストン
BA-THMP
BA-THMP
BA-THMP
ゴロ
RMBL
ゴロ
RMBL
THAT'S WHY TONIGHT...

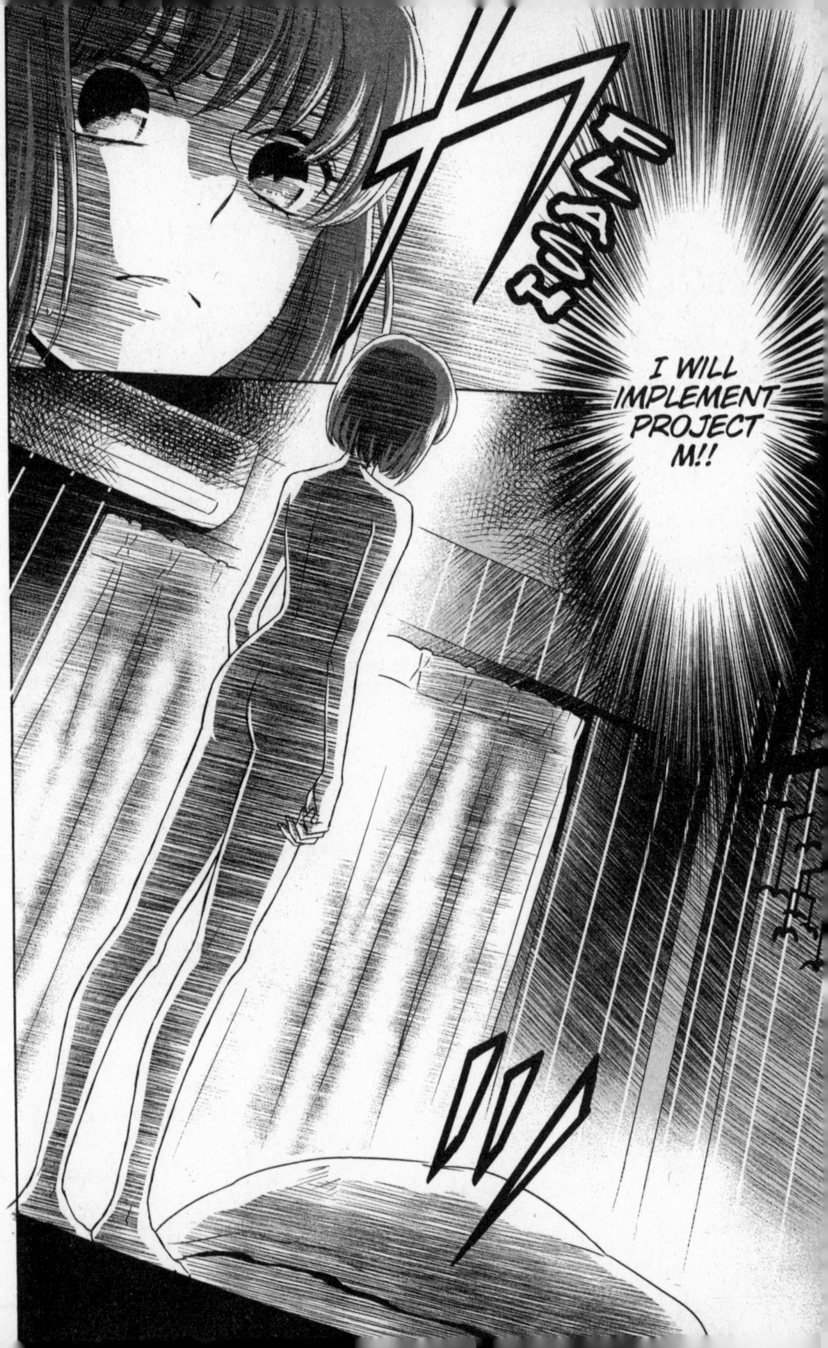
FLASH!
I WILL IMPLEMENT PROJECT M!!

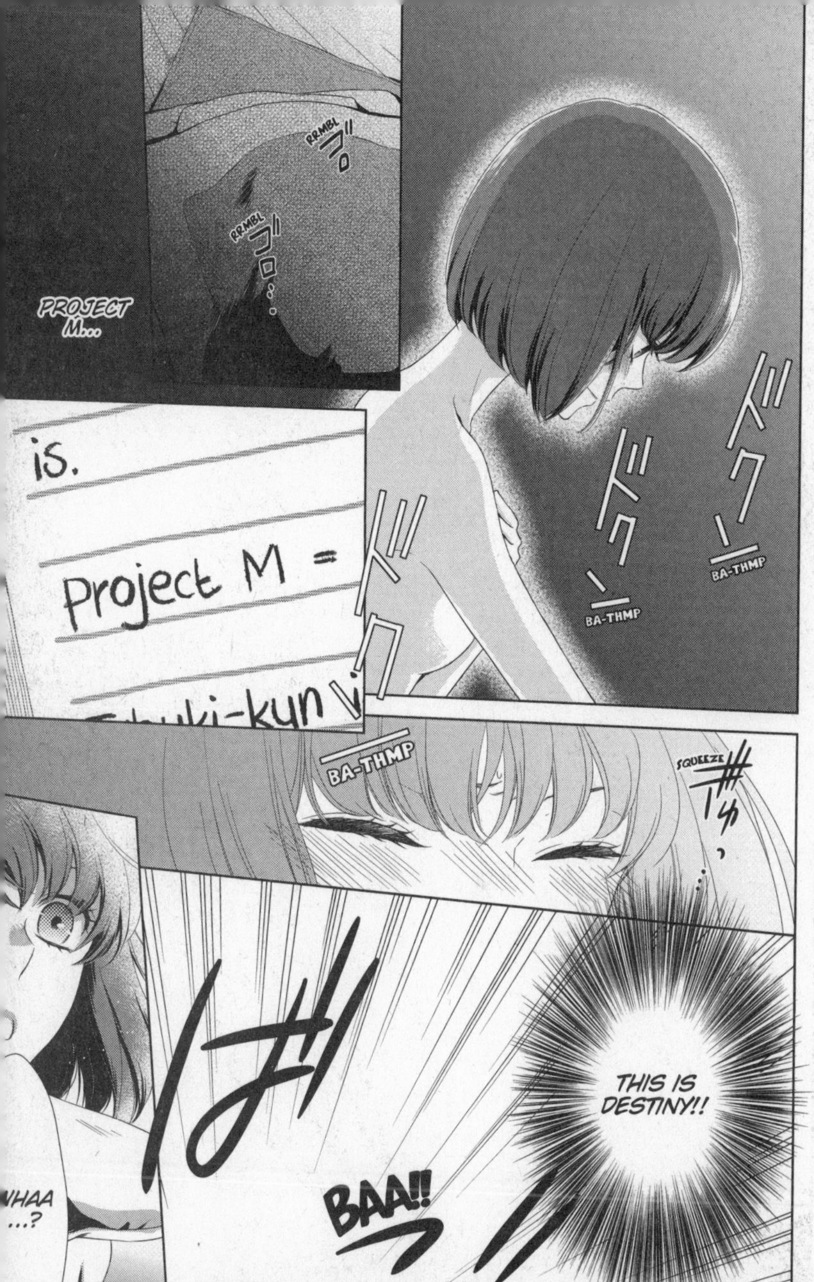
BA-THMP
BA-THMP
RRMBL
RRMBL
PROJECT M...
is.
Project M =
BA-THMP
SQUEEZE
THIS IS DESTINY!!
BAA!!
WHAA ...?

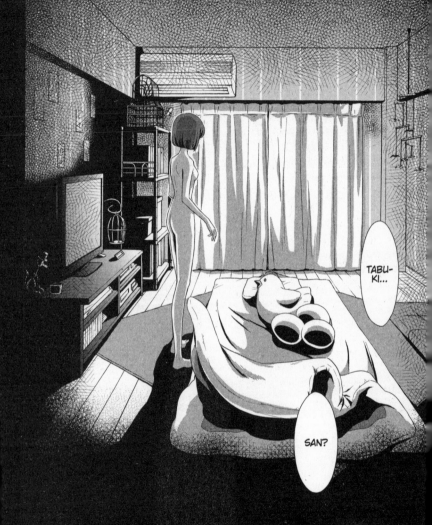

TABU-
KI...

SAN?

9

9TH STATION

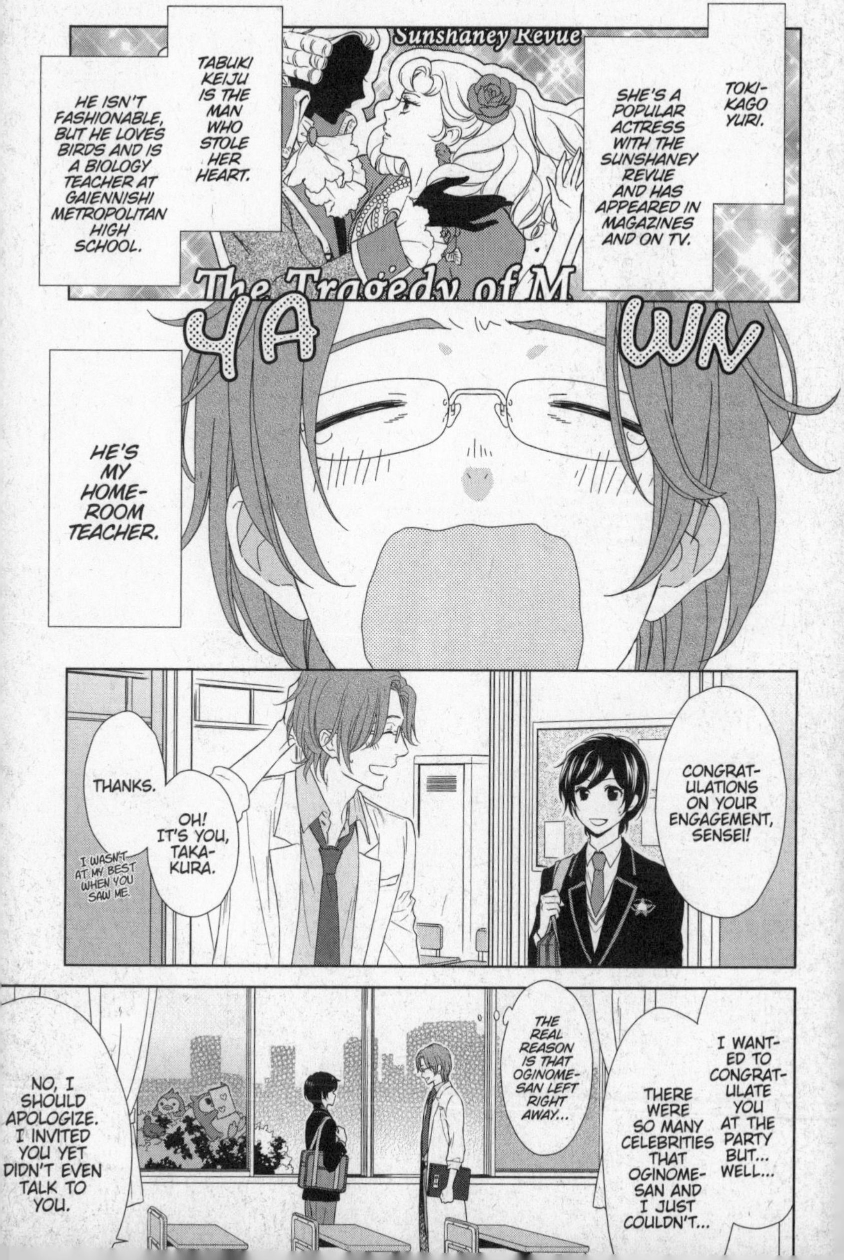

Sunshaney Revue
TOKI-KAGO YURI.
SHE'S A POPULAR ACTRESS WITH THE SUNSHANEY REVUE AND HAS APPEARED IN MAGAZINES AND ON TV.
TABUKI KEIJU IS THE MAN WHO STOLE HER HEART.
HE ISN'T FASHIONABLE, BUT HE LOVES BIRDS AND IS A BIOLOGY TEACHER AT GAIENNISHI METROPOLITAN HIGH SCHOOL.
The Tragedy of M
YAWN
HE'S MY HOME-ROOM TEACHER.
CONGRAT-ULATIONS ON YOUR ENGAGEMENT, SENSEI!
OH! IT'S YOU, TAKA-KURA.
THANKS.
I WASN'T AT MY BEST WHEN YOU SAW ME.
I WANT-ED TO CONGRAT-ULATE YOU AT THE PARTY BUT... WELL...
THERE WERE SO MANY CELEBRITIES THAT OGINOME-SAN AND I JUST COULDN'T...
THE REAL REASON IS THAT OGINOME-SAN LEFT RIGHT AWAY...
NO, I SHOULD APOLOGIZE. I INVITED YOU YET DIDN'T EVEN TALK TO YOU.

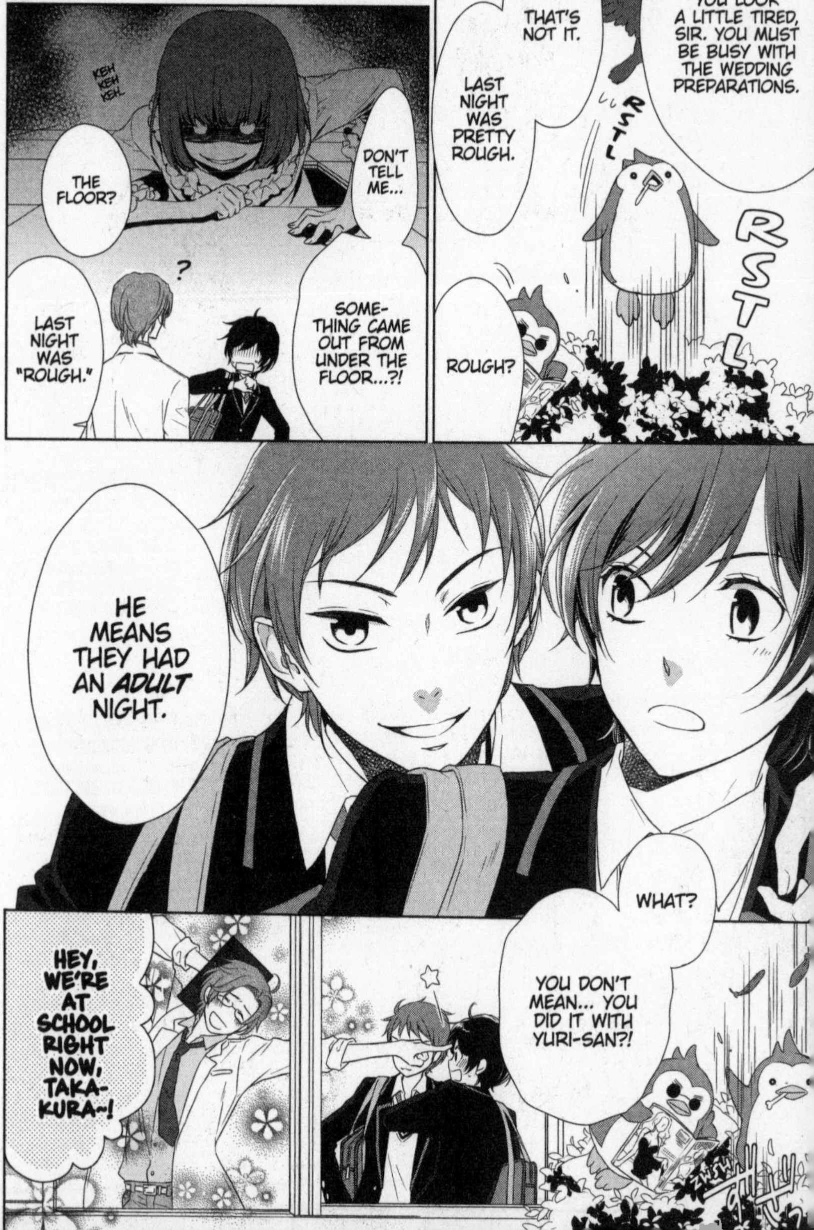
YOU LOOK A LITTLE TIRED, SIR. YOU MUST BE BUSY WITH THE WEDDING PREPARATIONS.
THAT'S NOT IT.
LAST NIGHT WAS PRETTY ROUGH.
RSTL
RSTL
ROUGH?
DON'T TELL ME...
KEH KEH KEH.
THE FLOOR?
SOME-THING CAME OUT FROM UNDER THE FLOOR...?!
?
LAST NIGHT WAS "ROUGH."
WHAT?
HE MEANS THEY HAD AN *ADULT* NIGHT.
YOU DON'T MEAN... YOU DID IT WITH YURI-SAN?!
ZWSH
HEY, WE'RE AT SCHOOL RIGHT NOW, TAKA-KURA~!

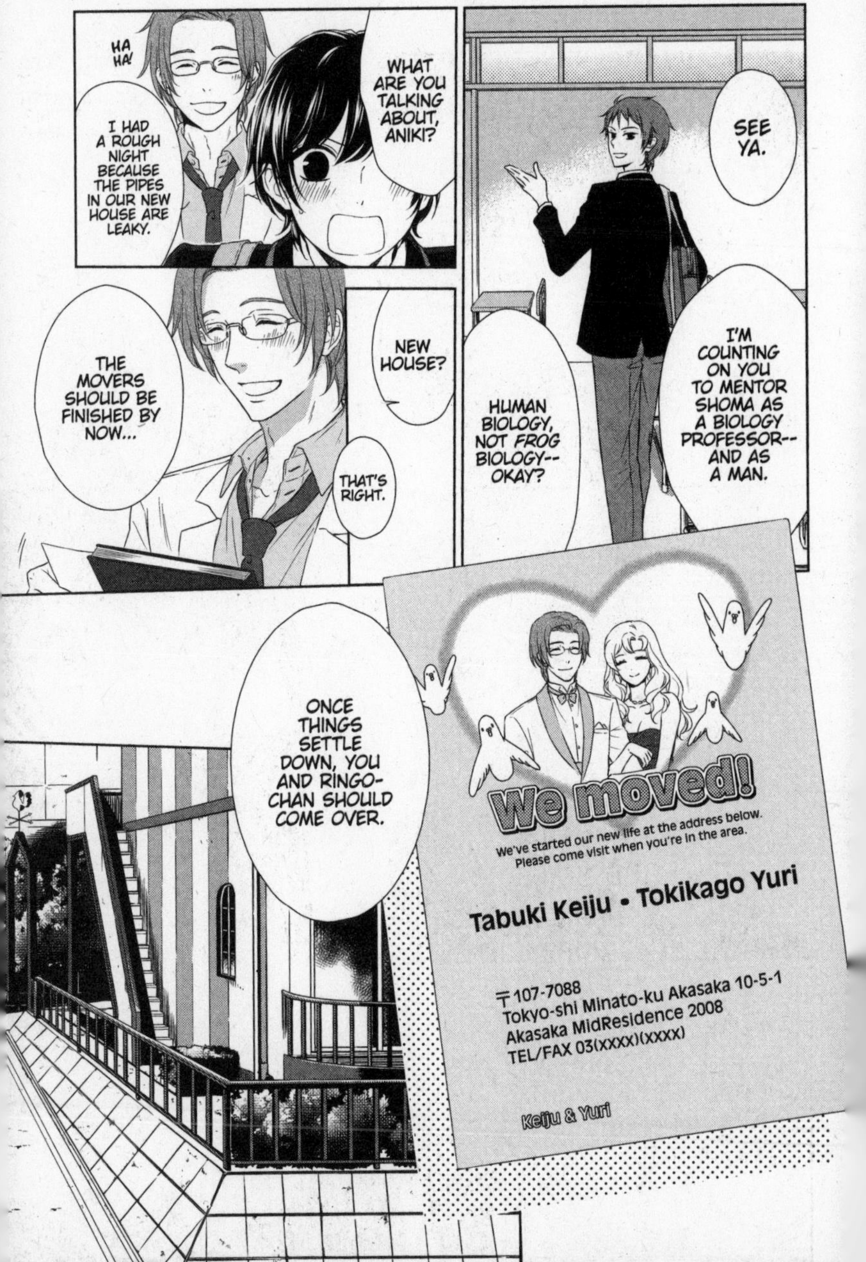
SEE YA.
I'M COUNTING ON YOU TO MENTOR SHOMA AS A BIOLOGY PROFESSOR--AND AS A MAN.
HUMAN BIOLOGY, NOT FROG BIOLOGY--OKAY?
WHAT ARE YOU TALKING ABOUT, ANIKI?
HA HA!
I HAD A ROUGH NIGHT BECAUSE THE PIPES IN OUR NEW HOUSE ARE LEAKY.
NEW HOUSE?
THAT'S RIGHT.
THE MOVERS SHOULD BE FINISHED BY NOW...
ONCE THINGS SETTLE DOWN, YOU AND RINGO-CHAN SHOULD COME OVER.
We moved!
We've started our new life at the address below.
Please come visit when you're in the area.
Tabuki Keiju • Tokikago Yuri
〒107-7088
Tokyo-shi Minato-ku Akasaka 10-5-1
Akasaka MidResidence 2008
TEL/FAX 03(XXXX)(XXXX)
Keiju & Yuri

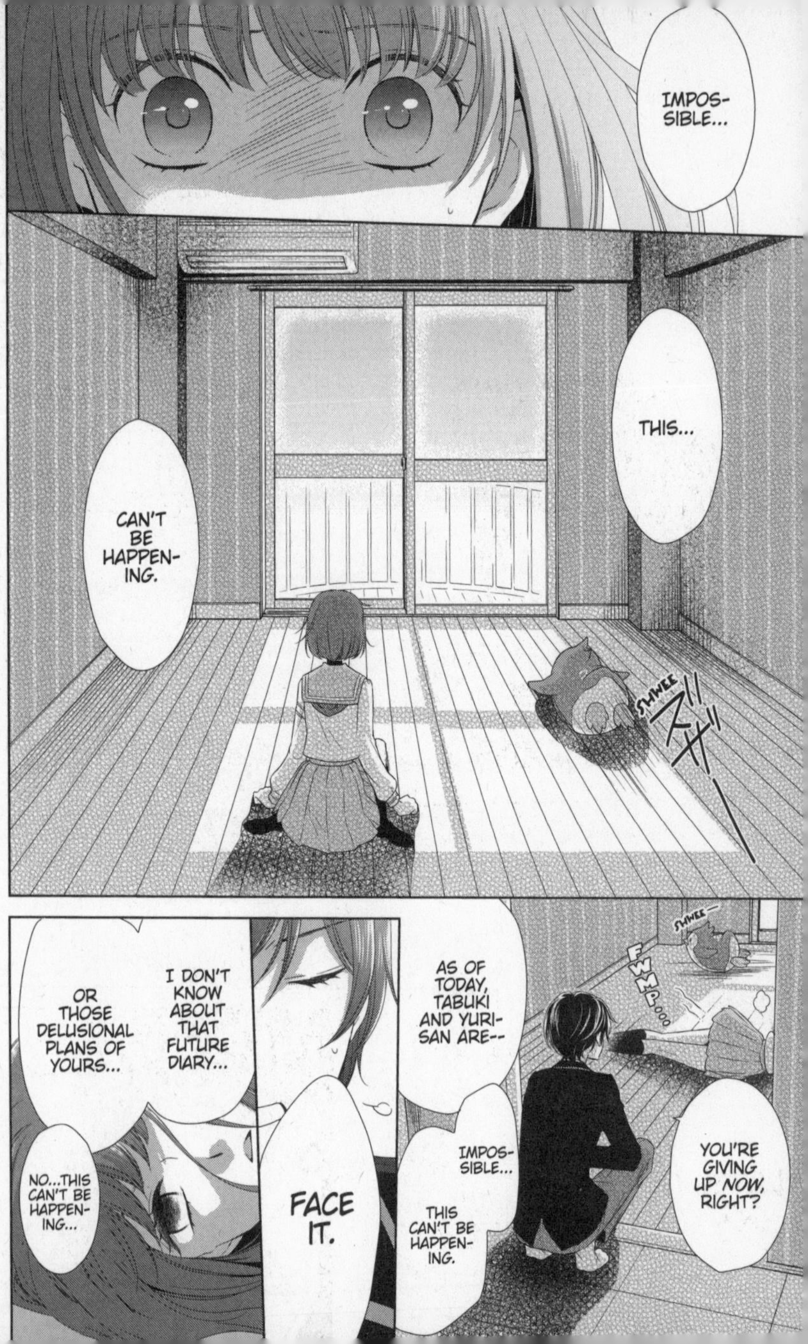
IMPOSSIBLE...
THIS...
CAN'T BE HAPPENING.
SWEE
YOU'RE GIVING UP NOW, RIGHT?
SWEE—
FWMP...
AS OF TODAY, TABUKI AND YURI-SAN ARE--
IMPOSSIBLE...
THIS CAN'T BE HAPPENING.
FACE IT.
I DON'T KNOW ABOUT THAT FUTURE DIARY...
OR THOSE DELUSIONAL PLANS OF YOURS...
NO...THIS CAN'T BE HAPPENING...

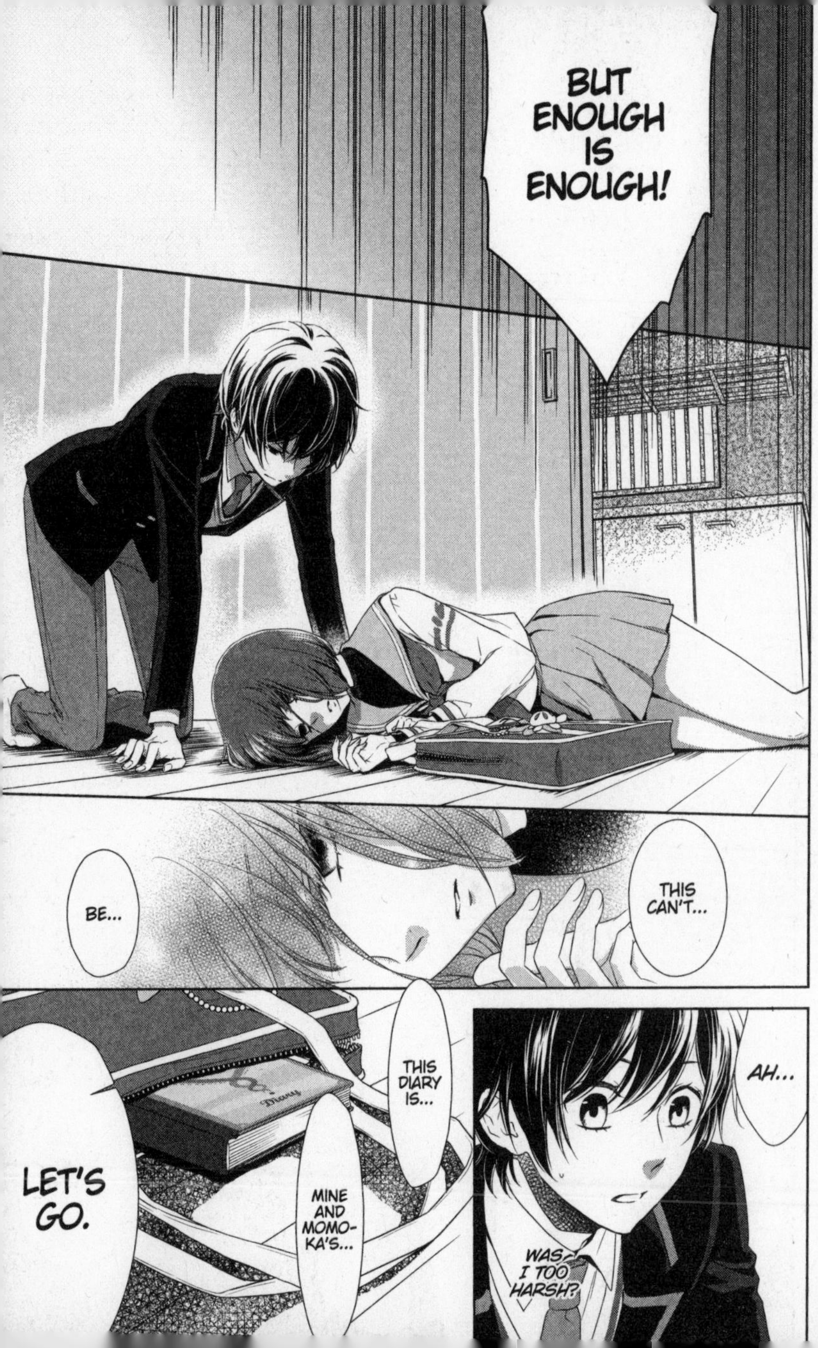
BUT ENOUGH IS ENOUGH!
THIS CAN'T...
BE...
AH...
WAS I TOO HARSH?
THIS DIARY IS...
MINE AND MOMOKA'S...
LET'S GO.

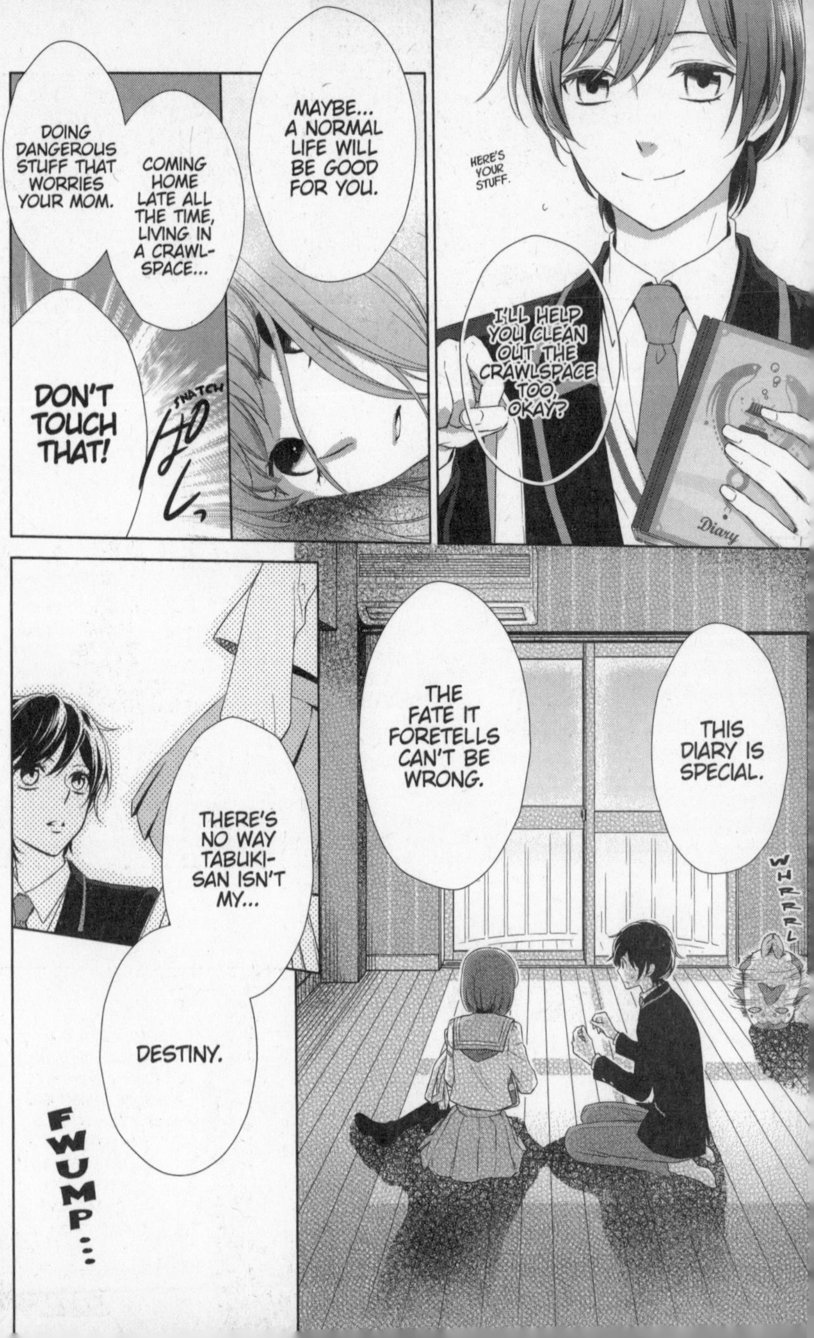
HERE'S YOUR STUFF.
I'LL HELP YOU CLEAN OUT THE CRAWLSPACE TOO, OKAY?
Diary
MAYBE... A NORMAL LIFE WILL BE GOOD FOR YOU.
COMING HOME LATE ALL THE TIME, LIVING IN A CRAWL-SPACE...
DOING DANGEROUS STUFF THAT WORRIES YOUR MOM.
SNATCH
DON'T TOUCH THAT!
WHRRRL
THIS DIARY IS SPECIAL.
THE FATE IT FORETELLS CAN'T BE WRONG.
THERE'S NO WAY TABUKI-SAN ISN'T MY...
DESTINY.
FWUMP...

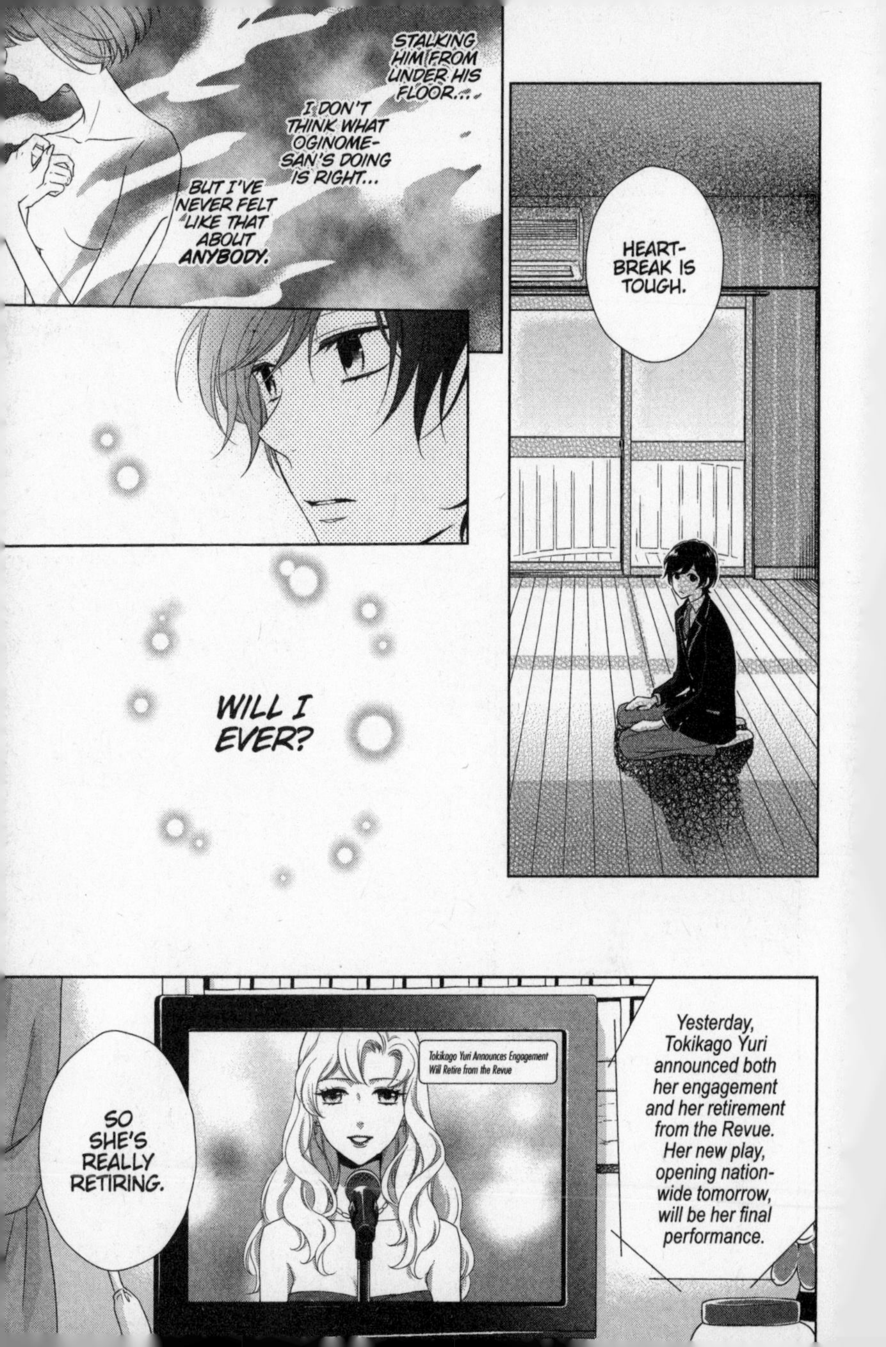
HEART-BREAK IS TOUGH.
STALKING HIM FROM UNDER HIS FLOOR...
I DON'T THINK WHAT OGINOME-SAN'S DOING IS RIGHT...
BUT I'VE NEVER FELT LIKE THAT ABOUT ANYBODY.
WILL I EVER?
Yesterday, Tokikago Yuri announced both her engagement and her retirement from the Revue. Her new play, opening nation-wide tomorrow, will be her final performance.
Tokikago Yuri Announces Engagement Will Retire from the Revue
SO SHE'S REALLY RETIRING.

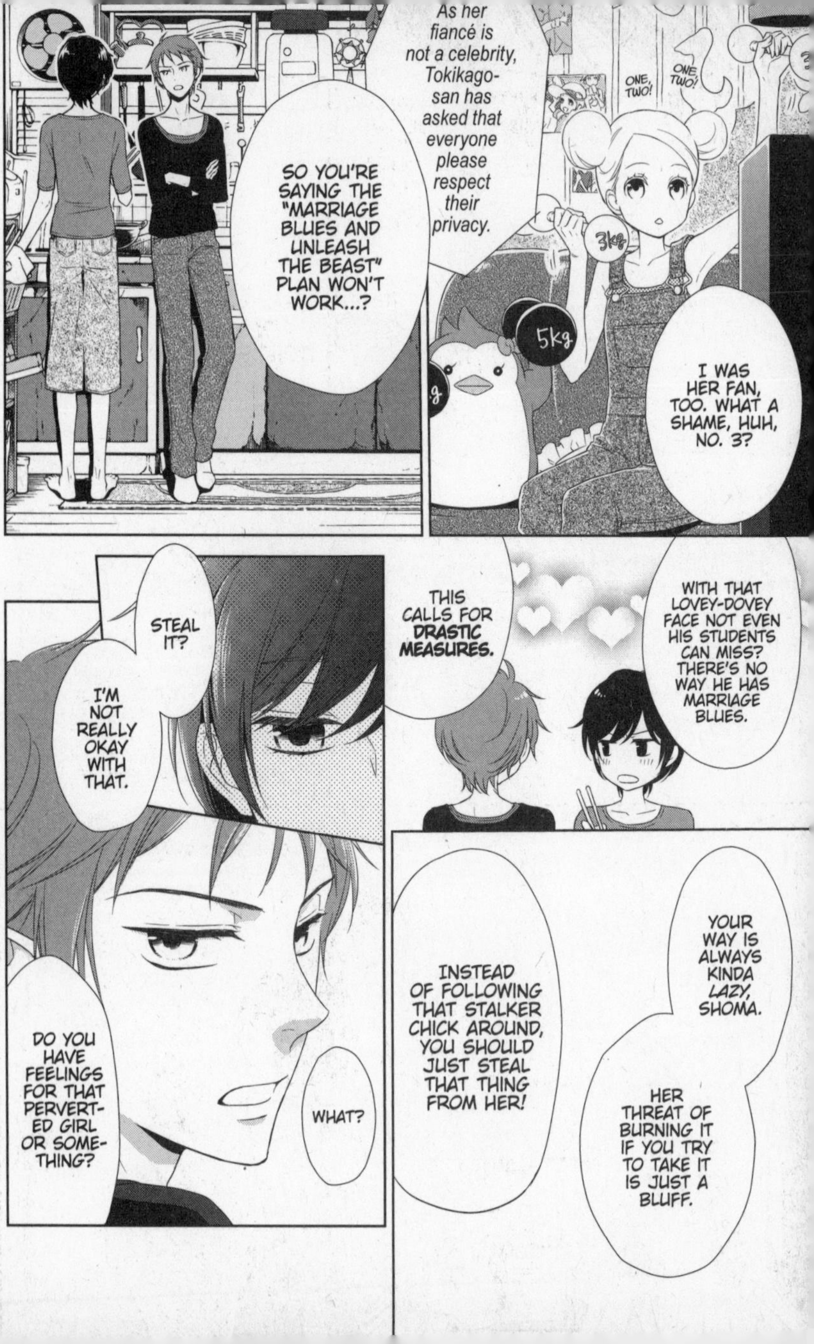
As her fiancé is not a celebrity, Tokikago-san has asked that everyone please respect their privacy.
ONE, TWO!
ONE, TWO!
3kg
5kg
I WAS HER FAN, TOO. WHAT A SHAME, HUH, NO. 3?
SO YOU'RE SAYING THE "MARRIAGE BLUES AND UNLEASH THE BEAST" PLAN WON'T WORK...?
WITH THAT LOVEY-DOVEY FACE NOT EVEN HIS STUDENTS CAN MISS? THERE'S NO WAY HE HAS MARRIAGE BLUES.
THIS CALLS FOR **DRASTIC MEASURES.**
YOUR WAY IS ALWAYS KINDA *LAZY,* SHOMA.
HER THREAT OF BURNING IT IF YOU TRY TO TAKE IT IS JUST A BLUFF.
INSTEAD OF FOLLOWING THAT STALKER CHICK AROUND, YOU SHOULD JUST STEAL THAT THING FROM HER!
STEAL IT?
I'M NOT REALLY OKAY WITH THAT.
WHAT?
DO YOU HAVE FEELINGS FOR THAT PERVERT-ED GIRL OR SOME-THING?

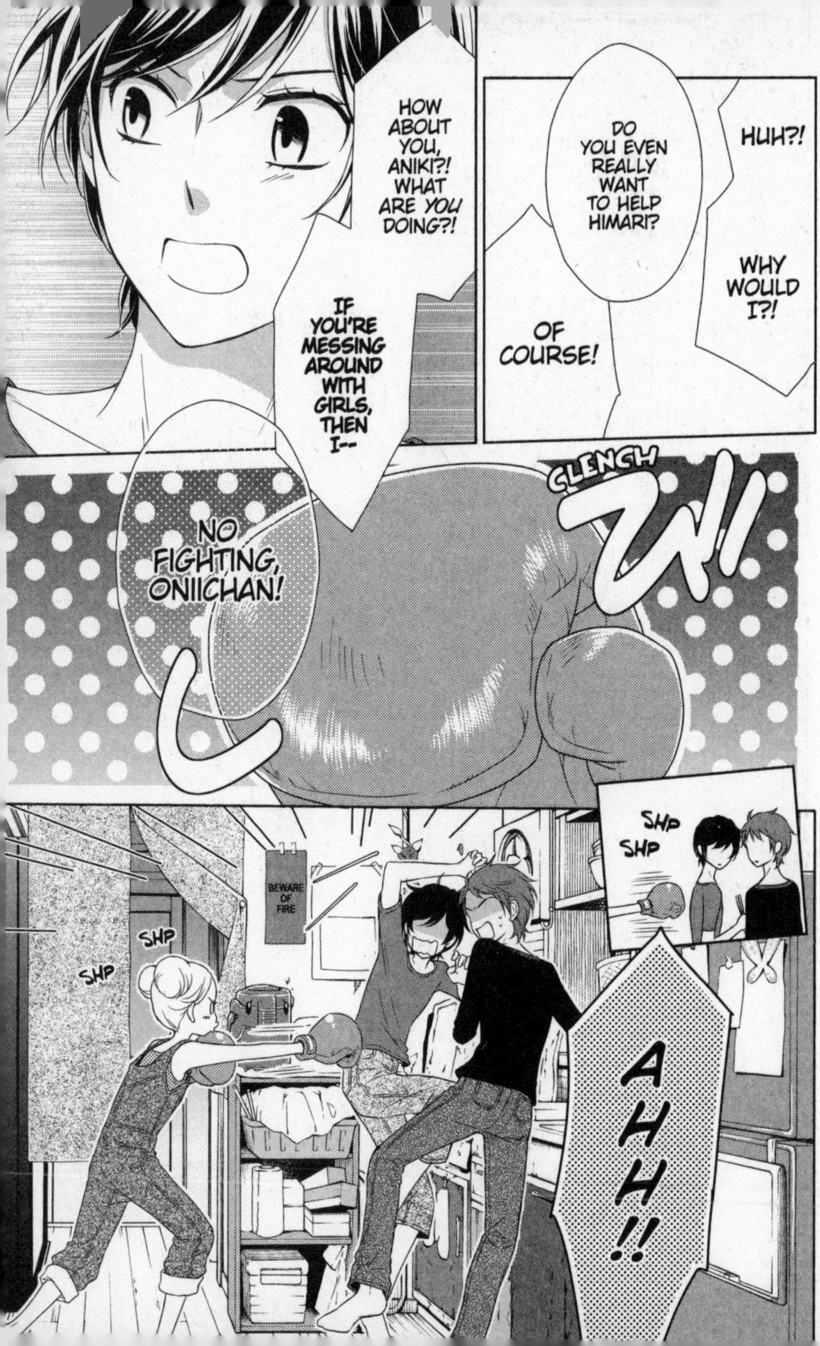
DO YOU EVEN REALLY WANT TO HELP HIMARI?
HUH?!
WHY WOULD I?!
OF COURSE!
HOW ABOUT YOU, ANIKI?! WHAT ARE YOU DOING?!
IF YOU'RE MESSING AROUND WITH GIRLS, THEN I--
CLENCH
NO FIGHTING, ONIICHAN!
SHP
SHP
AHH!!
BEWARE OF FIRE
SHP
SHP

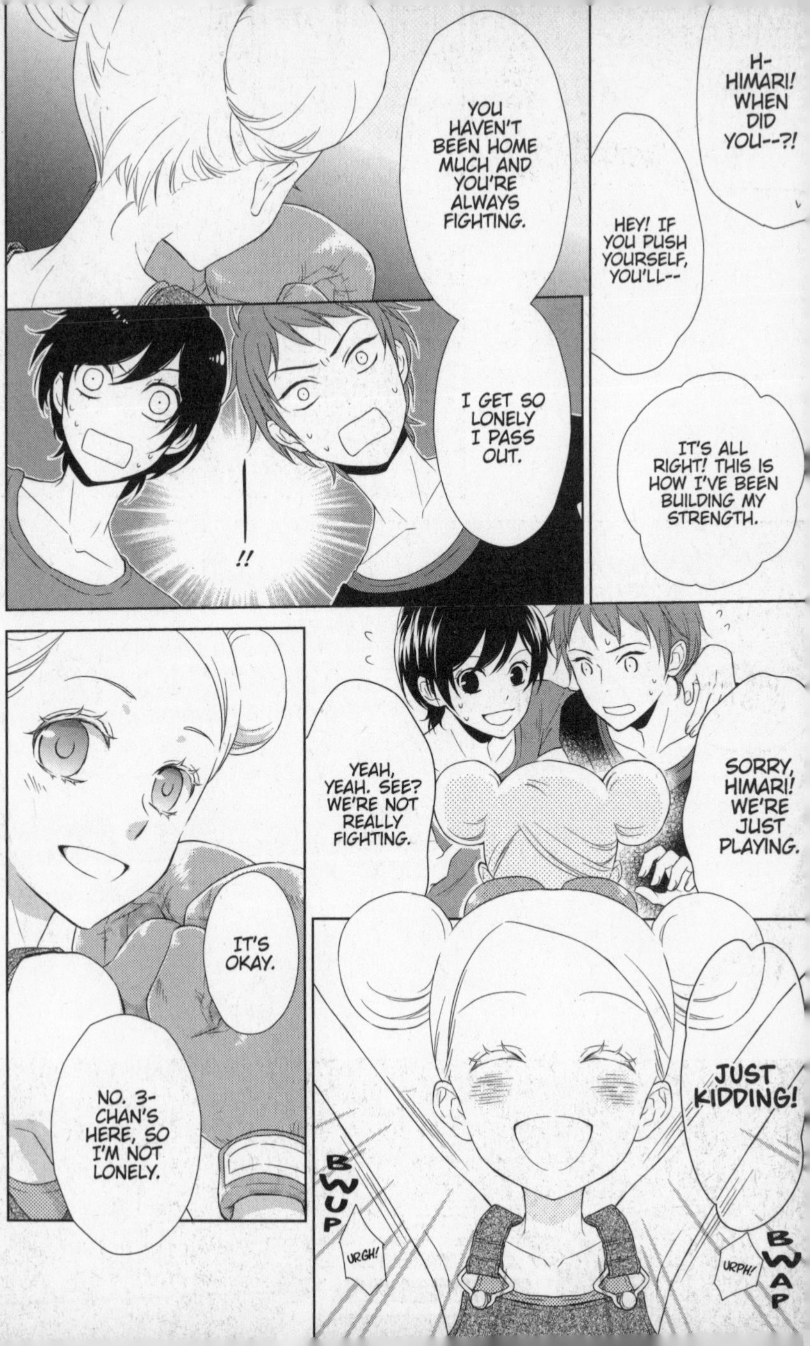
H-HIMARI! WHEN DID YOU--?!
HEY! IF YOU PUSH YOURSELF, YOU'LL--
IT'S ALL RIGHT! THIS IS HOW I'VE BEEN BUILDING MY STRENGTH.
YOU HAVEN'T BEEN HOME MUCH AND YOU'RE ALWAYS FIGHTING.
I GET SO LONELY I PASS OUT.
--!!
SORRY, HIMARI! WE'RE JUST PLAYING.
YEAH, YEAH. SEE? WE'RE NOT REALLY FIGHTING.
JUST KIDDING!
BWAP
URPH!
BWUP
URGH!
IT'S OKAY.
NO. 3-CHAN'S HERE, SO I'M NOT LONELY.

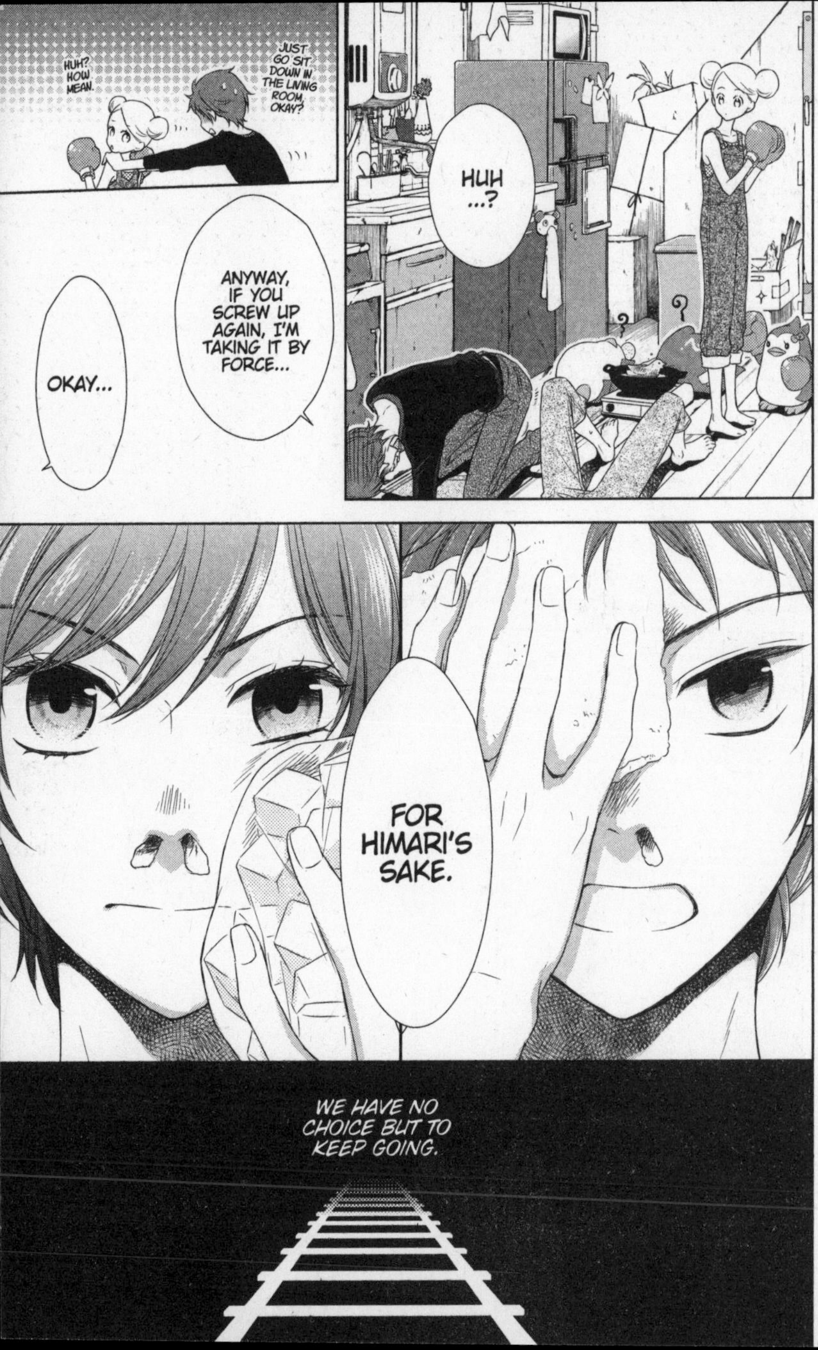
HUH ...?
JUST GO SIT DOWN IN THE LIVING ROOM, OKAY?
HUH? HOW MEAN.
ANYWAY, IF YOU SCREW UP AGAIN, I'M TAKING IT BY FORCE...
OKAY...
FOR HIMARI'S SAKE.
WE HAVE NO CHOICE BUT TO KEEP GOING.

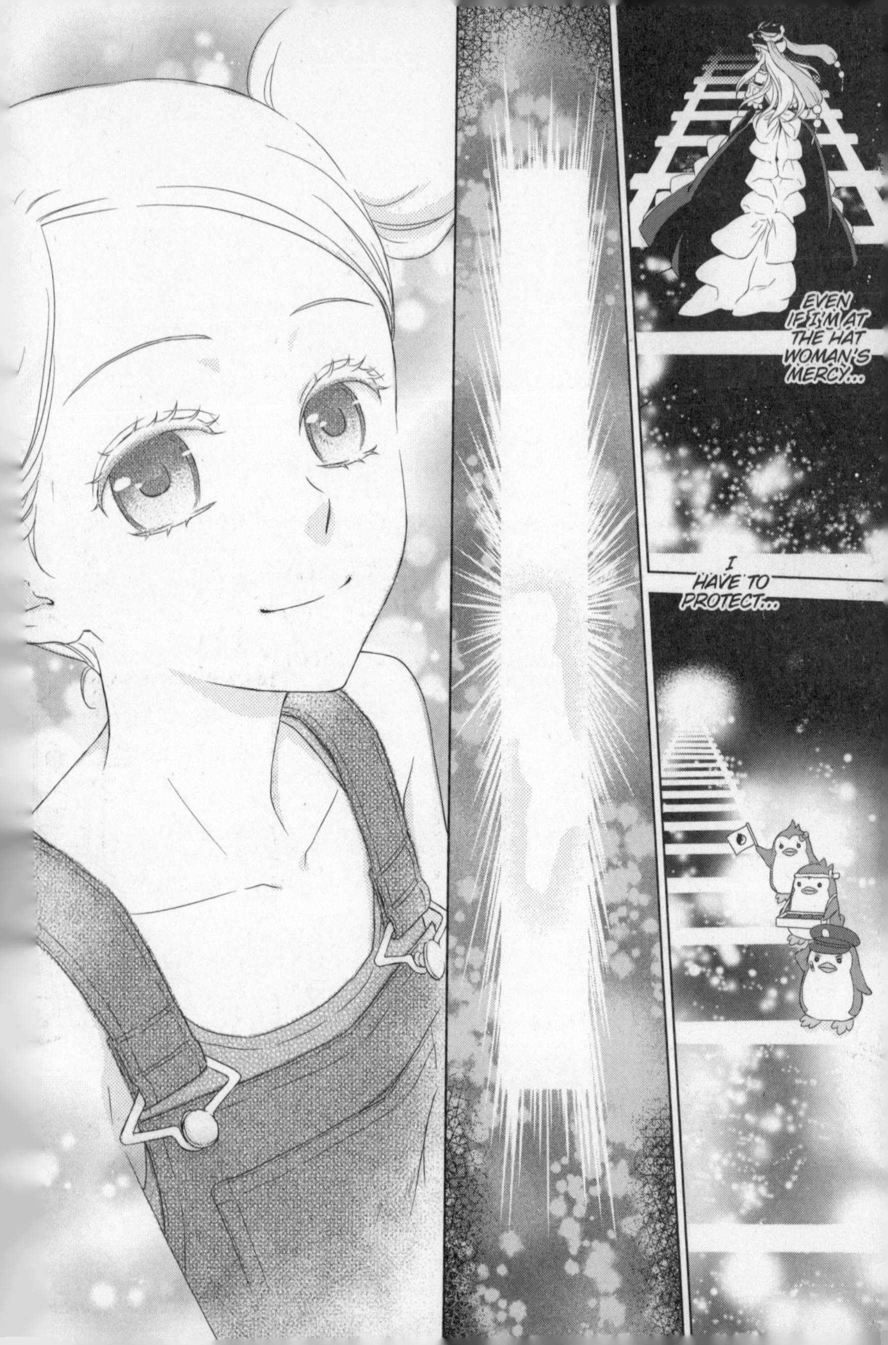
EVEN IF I'M AT THE HAT WOMAN'S MERCY...
I HAVE TO PROTECT...

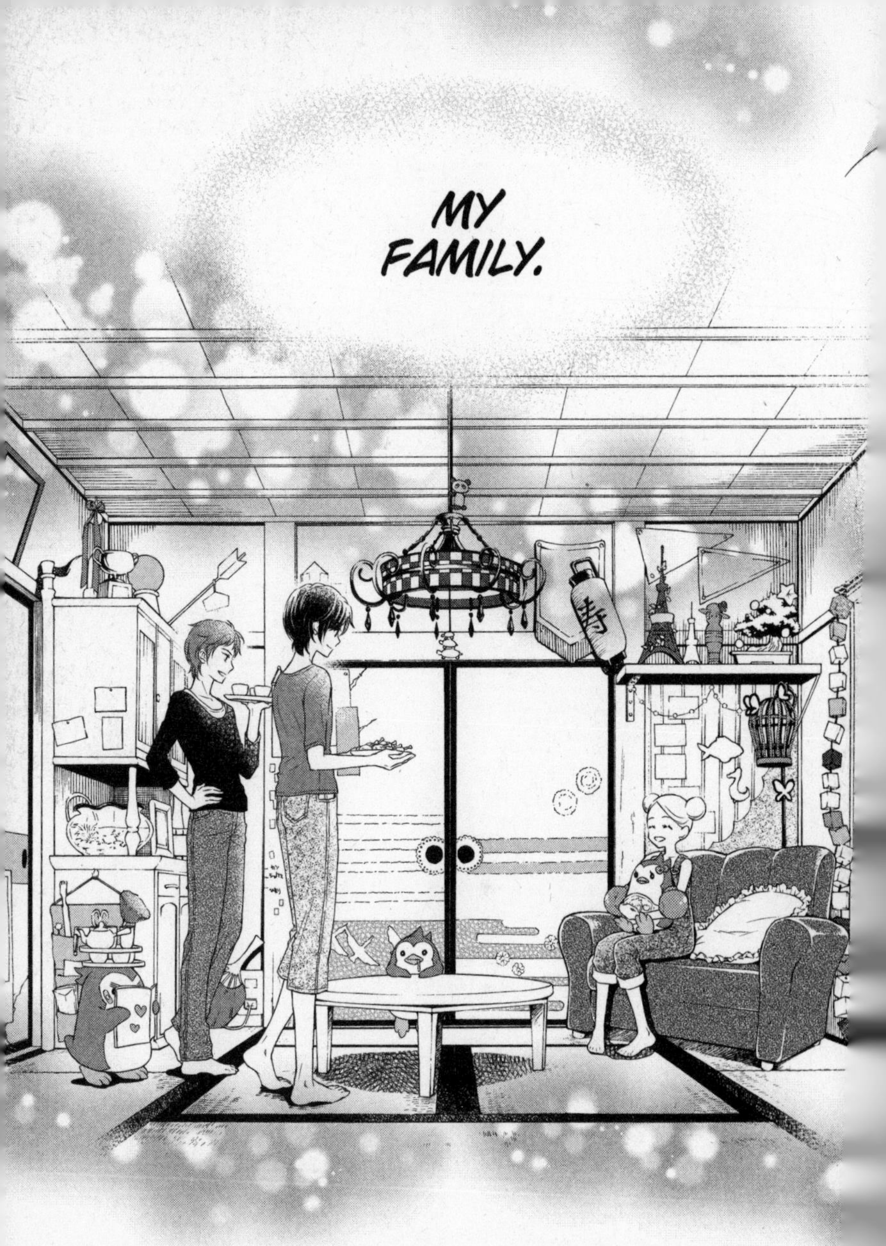
MY FAMILY.

Lantern: best wish

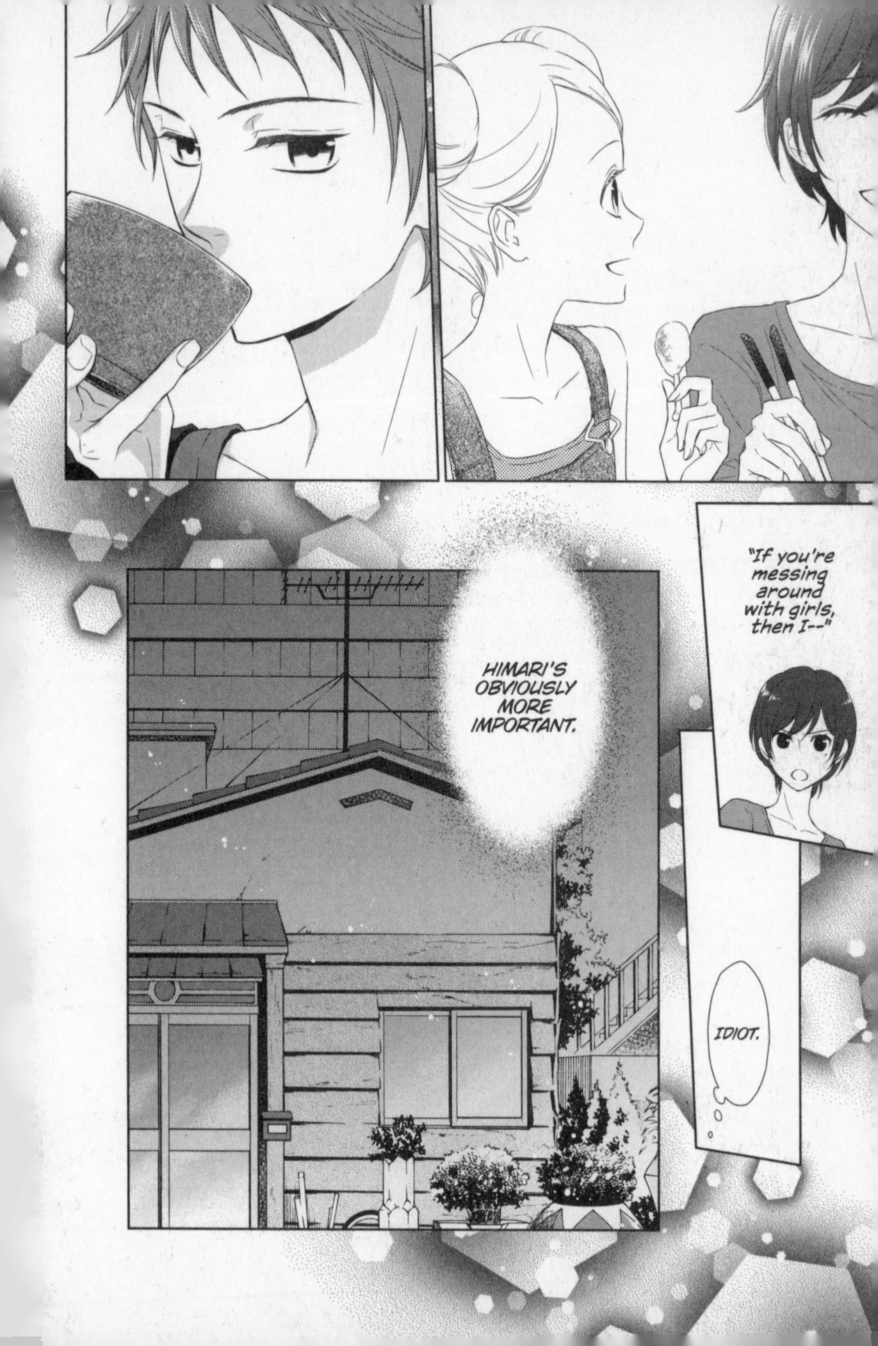
"If you're messing around with girls, then I--"
IDIOT.
HIMARI'S OBVIOUSLY MORE IMPORTANT.

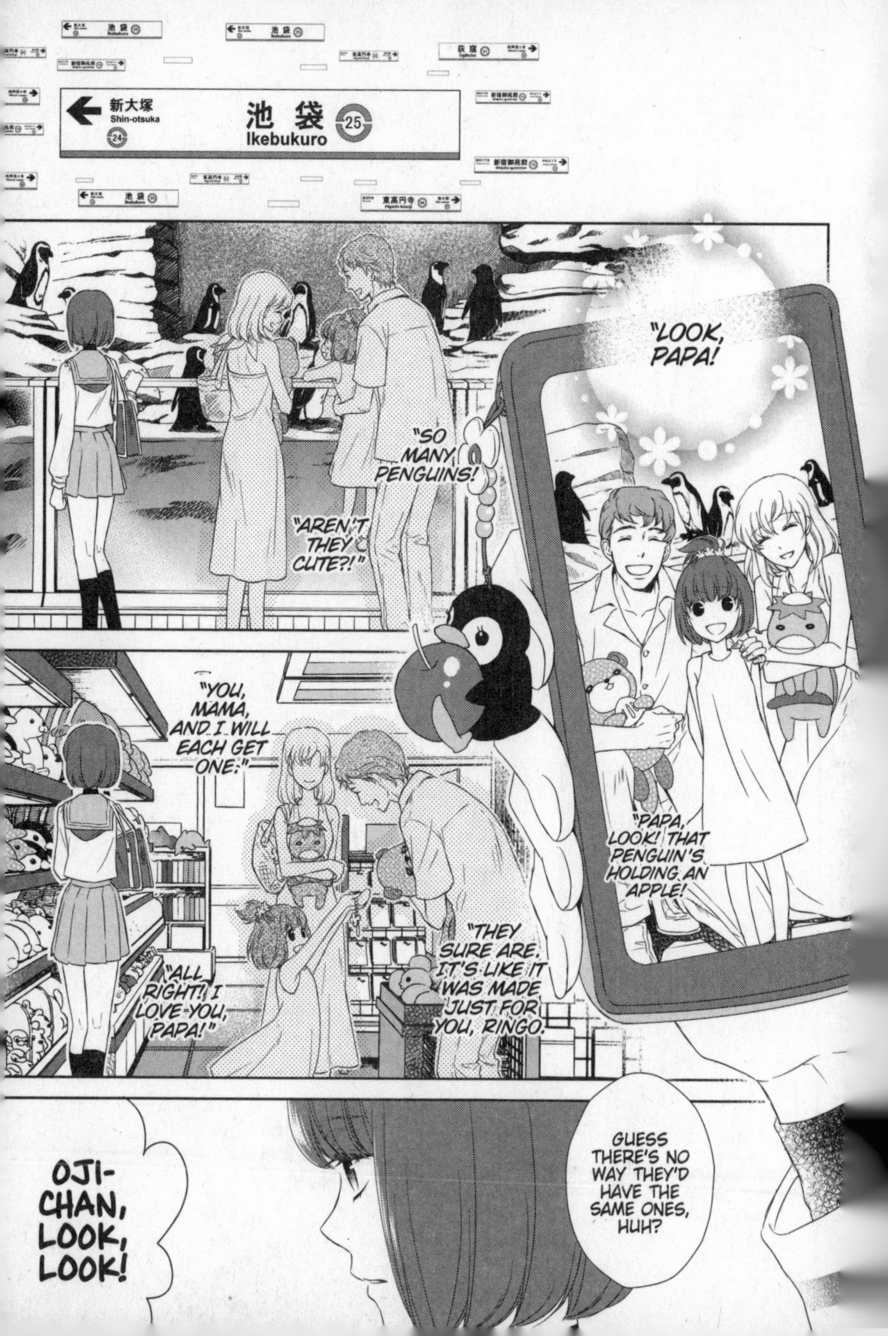

新大塚
Shin-otsuka
24
池袋
Ikebukuro
25
"LOOK, PAPA!
"PAPA, LOOK! THAT PENGUIN'S HOLDING AN APPLE!
"SO MANY PENGUINS!
"AREN'T THEY CUTE?!"
"THEY SURE ARE. IT'S LIKE IT WAS MADE JUST FOR YOU, RINGO.
"YOU, MAMA, AND I WILL EACH GET ONE."
"ALL RIGHT! I LOVE YOU, PAPA!"
GUESS THERE'S NO WAY THEY'D HAVE THE SAME ONES, HUH?
OJI-CHAN, LOOK, LOOK!

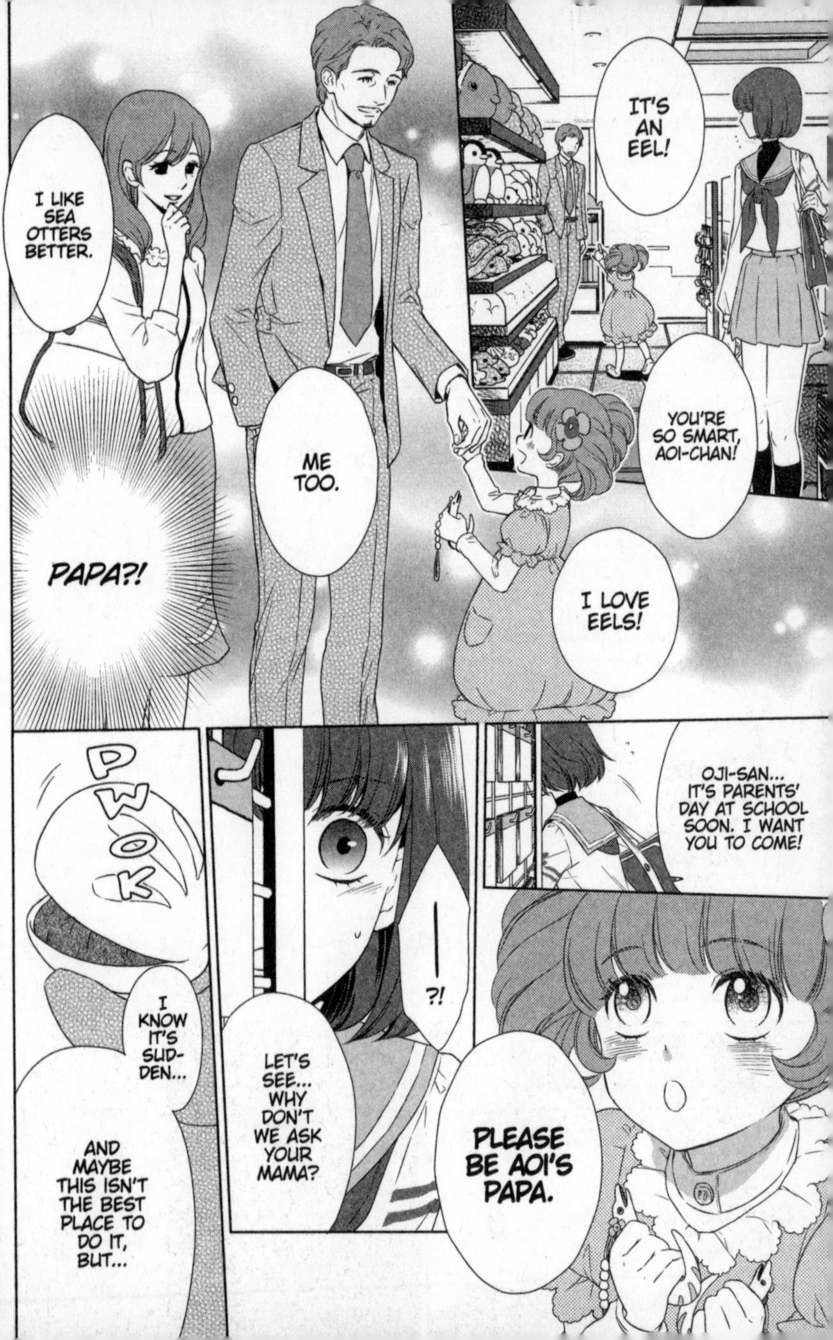
IT'S AN EEL!
YOU'RE SO SMART, AOI-CHAN!
I LOVE EELS!
ME TOO.
I LIKE SEA OTTERS BETTER.
PAPA?!
OJI-SAN... IT'S PARENTS' DAY AT SCHOOL SOON. I WANT YOU TO COME!
PLEASE BE AOI'S PAPA.
?!
LET'S SEE... WHY DON'T WE ASK YOUR MAMA?
PWOK
I KNOW IT'S SUD-DEN...
AND MAYBE THIS ISN'T THE BEST PLACE TO DO IT, BUT...

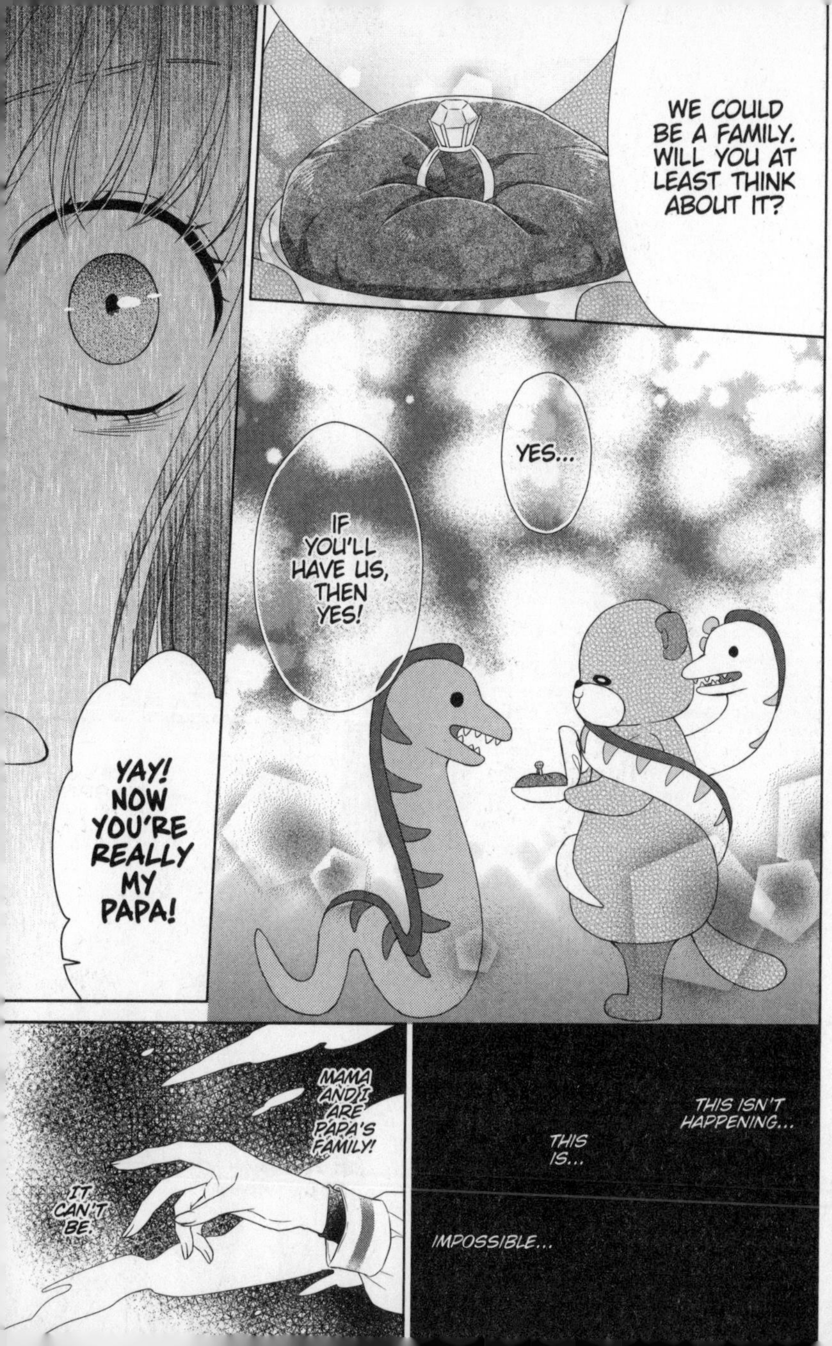
WE COULD BE A FAMILY. WILL YOU AT LEAST THINK ABOUT IT?
YES...
IF YOU'LL HAVE US, THEN YES!
YAY! NOW YOU'RE REALLY MY PAPA!
THIS ISN'T HAPPENING...
THIS IS...
IMPOSSIBLE...
MAMA AND I ARE PAPA'S FAMILY!
IT CAN'T BE.

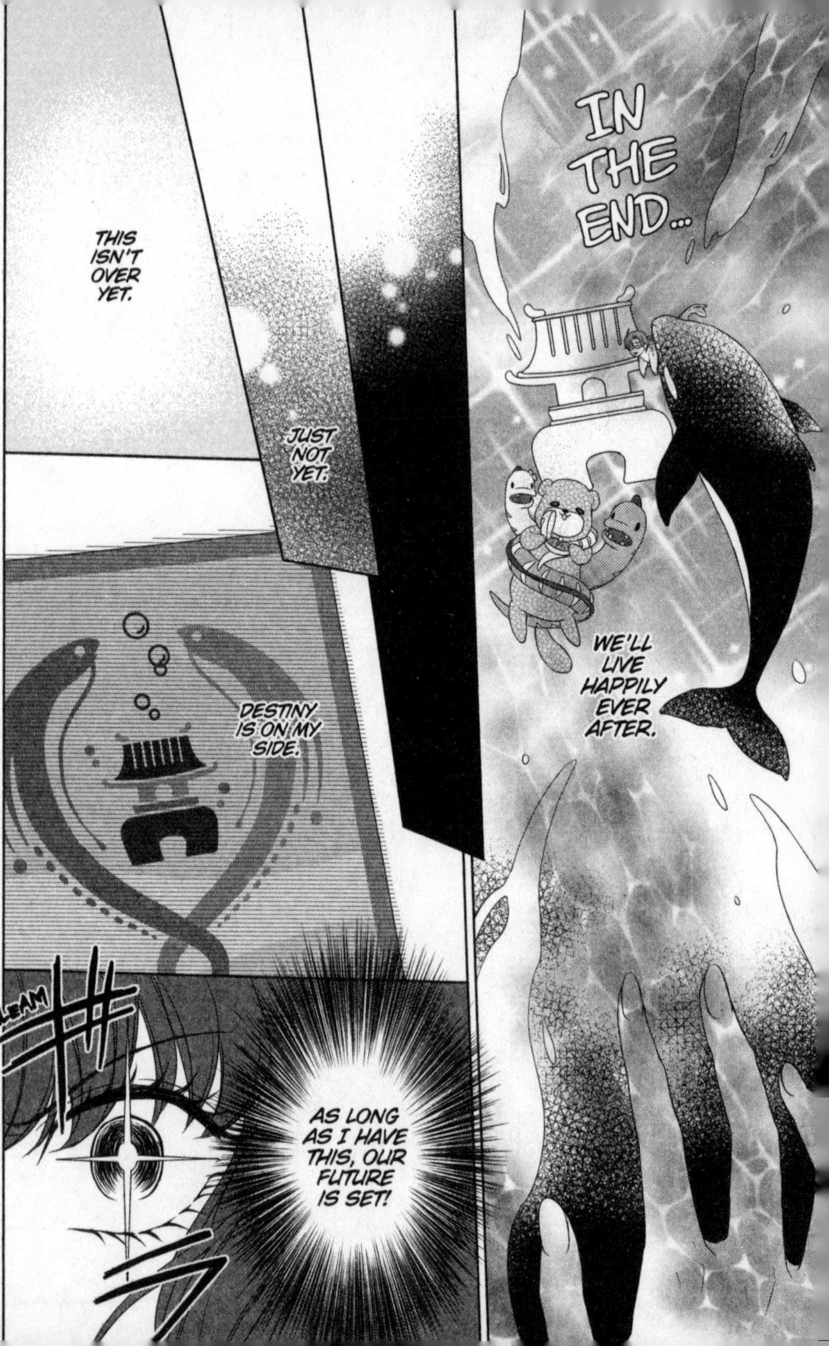
IN THE END...
WE'LL LIVE HAPPILY EVER AFTER.
THIS ISN'T OVER YET.
JUST NOT YET.
DESTINY IS ON MY SIDE.
GLEAM
AS LONG AS I HAVE THIS, OUR FUTURE IS SET!

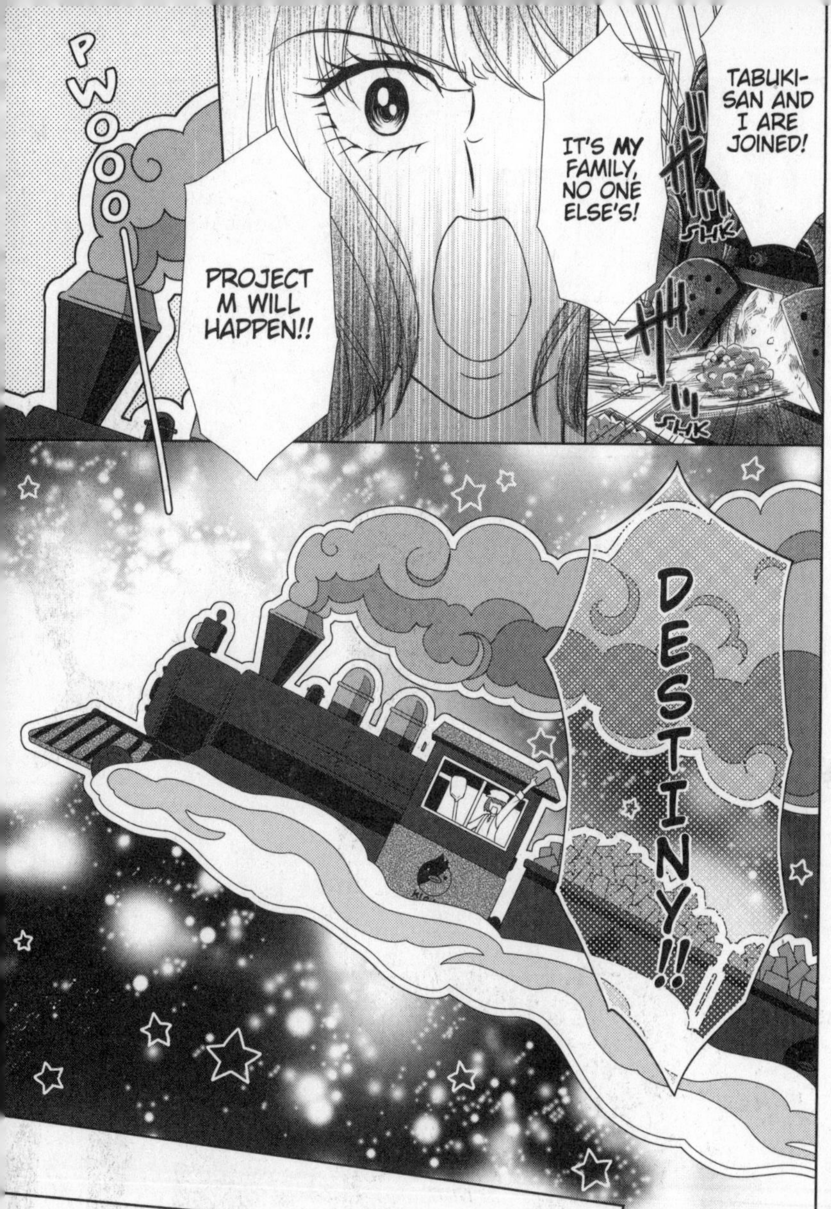
TABUKI-SAN AND I ARE JOINED!
SHK
SHK
IT'S MY FAMILY, NO ONE ELSE'S!
PROJECT M WILL HAPPEN!!
PWOOO
DESTINY!!

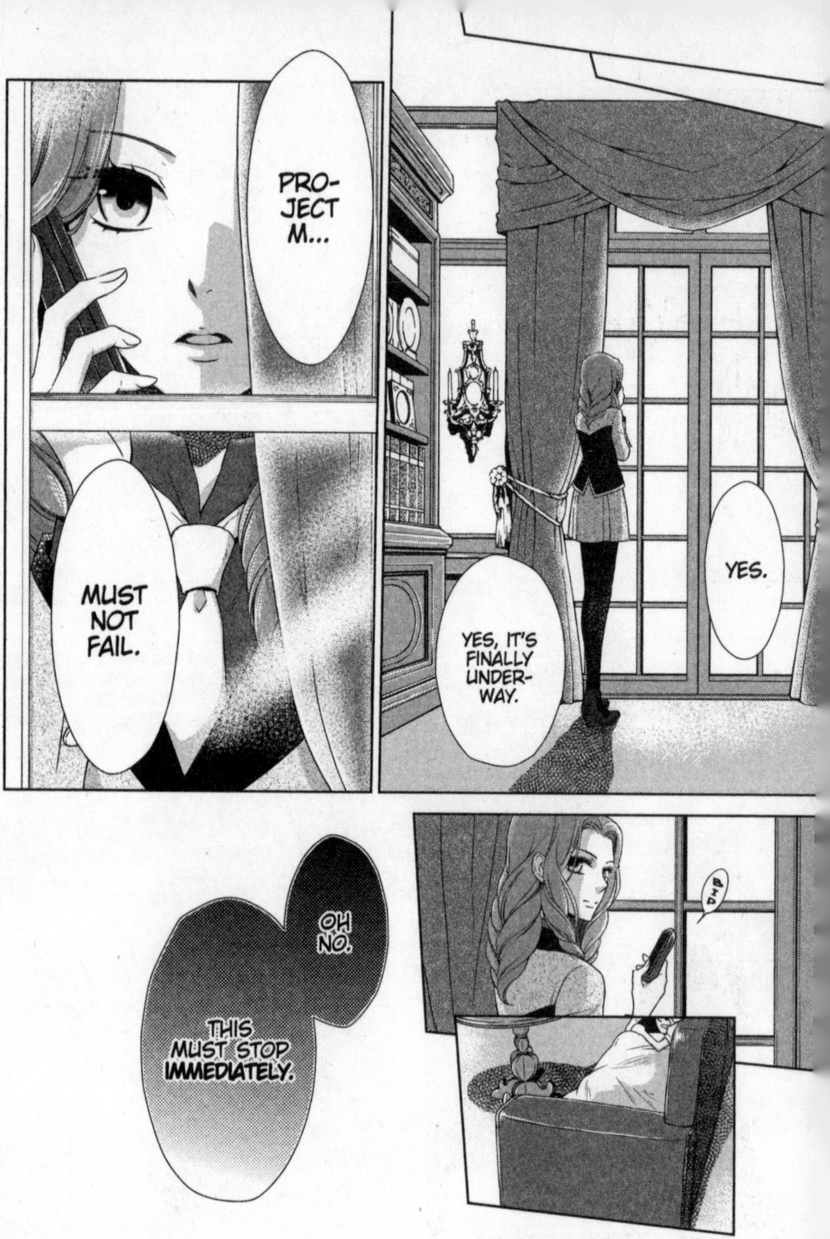
YES.
YES, IT'S FINALLY UNDERWAY.
PROJECT M...
MUST NOT FAIL.
BIP
OH NO.
THIS MUST STOP IMMEDIATELY.

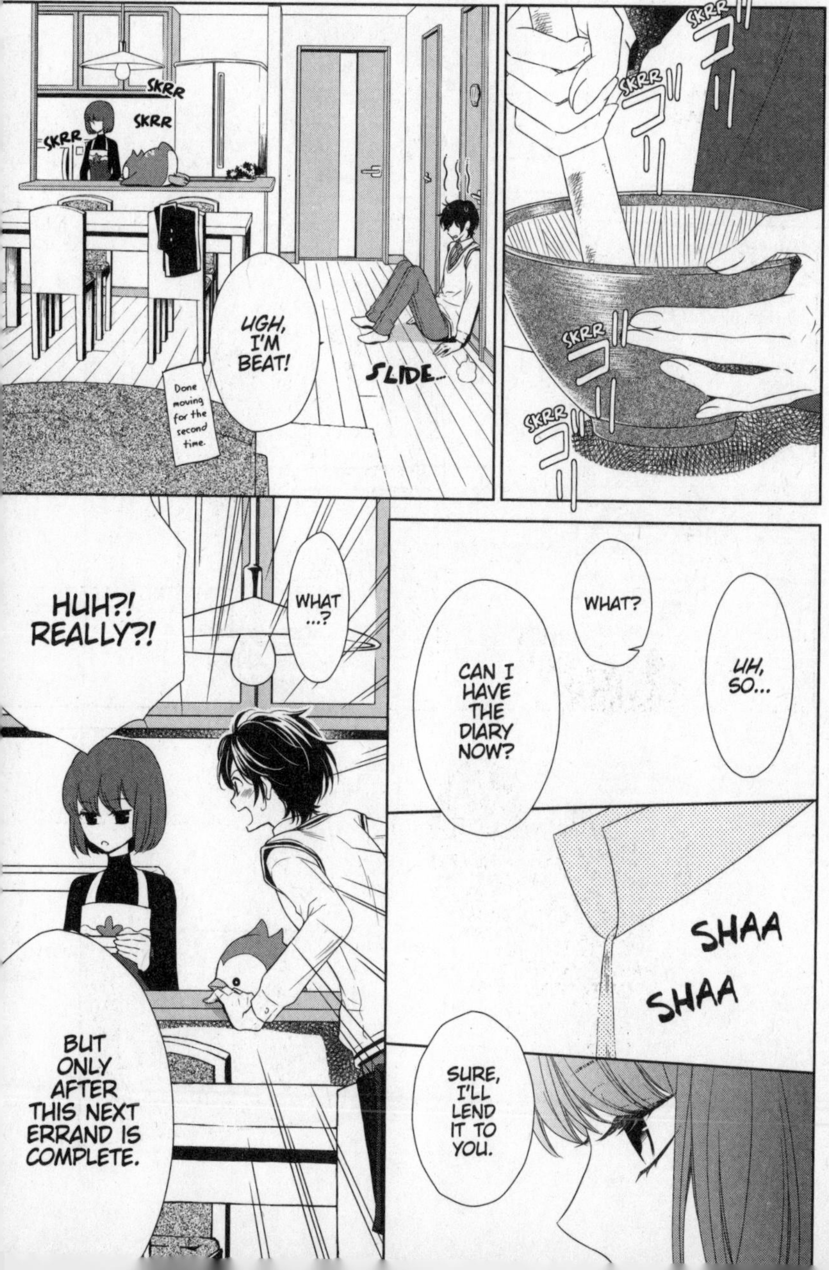
SKRR
SKRR
SKRR
SKRR
SKRR
SKRR
SKRR
UGH, I'M BEAT!
SLIDE...
Done moving for the second time.
UH, SO...
WHAT?
CAN I HAVE THE DIARY NOW?
SHAA
SHAA
SURE, I'LL LEND IT TO YOU.
WHAT ...?
HUH?! REALLY?!
BUT ONLY AFTER THIS NEXT ERRAND IS COMPLETE.

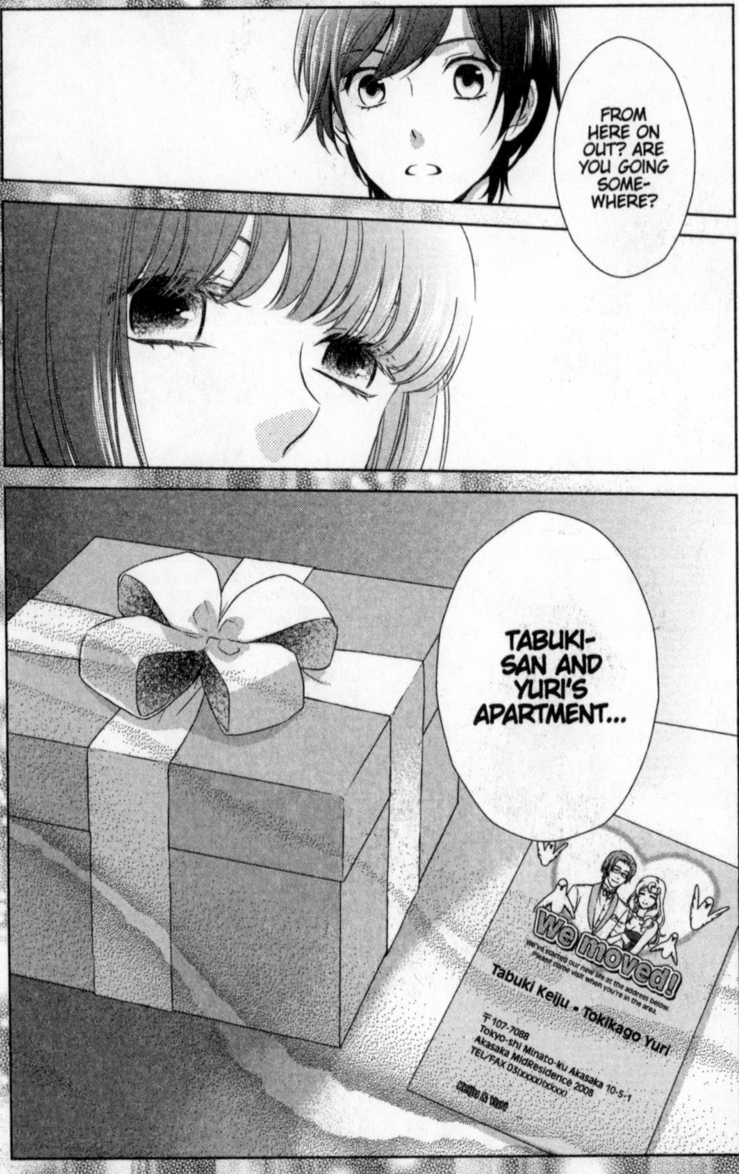
FROM HERE ON OUT? ARE YOU GOING SOME-WHERE?
TABUKI-SAN AND YURI'S APARTMENT...
We moved!
We've started our new life at the address below. Please come visit when you're in the area.
Tabuki Keiju ■ Tokikago Yuri
〒107-7088
Tokyo-shi Minato-ku Akasaka 10-5-1
Akasaka MidResidence 2008
TEL/FAX 03(xxxx)(xxxx)
Keiju & Yuri

10

10TH STATION

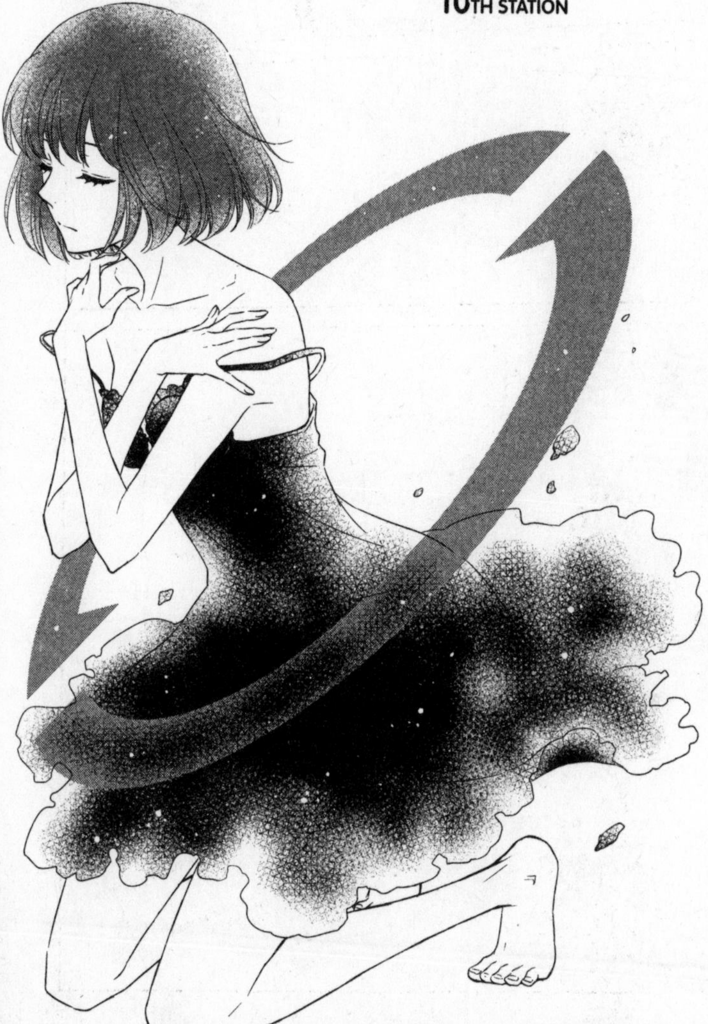

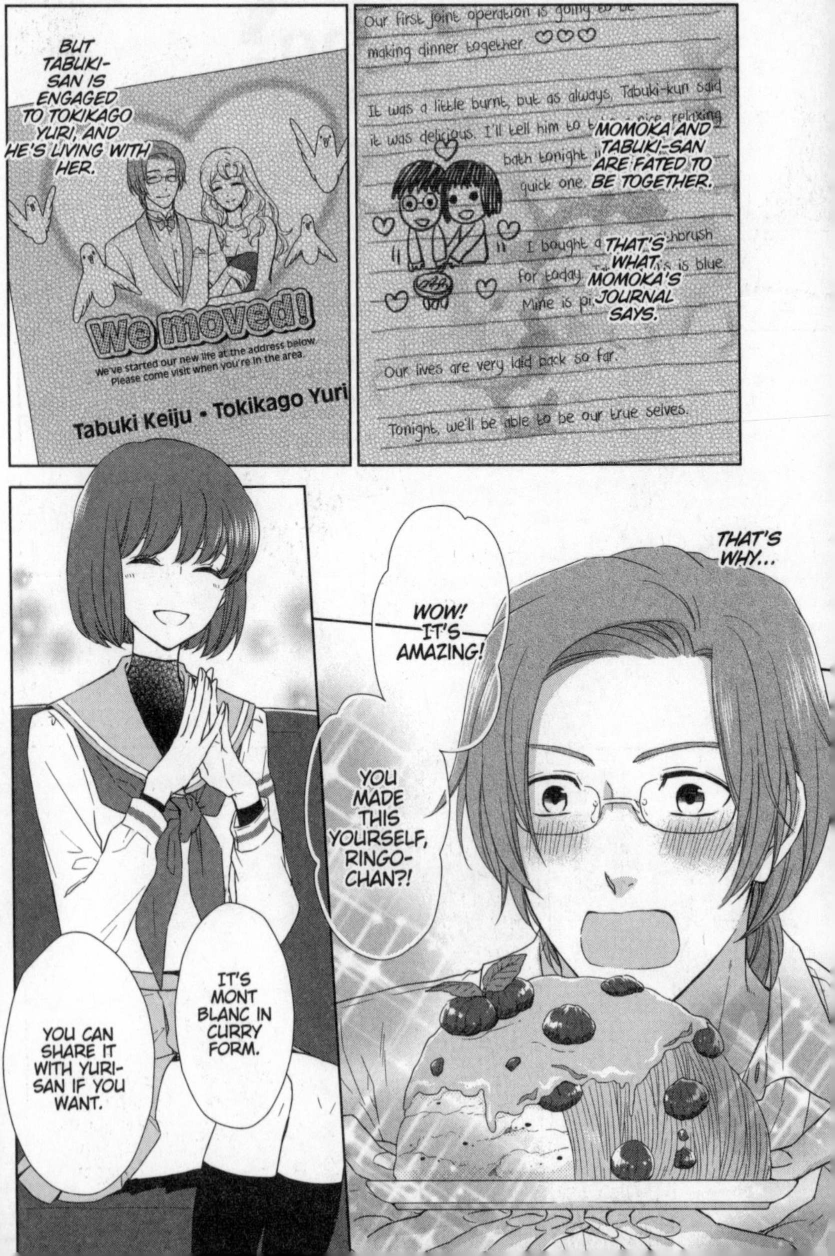

Our first joint operation is going to be
making dinner together.
It was a little burnt, but as always, Tabuki-kun said
Our lives are very laid back so far.
Tonight, we'll be able to be our true selves.
MOMOKA AND TABUKI-SAN ARE FATED TO BE TOGETHER.
THAT'S WHAT MOMOKA'S JOURNAL SAYS.
BUT TABUKI-SAN IS ENGAGED TO TOKIKAGO YURI, AND HE'S LIVING WITH HER.
We moved!
We've started our new life at the address below
Please come visit when you're in the area.
Tabuki Keiju • Tokikago Yuri
THAT'S WHY...
WOW! IT'S AMAZING!
YOU MADE THIS YOURSELF, RINGO-CHAN?!
IT'S MONT BLANC IN CURRY FORM.
YOU CAN SHARE IT WITH YURI-SAN IF YOU WANT.

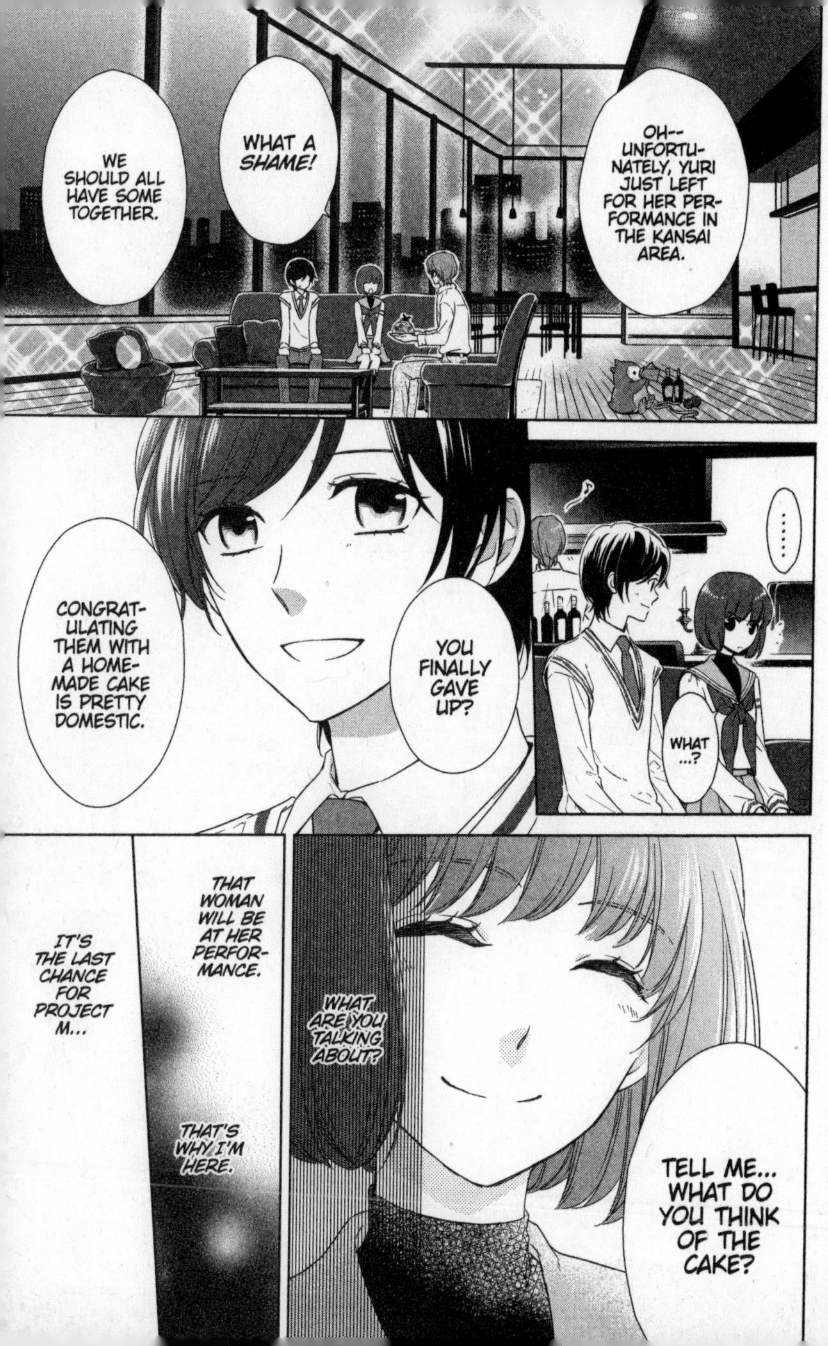
OH-- UNFORTUNATELY, YURI JUST LEFT FOR HER PERFORMANCE IN THE KANSAI AREA.
WHAT A SHAME!
WE SHOULD ALL HAVE SOME TOGETHER.
......
WHAT ...?
YOU FINALLY GAVE UP?
CONGRATULATING THEM WITH A HOMEMADE CAKE IS PRETTY DOMESTIC.
TELL ME... WHAT DO YOU THINK OF THE CAKE?
WHAT ARE YOU TALKING ABOUT?
THAT WOMAN WILL BE AT HER PERFORMANCE.
IT'S THE LAST CHANCE FOR PROJECT M...
THAT'S WHY I'M HERE.

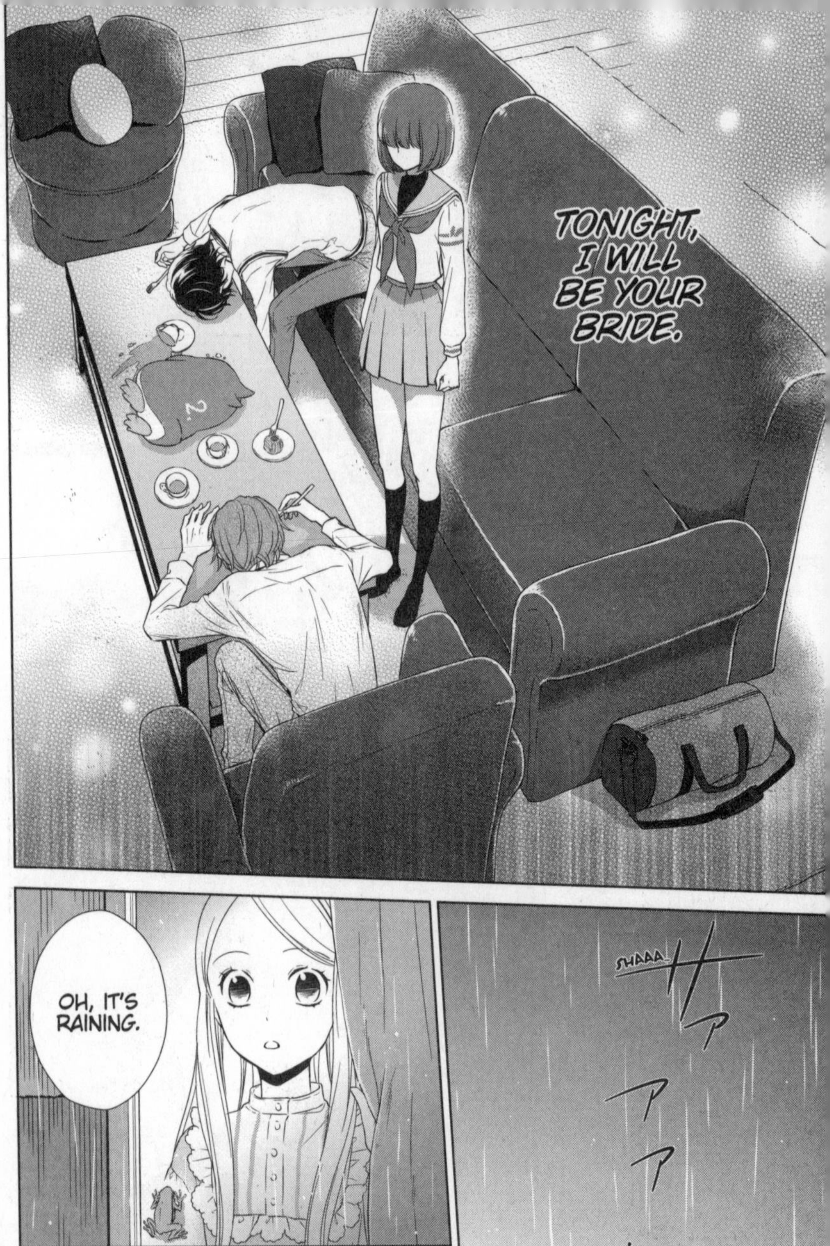
TONIGHT, I WILL BE YOUR BRIDE.
SHAAA...
OH, IT'S RAINING.

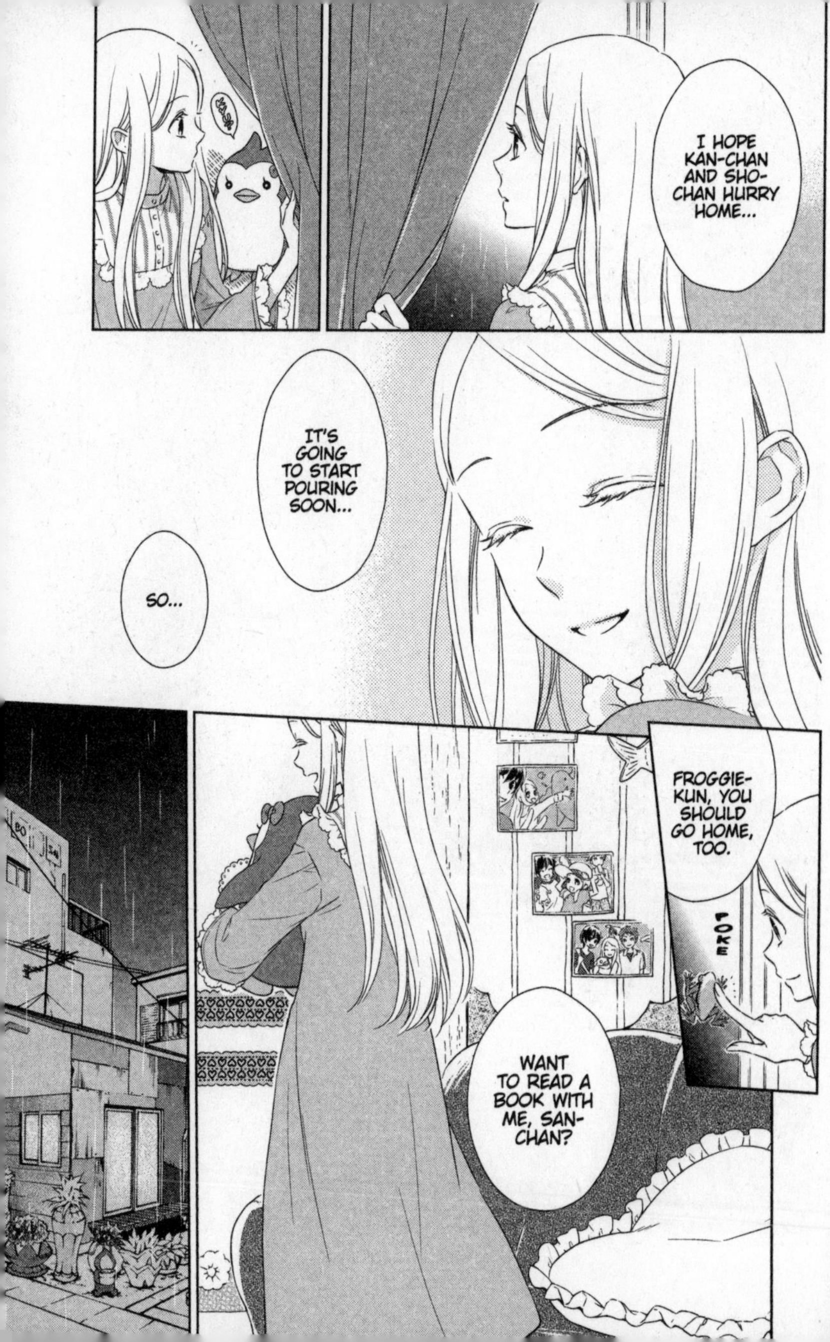
I HOPE KAN-CHAN AND SHO-CHAN HURRY HOME...
IT'S GOING TO START POURING SOON...
SO...
FROGGIE-KUN, YOU SHOULD GO HOME, TOO.
POKE
WANT TO READ A BOOK WITH ME, SAN-CHAN?

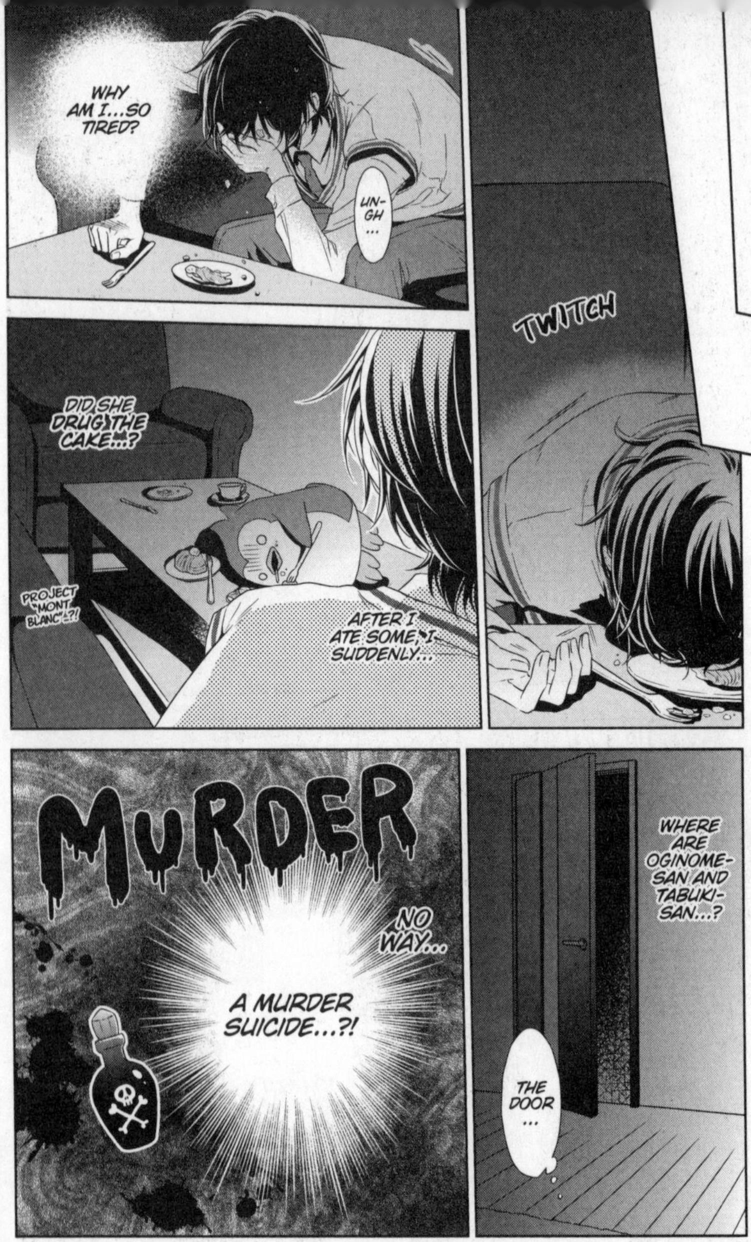
TWITCH
UN-GH...
WHY AM I...SO TIRED?
AFTER I ATE SOME, I SUDDENLY...
DID SHE DRUG THE CAKE...?
PROJECT "MONT BLANC"-?!
WHERE ARE OGINOME-SAN AND TABUKI-SAN...?
THE DOOR...
NO WAY...
MURDER
A MURDER SUICIDE...?!

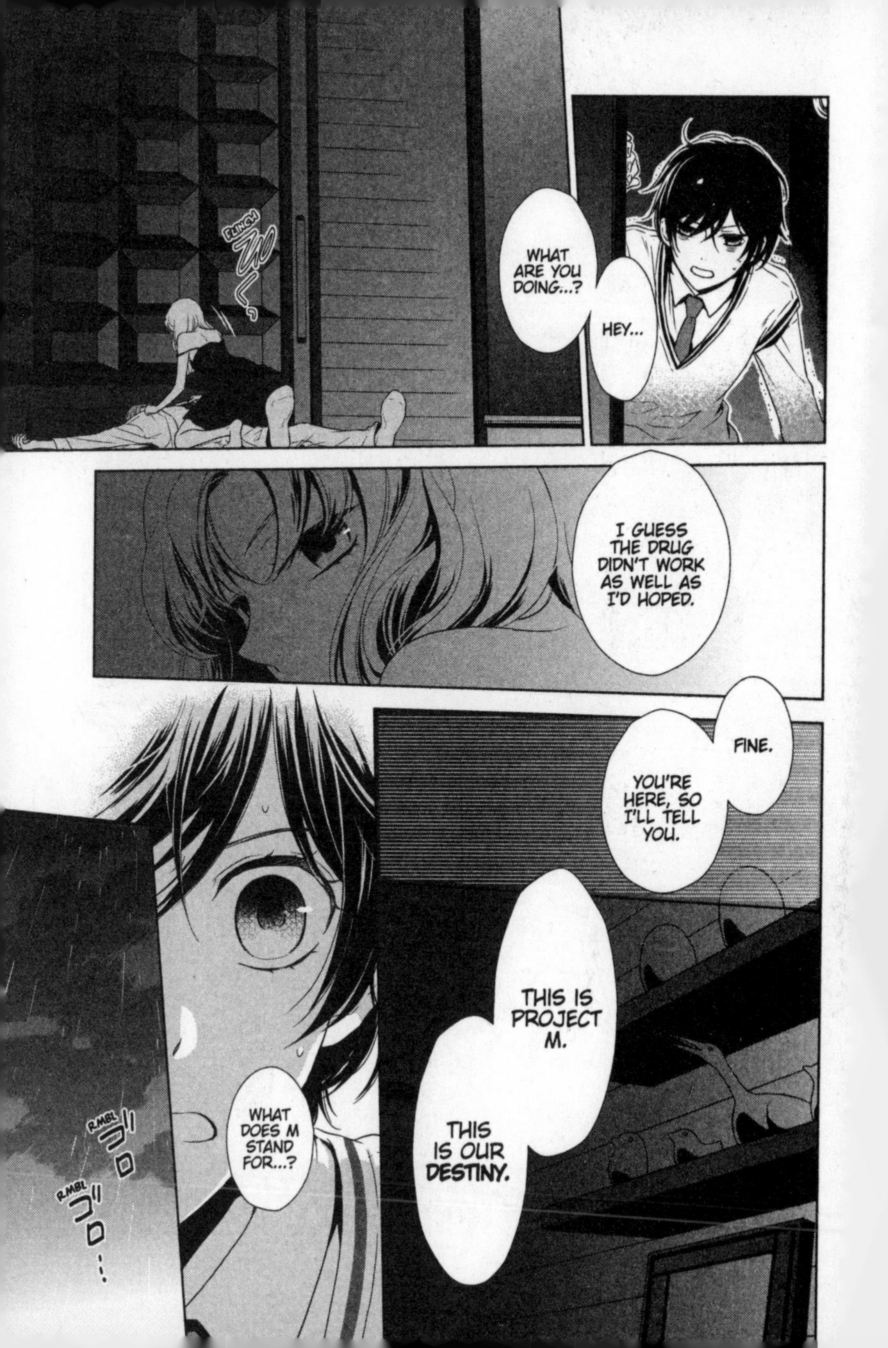
HEY...
WHAT ARE YOU DOING...?
FLINCH
I GUESS THE DRUG DIDN'T WORK AS WELL AS I'D HOPED.
FINE.
YOU'RE HERE, SO I'LL TELL YOU.
THIS IS PROJECT M.
THIS IS OUR DESTINY.
WHAT DOES M STAND FOR...?
RMBL
RMBL

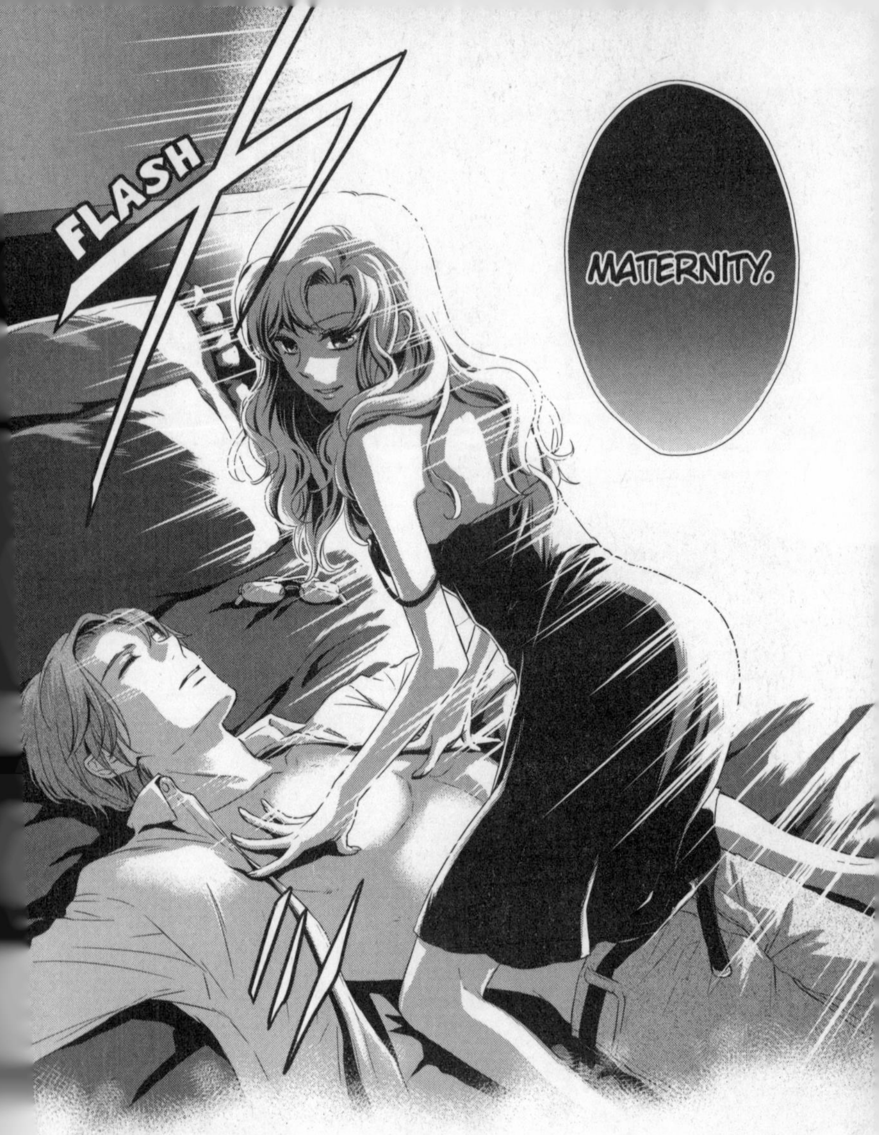
MATERNITY.
FLASH

Project M = Operation Maternity!

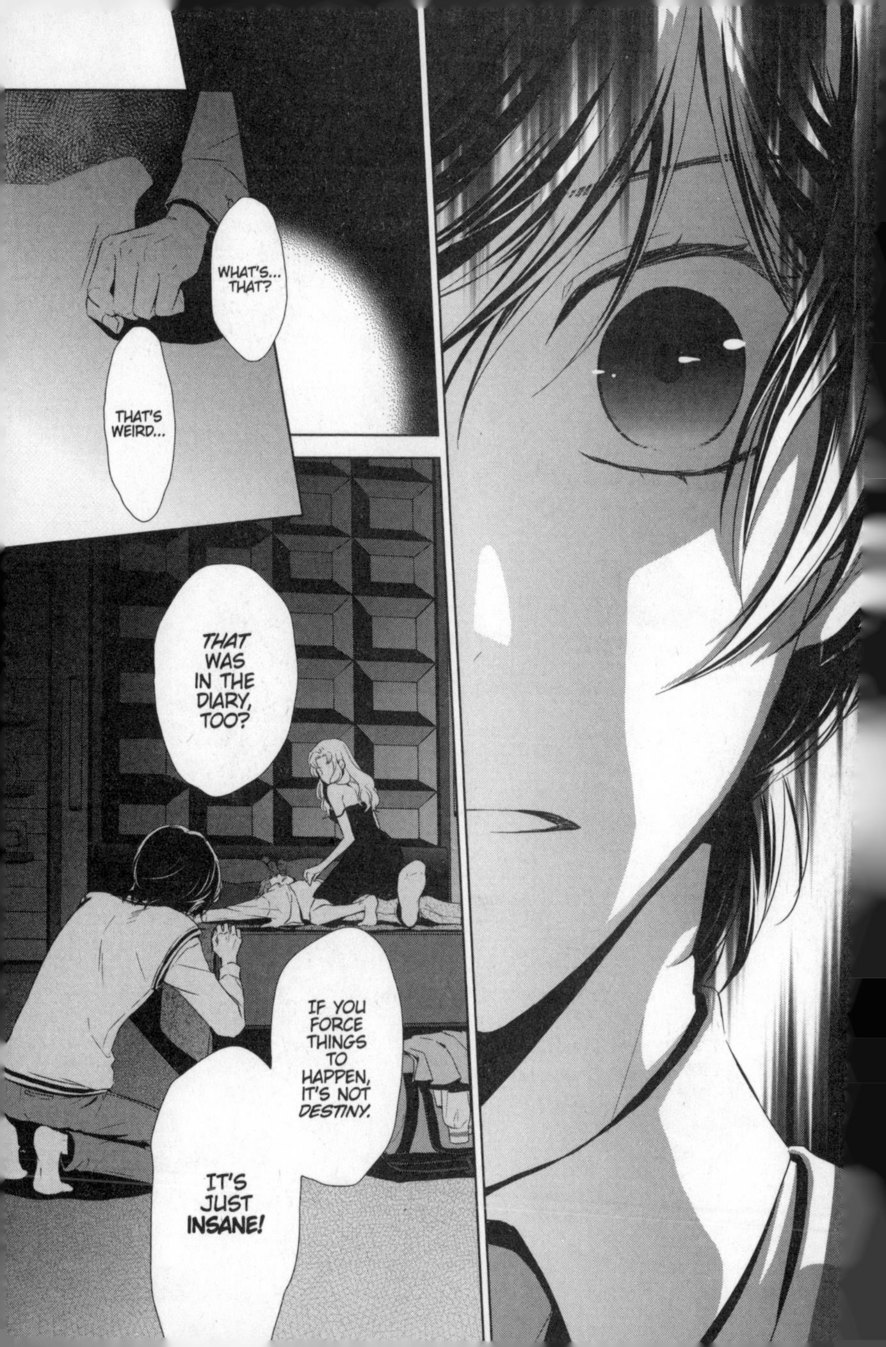
WHAT'S... THAT?
THAT'S WEIRD...
THAT WAS IN THE DIARY, TOO?
IF YOU FORCE THINGS TO HAPPEN, IT'S NOT *DESTINY.*
IT'S JUST **INSANE!**

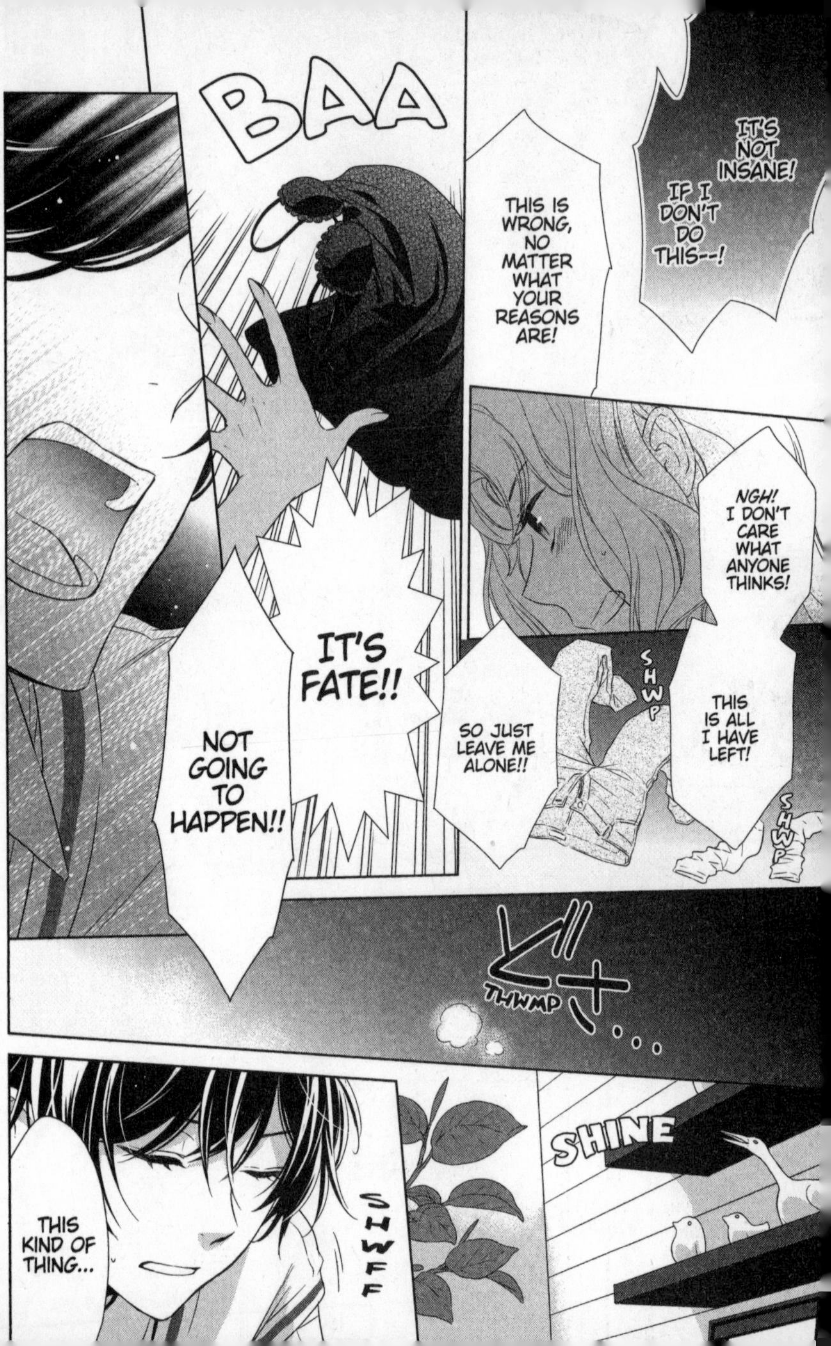
IT'S NOT INSANE!
IF I DON'T DO THIS--!
THIS IS WRONG, NO MATTER WHAT YOUR REASONS ARE!
NGH! I DON'T CARE WHAT ANYONE THINKS!
THIS IS ALL I HAVE LEFT!
SHWP
SHWP
SO JUST LEAVE ME ALONE!!
BAA
IT'S FATE!!
NOT GOING TO HAPPEN!!
THWMP
...
SHINE
SHWFF
THIS KIND OF THING...

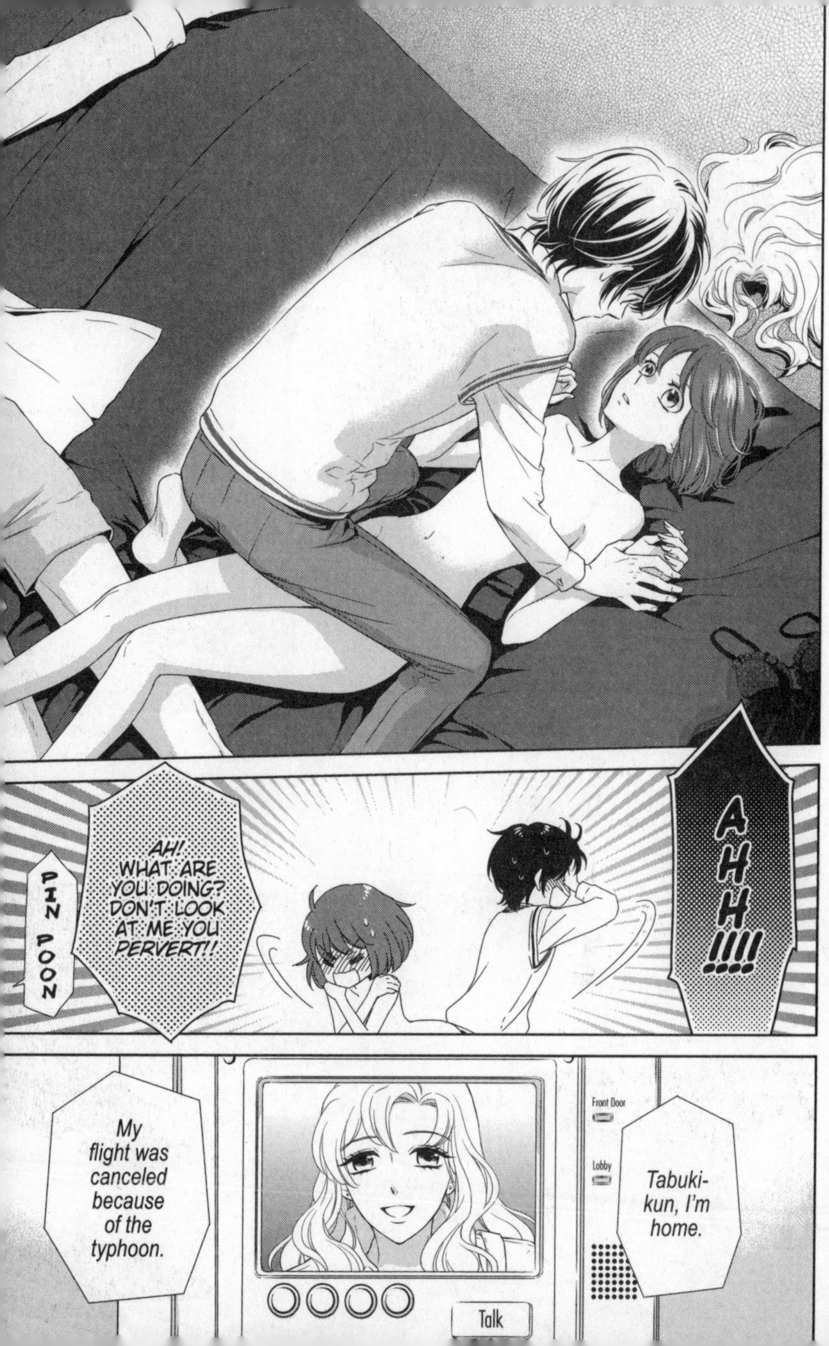
AHH!!!!
AH! WHAT ARE YOU DOING? DON'T LOOK AT ME YOU PERVERT!!
PIN POON
Tabuki-kun, I'm home.
Front Door
Lobby
Talk
My flight was canceled because of the typhoon.

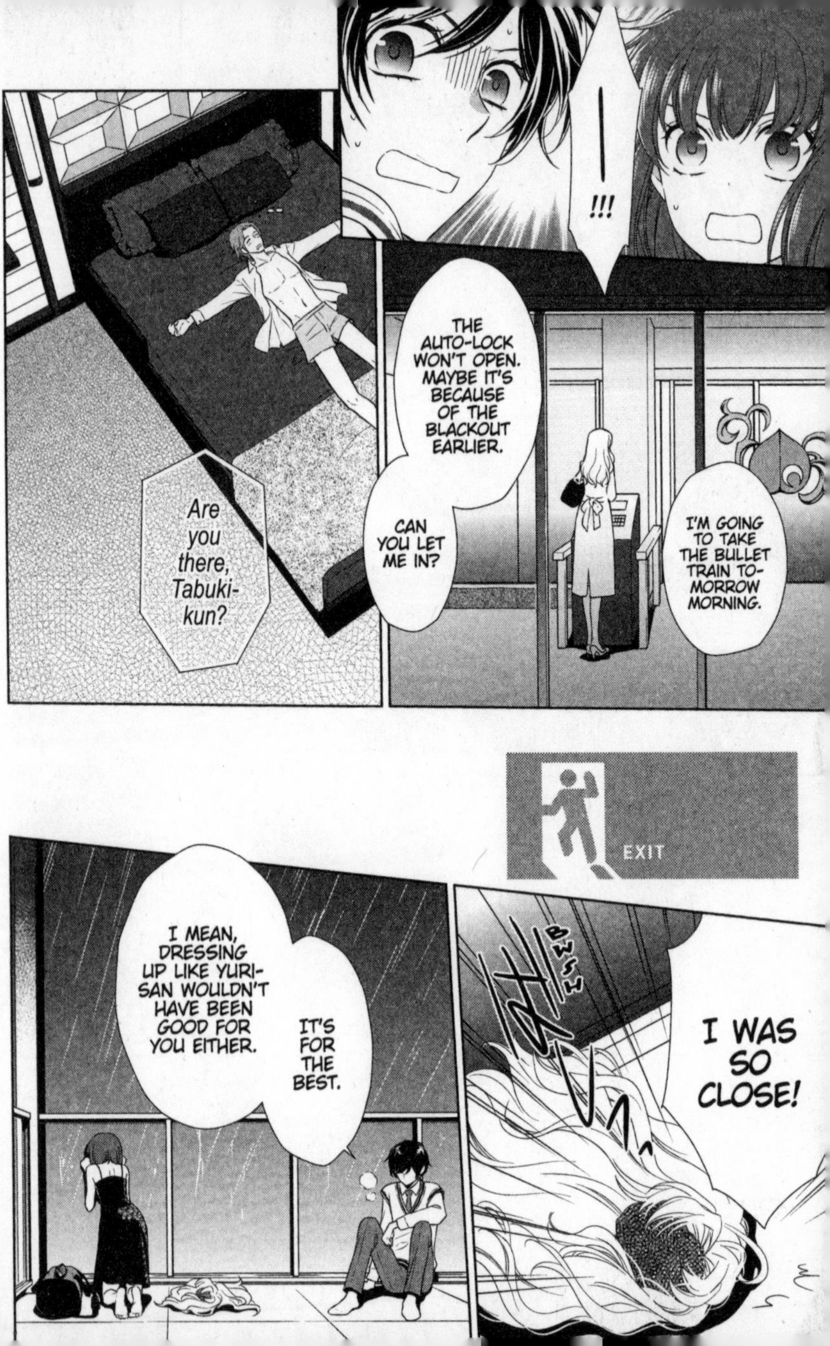
!!!
THE AUTO-LOCK WON'T OPEN. MAYBE IT'S BECAUSE OF THE BLACKOUT EARLIER.
CAN YOU LET ME IN?
I'M GOING TO TAKE THE BULLET TRAIN TO-MORROW MORNING.
Are you there, Tabuki-kun?
EXIT
BWSH
I WAS SO CLOSE!
I MEAN, DRESSING UP LIKE YURI-SAN WOULDN'T HAVE BEEN GOOD FOR YOU EITHER.
IT'S FOR THE BEST.

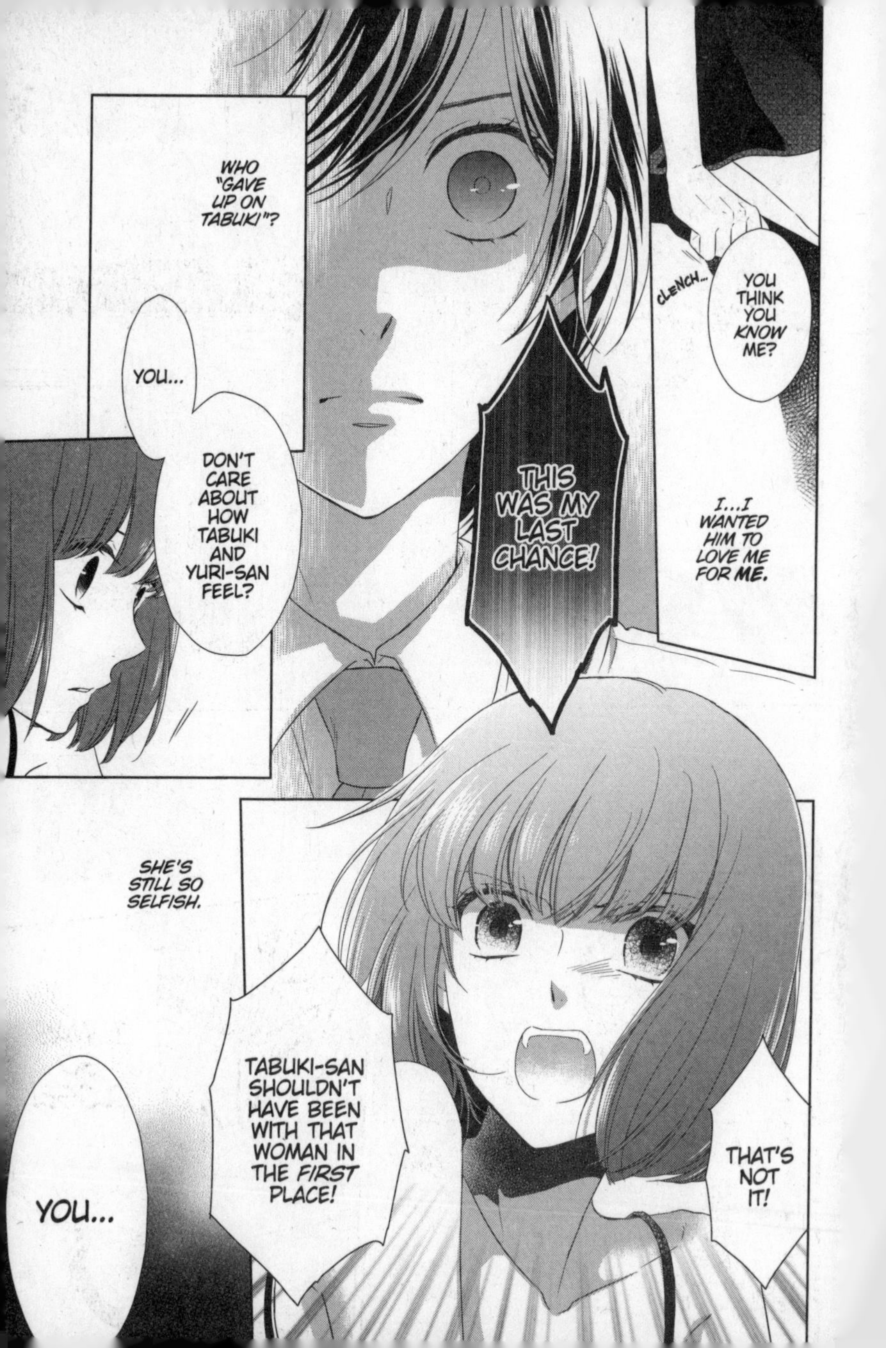
CLENCH...
YOU THINK YOU KNOW ME?
I...I WANTED HIM TO LOVE ME FOR ME.
THIS WAS MY LAST CHANCE!
WHO "GAVE UP ON TABUKI"?
YOU...
DON'T CARE ABOUT HOW TABUKI AND YURI-SAN FEEL?
THAT'S NOT IT!
TABUKI-SAN SHOULDN'T HAVE BEEN WITH THAT WOMAN IN THE FIRST PLACE!
SHE'S STILL SO SELFISH.
YOU...

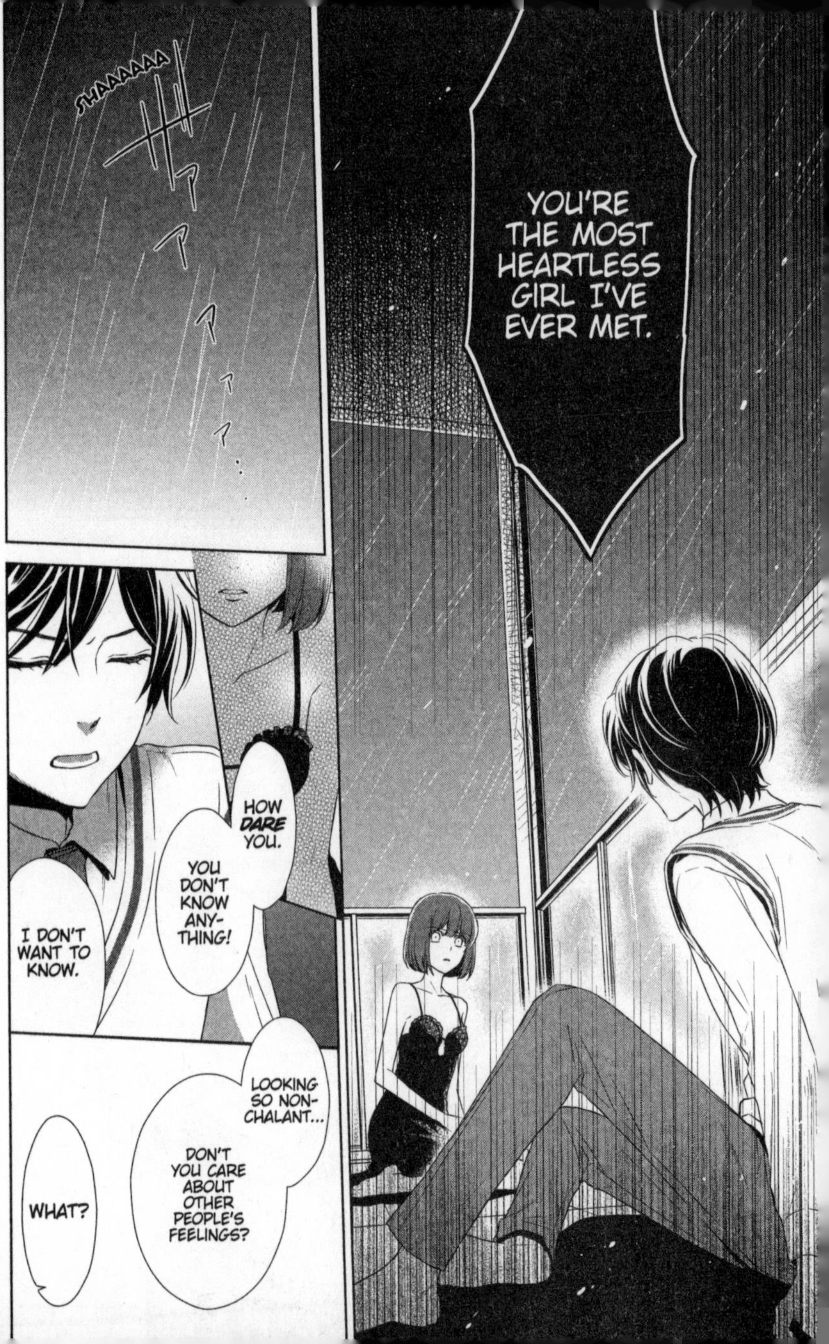
YOU'RE THE MOST HEARTLESS GIRL I'VE EVER MET.
SHAAAAAA
HOW DARE YOU.
YOU DON'T KNOW ANYTHING!
I DON'T WANT TO KNOW.
LOOKING SO NON-CHALANT...
DON'T YOU CARE ABOUT OTHER PEOPLE'S FEELINGS?
WHAT?

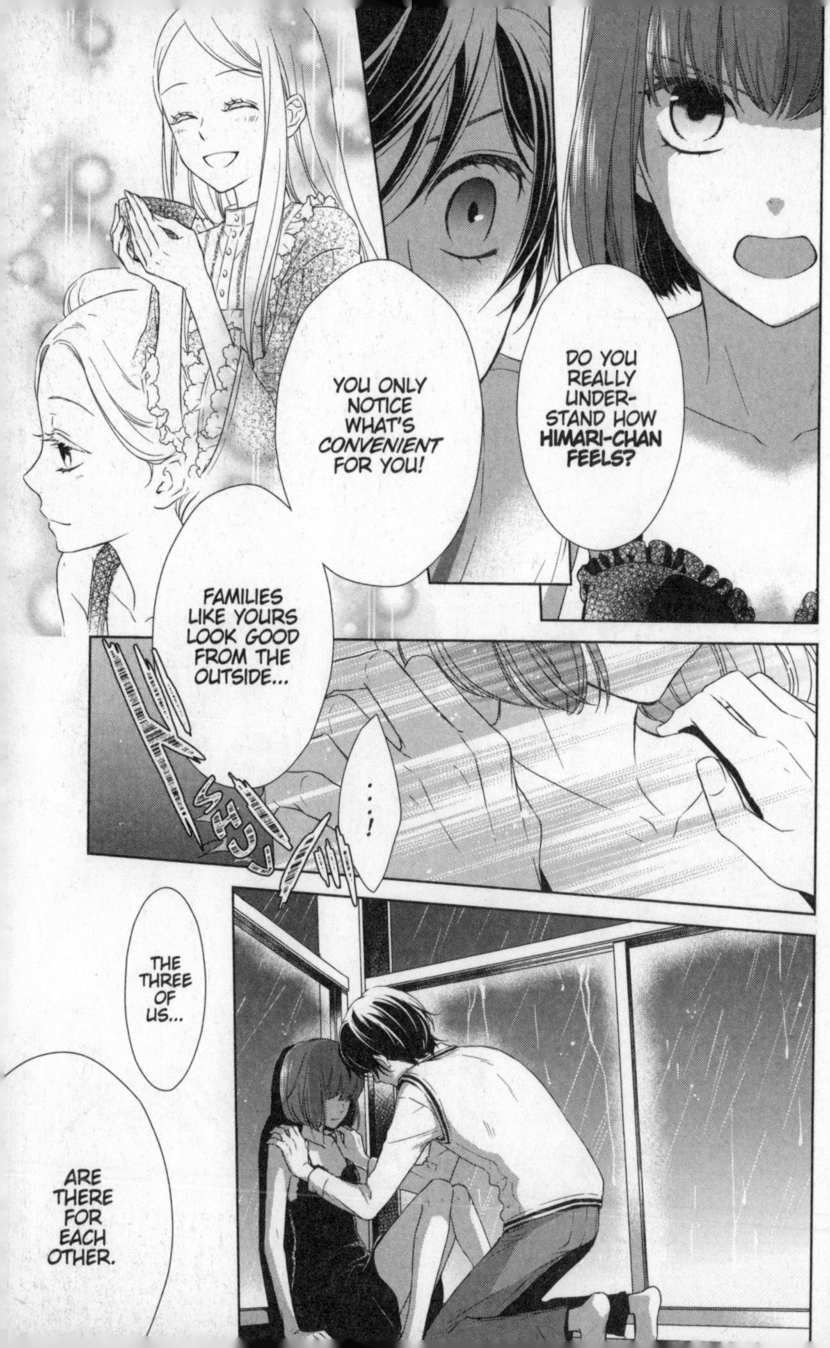
DO YOU REALLY UNDER-STAND HOW HIMARI-CHAN FEELS?
YOU ONLY NOTICE WHAT'S CONVENIENT FOR YOU!
FAMILIES LIKE YOURS LOOK GOOD FROM THE OUTSIDE...
...!
THE THREE OF US...
ARE THERE FOR EACH OTHER.

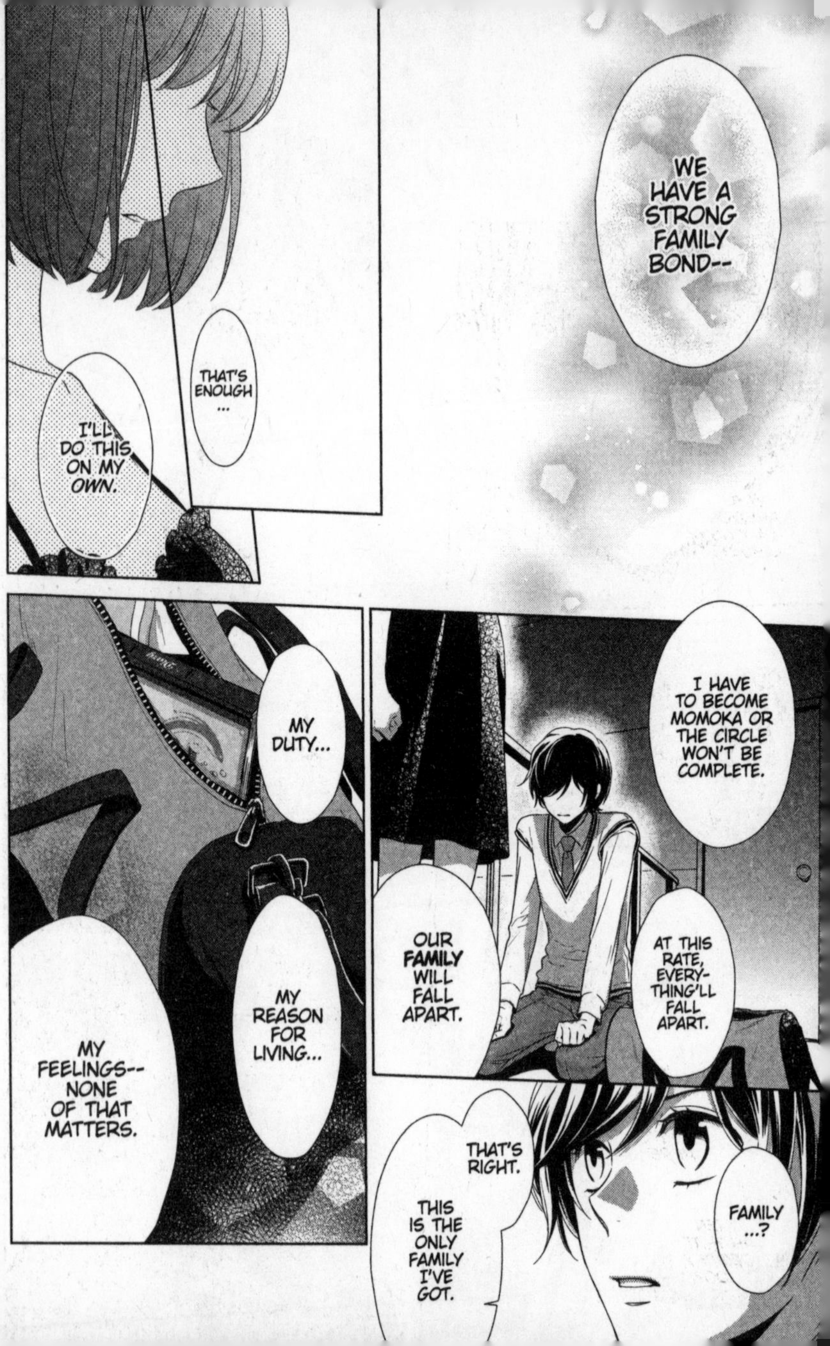
WE HAVE A STRONG FAMILY BOND--
THAT'S ENOUGH...
I'LL DO THIS ON MY OWN.
I HAVE TO BECOME MOMOKA OR THE CIRCLE WON'T BE COMPLETE.
AT THIS RATE, EVERY-THING'LL FALL APART.
OUR FAMILY WILL FALL APART.
FAMILY...?
THAT'S RIGHT.
THIS IS THE ONLY FAMILY I'VE GOT.
MY DUTY...
MY REASON FOR LIVING...
MY FEELINGS--NONE OF THAT MATTERS.

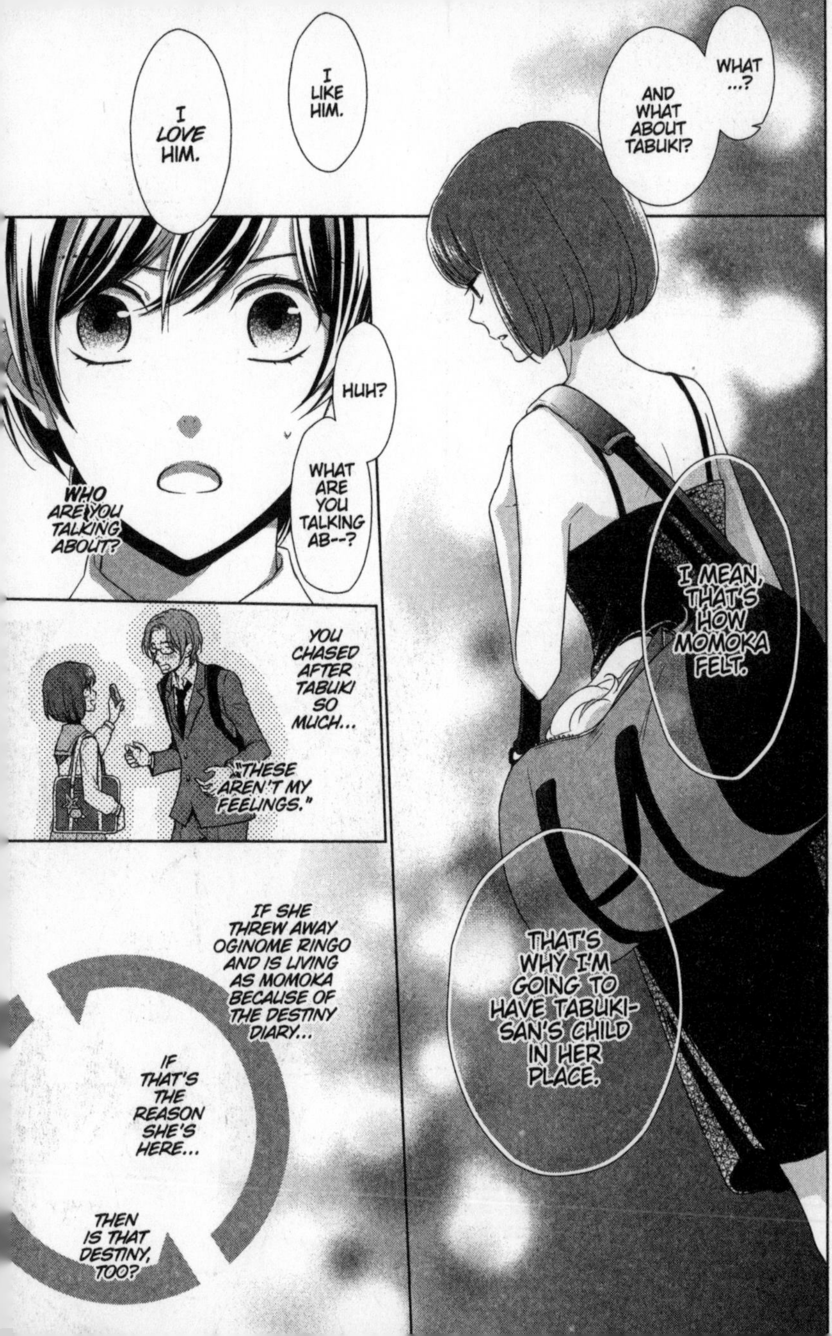

WHAT ...?
AND WHAT ABOUT TABUKI?
I LIKE HIM.
I LOVE HIM.
I MEAN, THAT'S HOW MOMOKA FELT.
THAT'S WHY I'M GOING TO HAVE TABUKI-SAN'S CHILD IN HER PLACE.
HUH?
WHAT ARE YOU TALKING AB--?
WHO ARE YOU TALKING ABOUT?
YOU CHASED AFTER TABUKI SO MUCH...
"THESE AREN'T MY FEELINGS."
IF SHE THREW AWAY OGINOME RINGO AND IS LIVING AS MOMOKA BECAUSE OF THE DESTINY DIARY...
IF THAT'S THE REASON SHE'S HERE...
THEN IS THAT DESTINY, TOO?

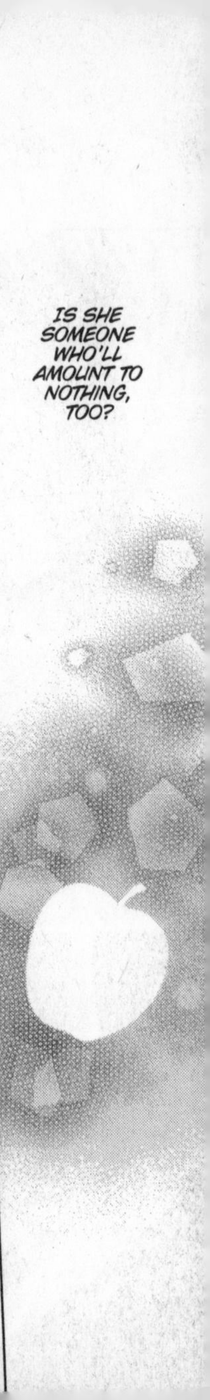
IS SHE SOMEONE WHO'LL AMOUNT TO NOTHING, TOO?

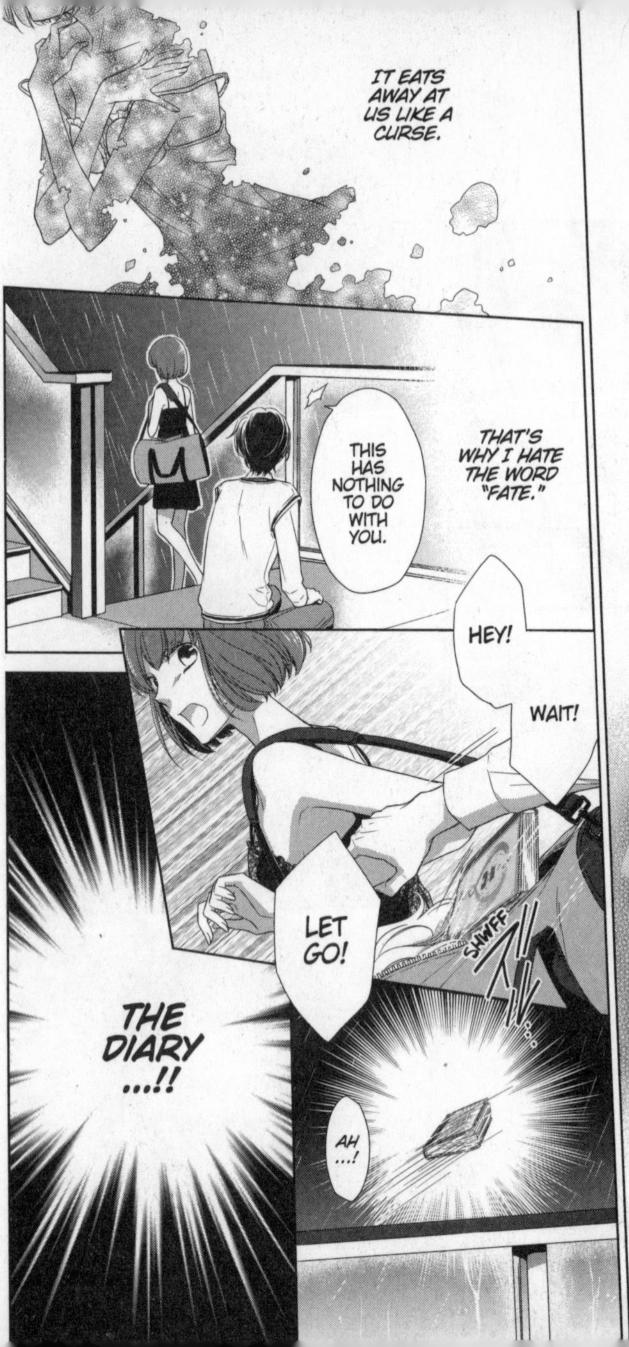
IT EATS AWAY AT US LIKE A CURSE.
THAT'S WHY I HATE THE WORD "FATE."
THIS HAS NOTHING TO DO WITH YOU.
HEY!
WAIT!
LET GO!
SHWFF
AH ...!
THE DIARY ...!!

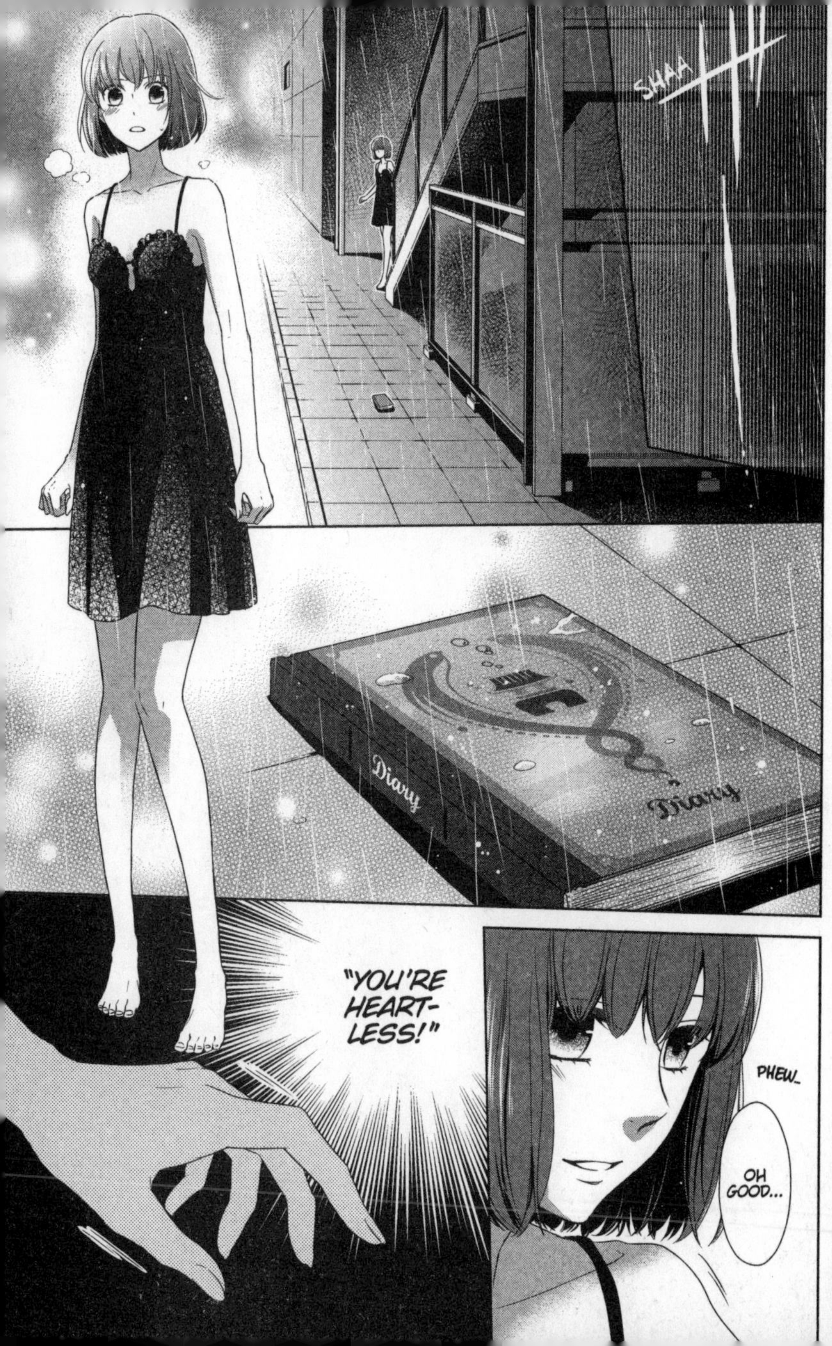
SHAA
Diary
Diary
PHEW_
OH GOOD...
"YOU'RE HEART-LESS!"

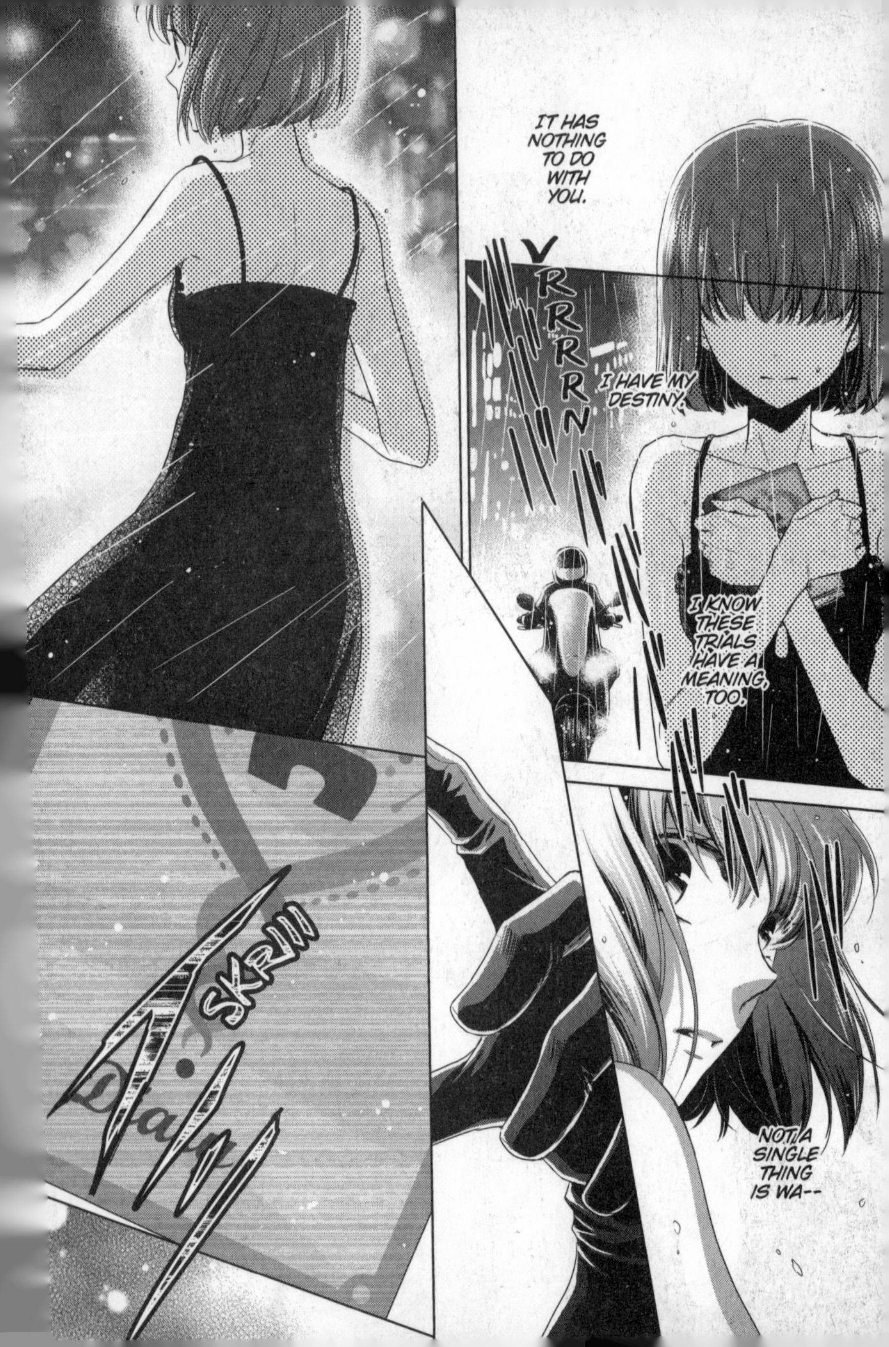
IT HAS NOTHING TO DO WITH YOU.
I HAVE MY DESTINY.
VRRRRN
I KNOW THESE TRIALS HAVE A MEANING, TOO.
NOT A SINGLE THING IS WA--
SKRIII

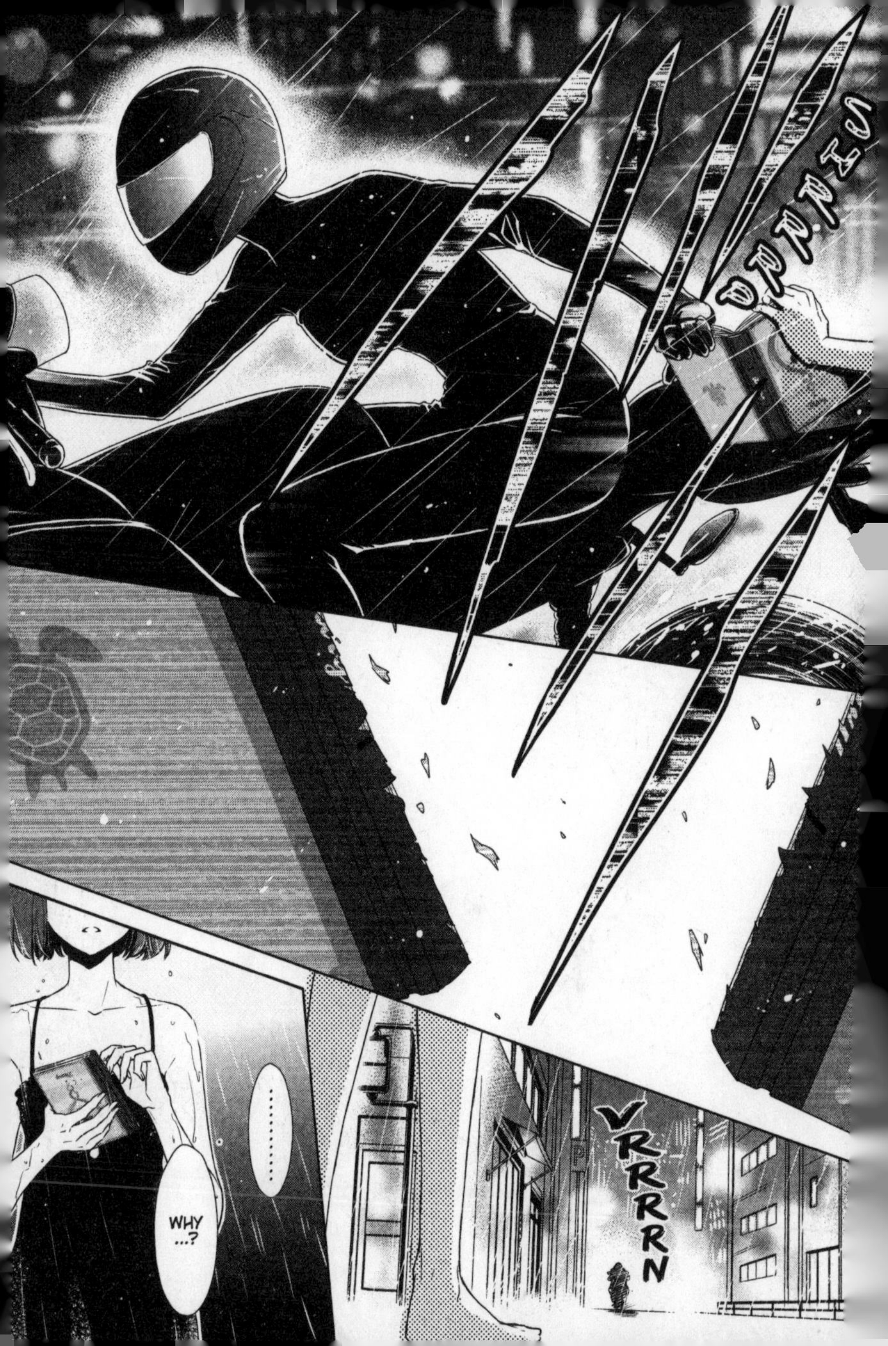

......
WHY ...?
VRRRRN

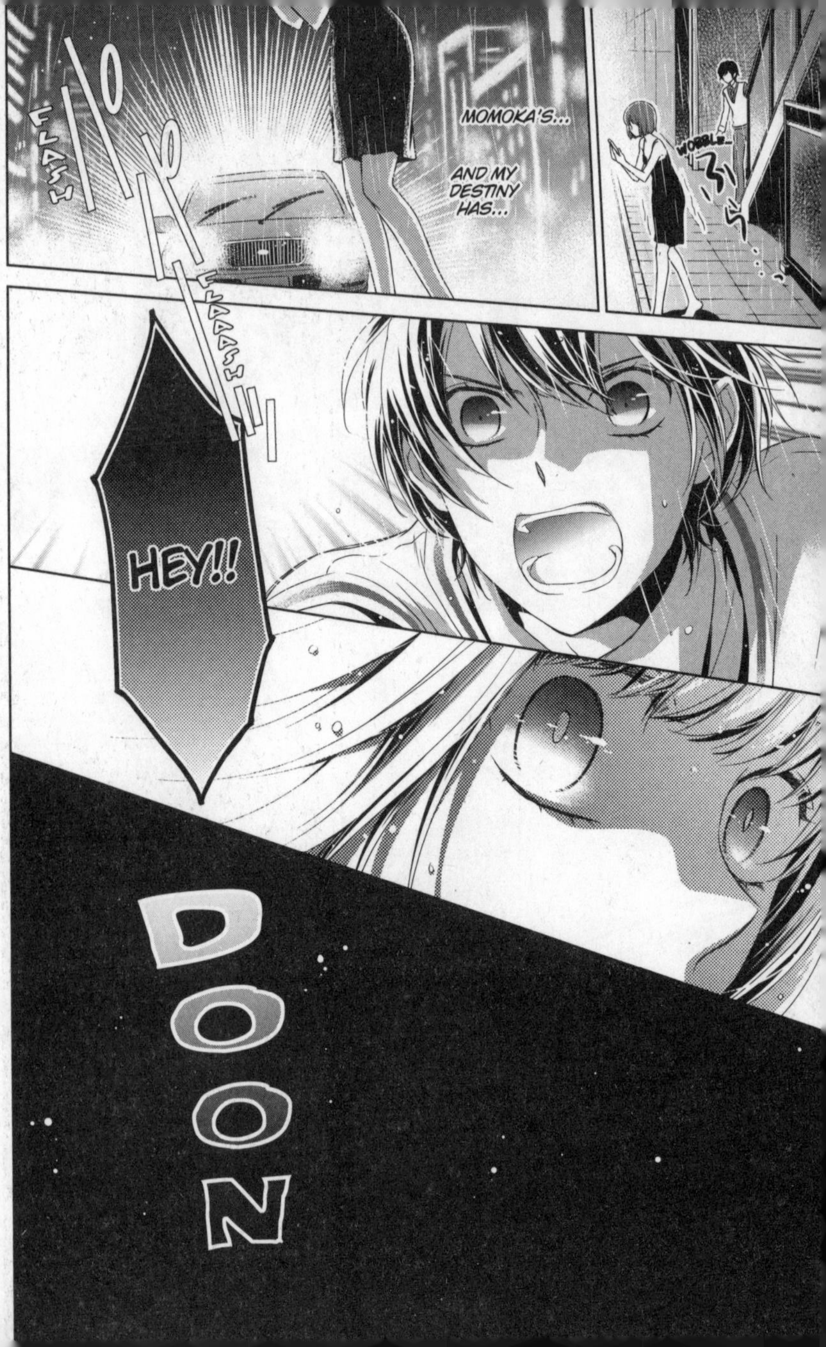
WOBBLE...
MOMOKA'S...
AND MY DESTINY HAS...
FLASH
FLAAASH
HEY!!
DOOON

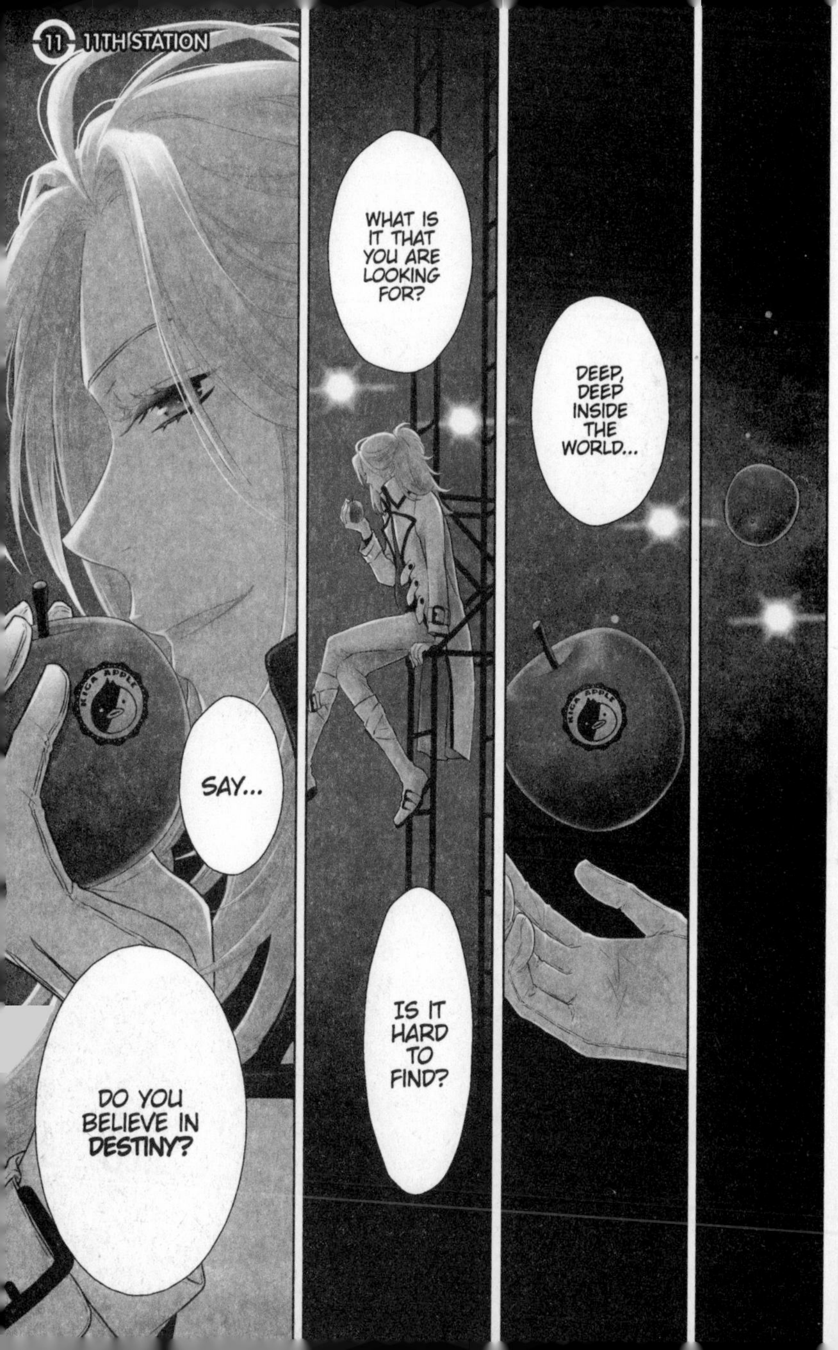
DEEP, DEEP INSIDE THE WORLD...
KIGA APPLE
WHAT IS IT THAT YOU ARE LOOKING FOR?
IS IT HARD TO FIND?
KIGA APPLE
SAY...
DO YOU BELIEVE IN DESTINY?

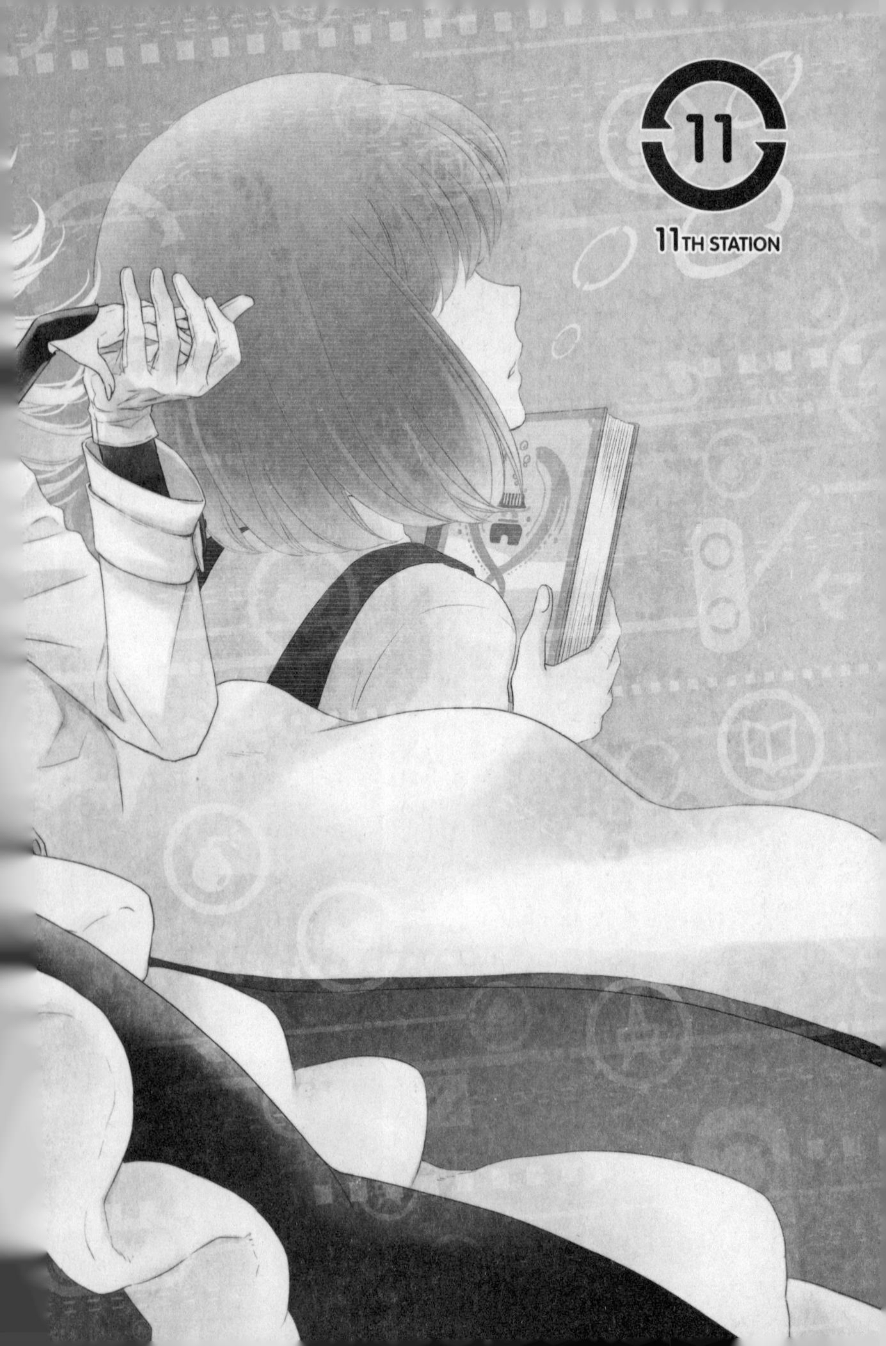
11
11TH STATION

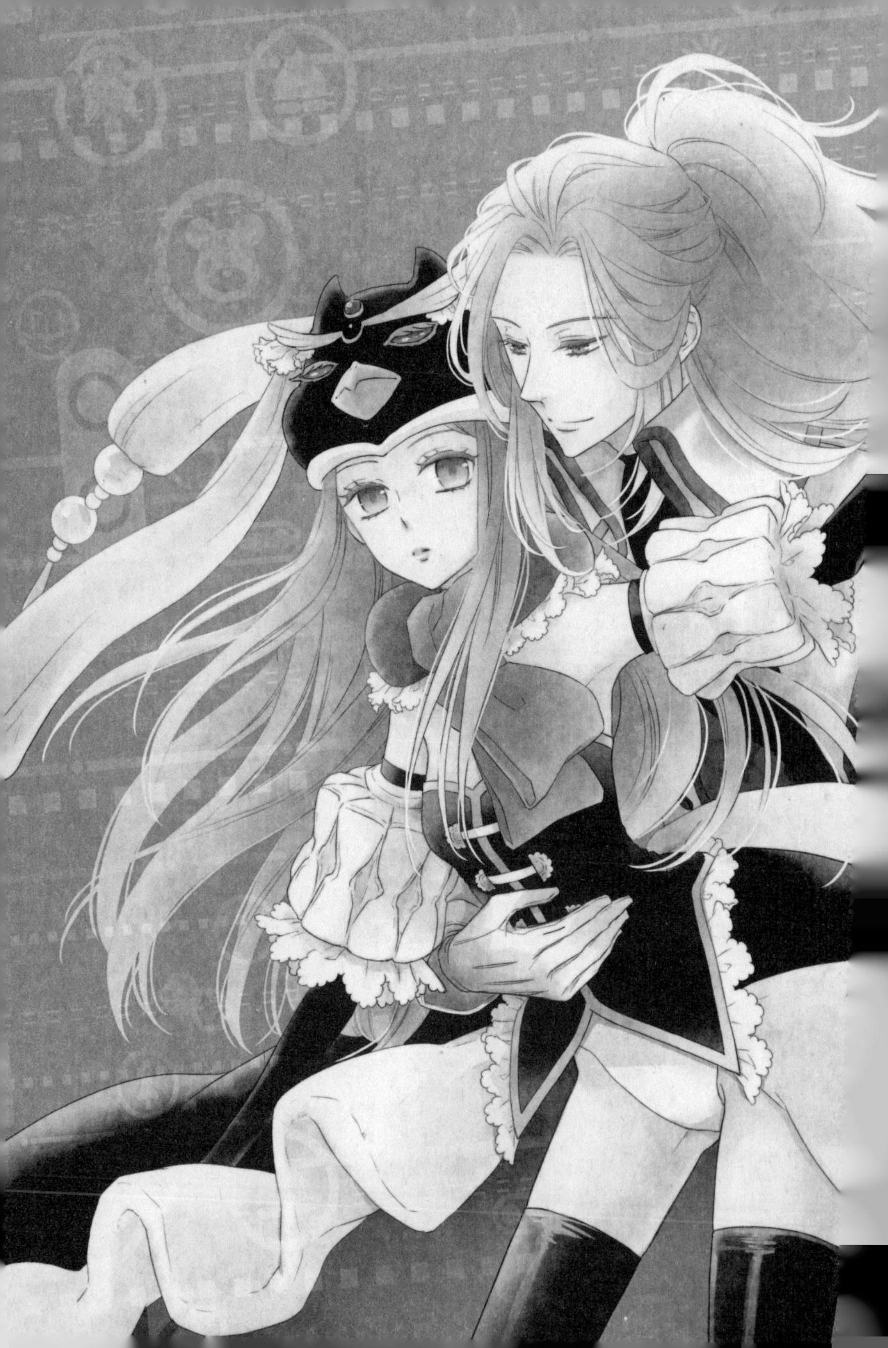

PENGUINDRUM

Based on the original anime
Manga by Isuzu Shibata

2

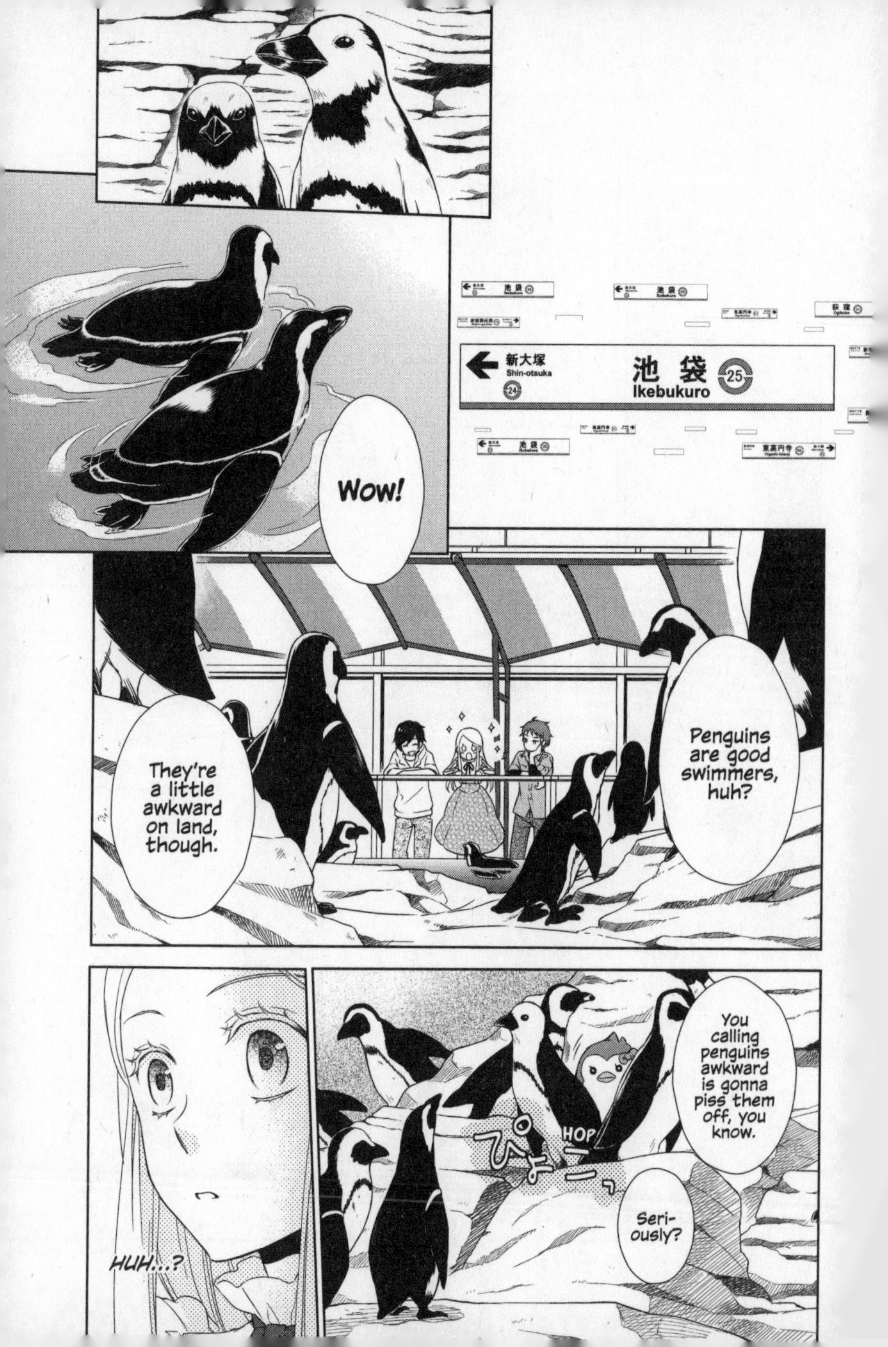

新大塚
Shin-otsuka
24
池袋
Ikebukuro
25
WOW!
Penguins are good swimmers, huh?
They're a little awkward on land, though.
You calling penguins awkward is gonna piss them off, you know.
HOP
Seri-ously?
HUH...?

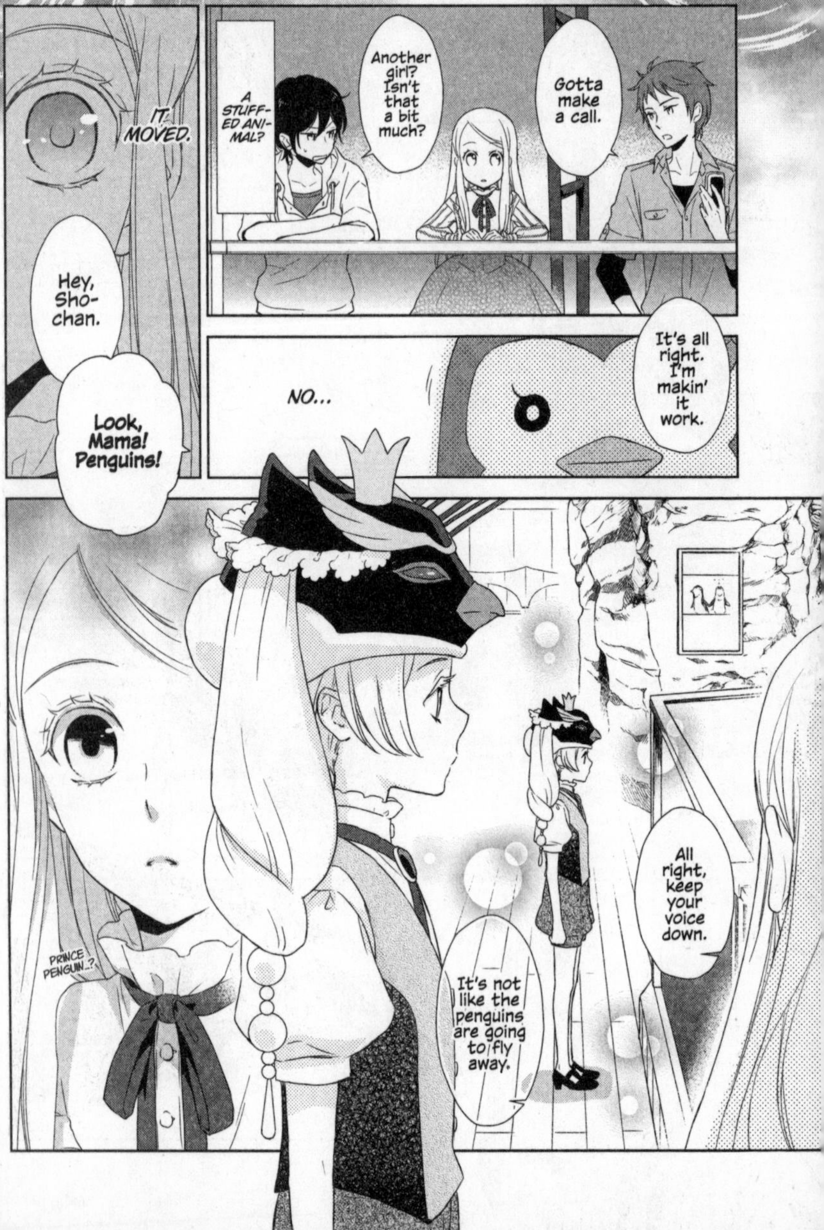
Gotta make a call.
Another girl? Isn't that a bit much?
A STUFFED ANIMAL?
It's all right. I'm makin' it work.
NO...
IT MOVED.
Hey, Sho-chan.
Look, Mama! Penguins!
All right, keep your voice down.
It's not like the penguins are going to fly away.
PRINCE PENGUIN...?

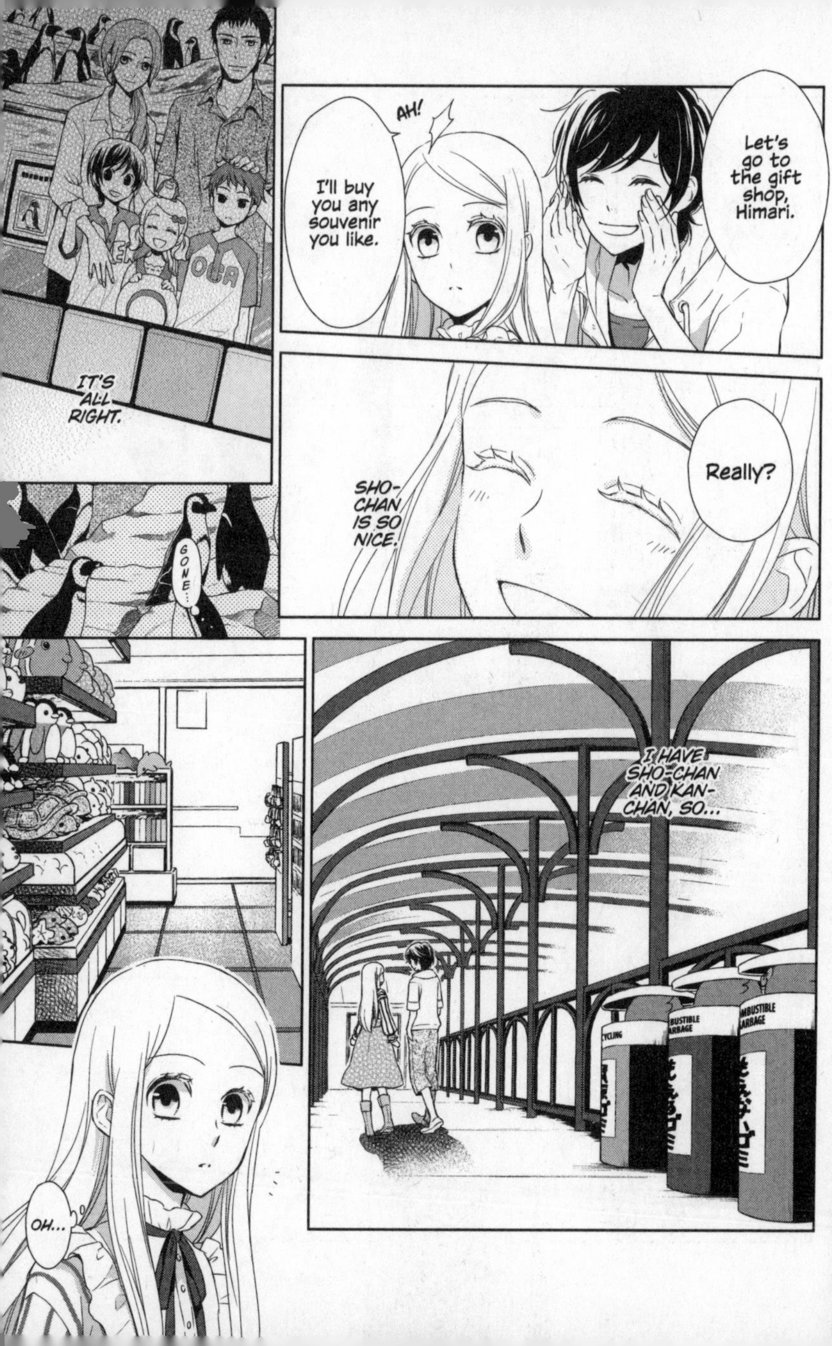
Let's go to the gift shop, Himari.
AH!
I'll buy you any souvenir you like.
IT'S ALL RIGHT.
Really?
SHO-CHAN IS SO NICE.
GONE...
I HAVE SHO-CHAN AND KAN-CHAN, SO...
OH...

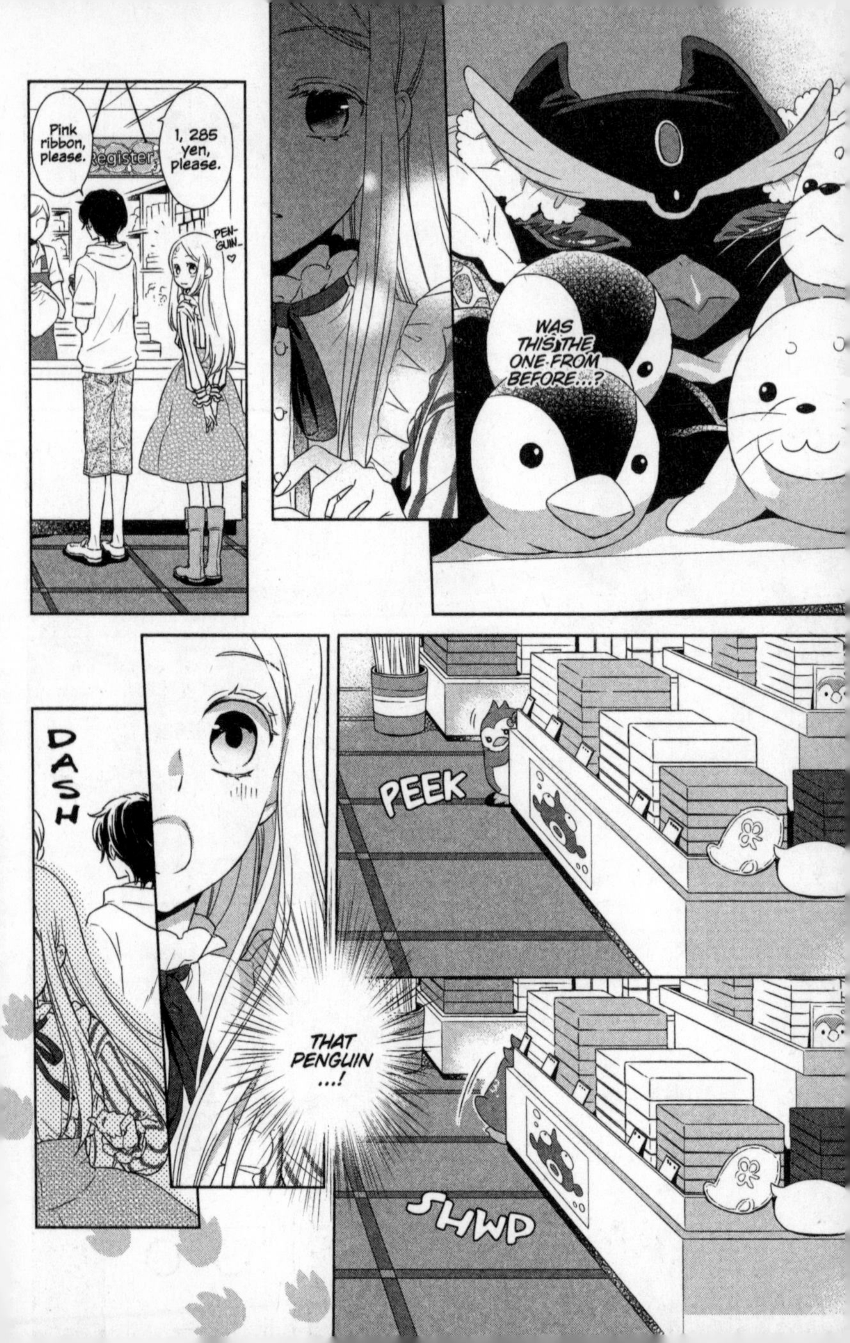
WAS THIS THE ONE FROM BEFORE...?
1, 285 yen, please.
Pink ribbon, please.
PEN-GUIN...♥
PEEK
SHWP
THAT PENGUIN ...!
DASH

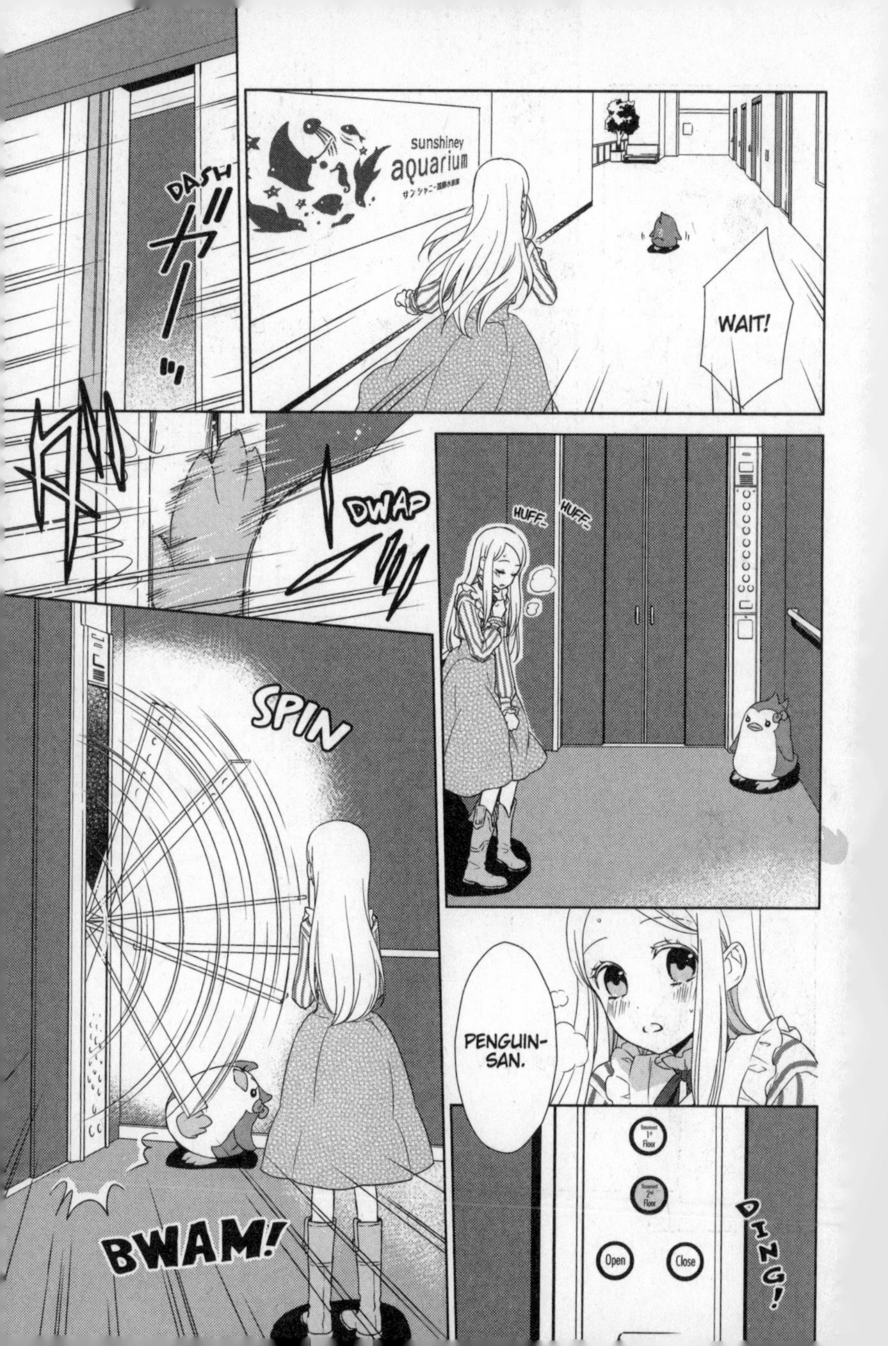
sunshiney
aquarium
WAIT!
DASH
HUFF-
HUFF-
DWAP
PENGUIN-SAN.
Open
Close
DING!
SPIN
BWAM!

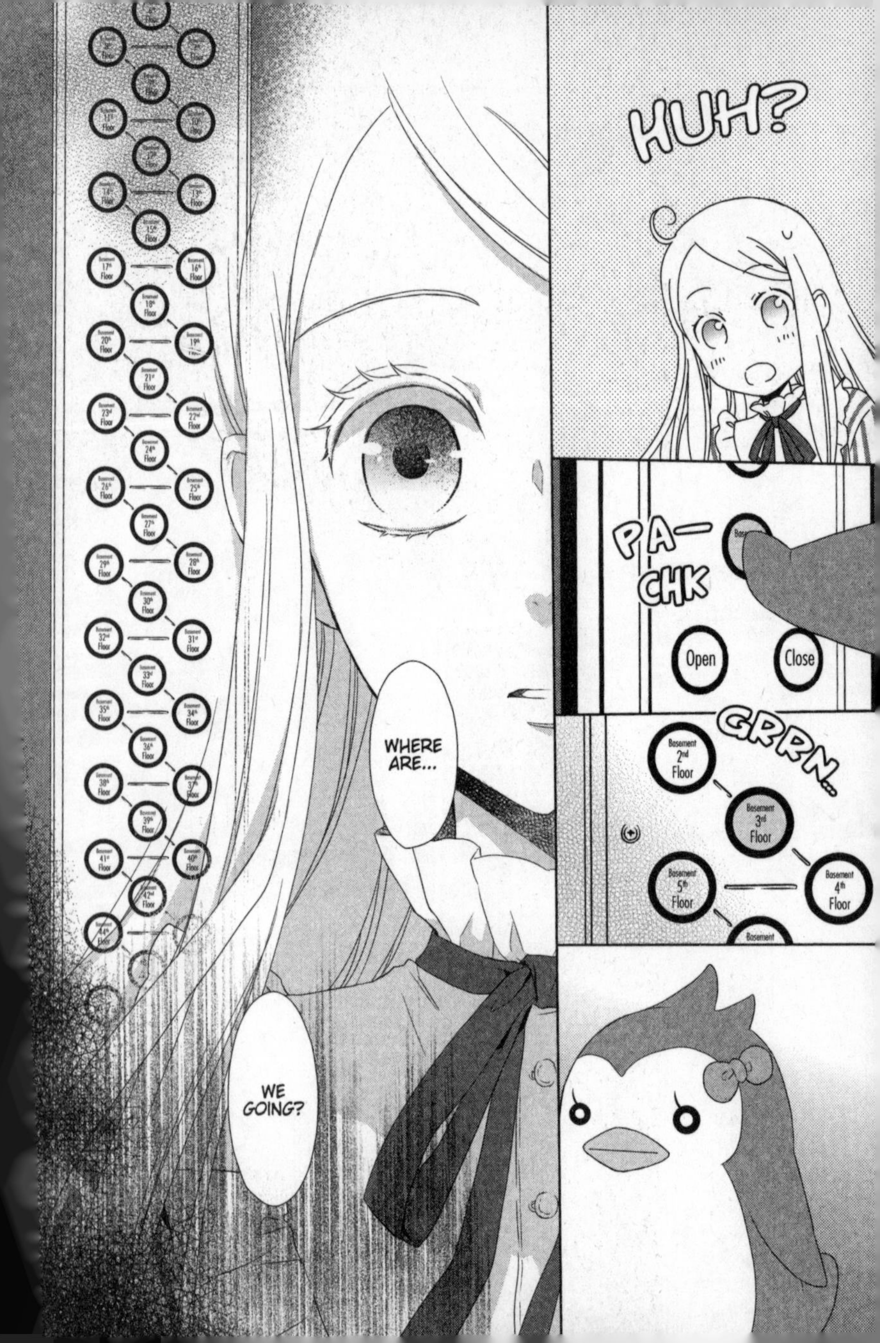
HUH?
PA-CHK
Open
Close
GRRN...
Basement 2nd Floor
Basement 3rd Floor
Basement 4th Floor
Basement 5th Floor
WHERE ARE...
WE GOING?

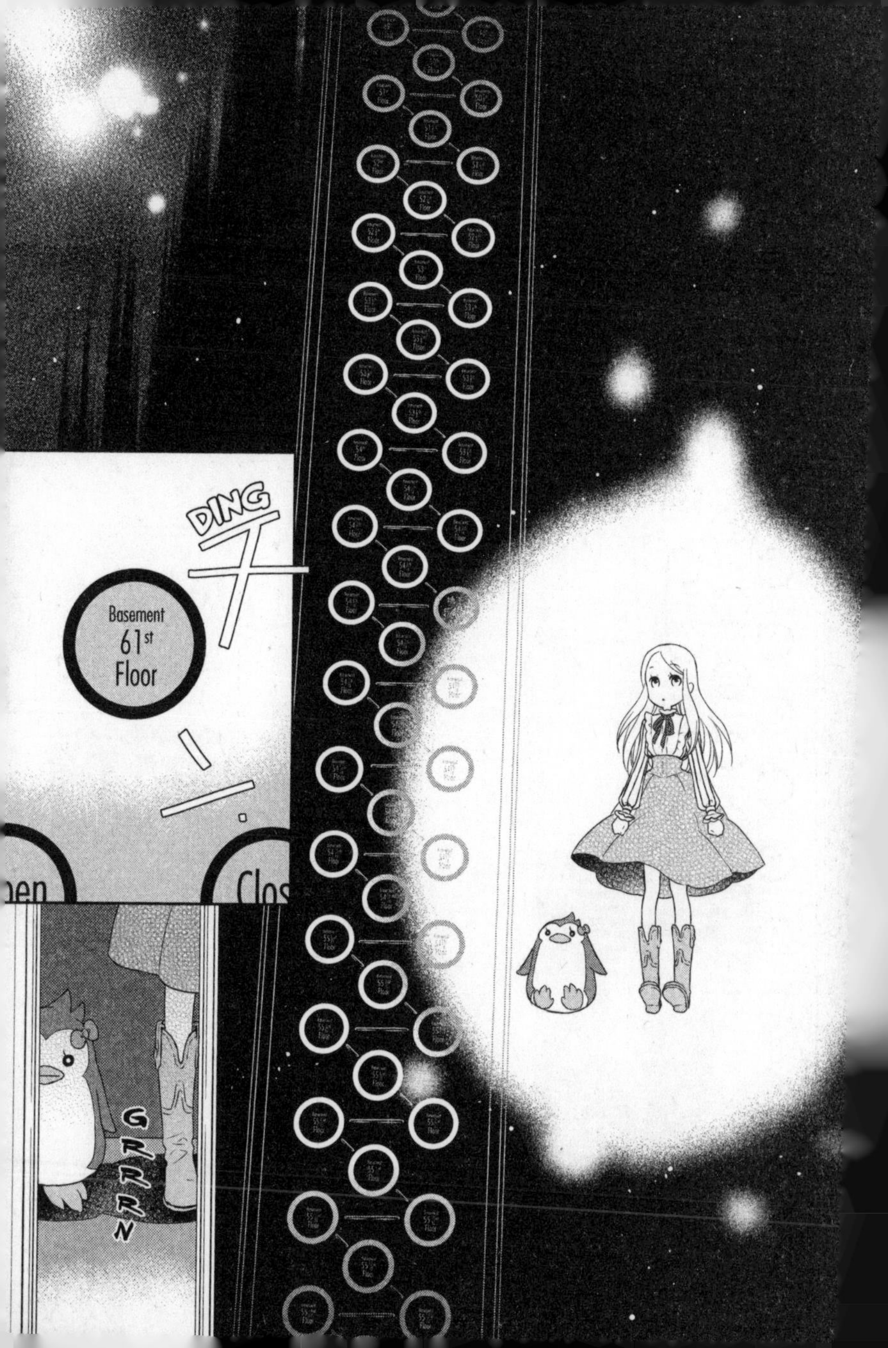
DING
Basement 61st Floor
GRRRN

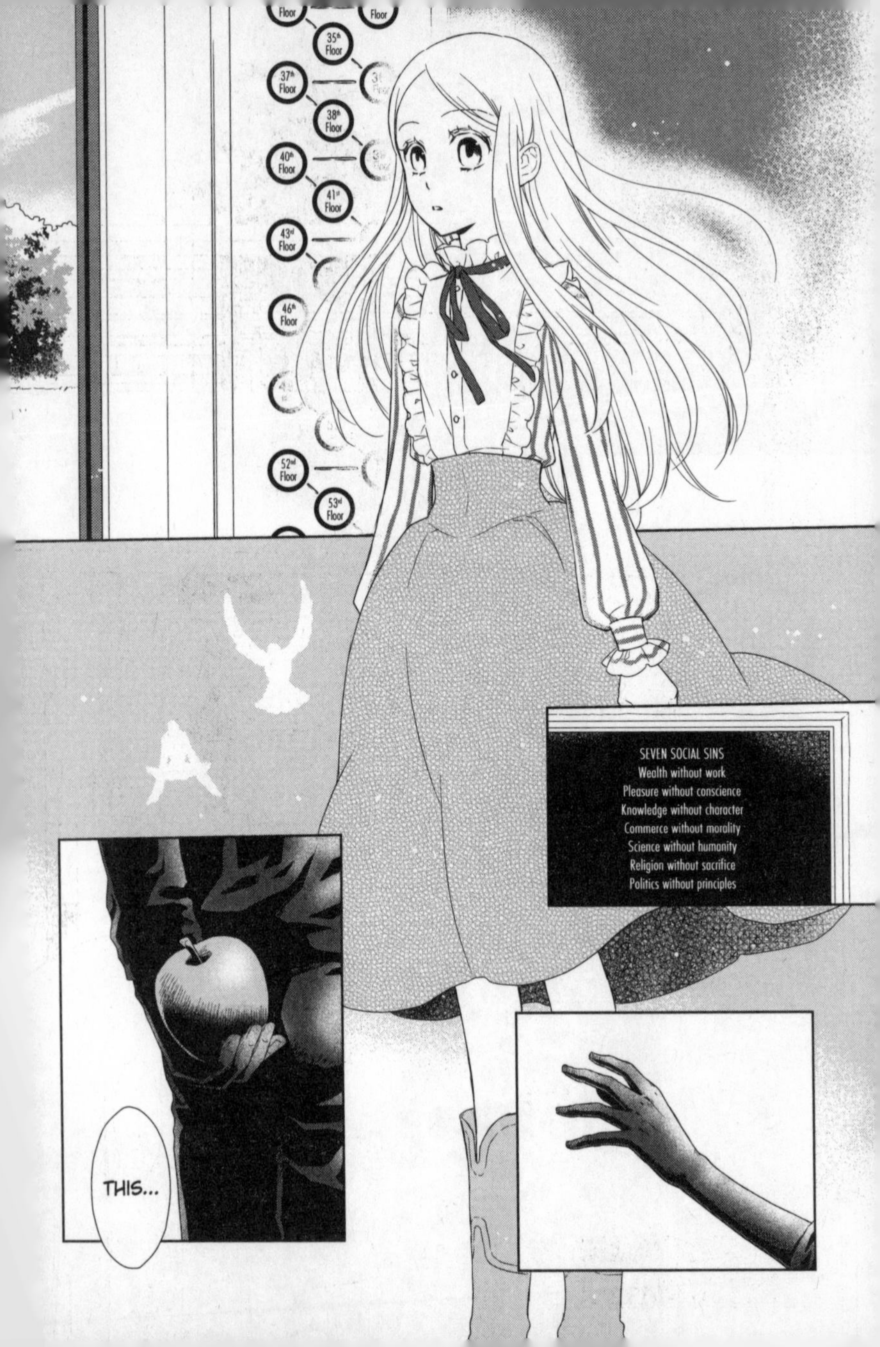
35th Floor
37th Floor
38th Floor
40th Floor
41st Floor
43rd Floor
46th Floor
52nd Floor
53rd Floor
SEVEN SOCIAL SINS
Wealth without work
Pleasure without conscience
Knowledge without character
Commerce without morality
Science without humanity
Religion without sacrifice
Politics without principles
THIS...

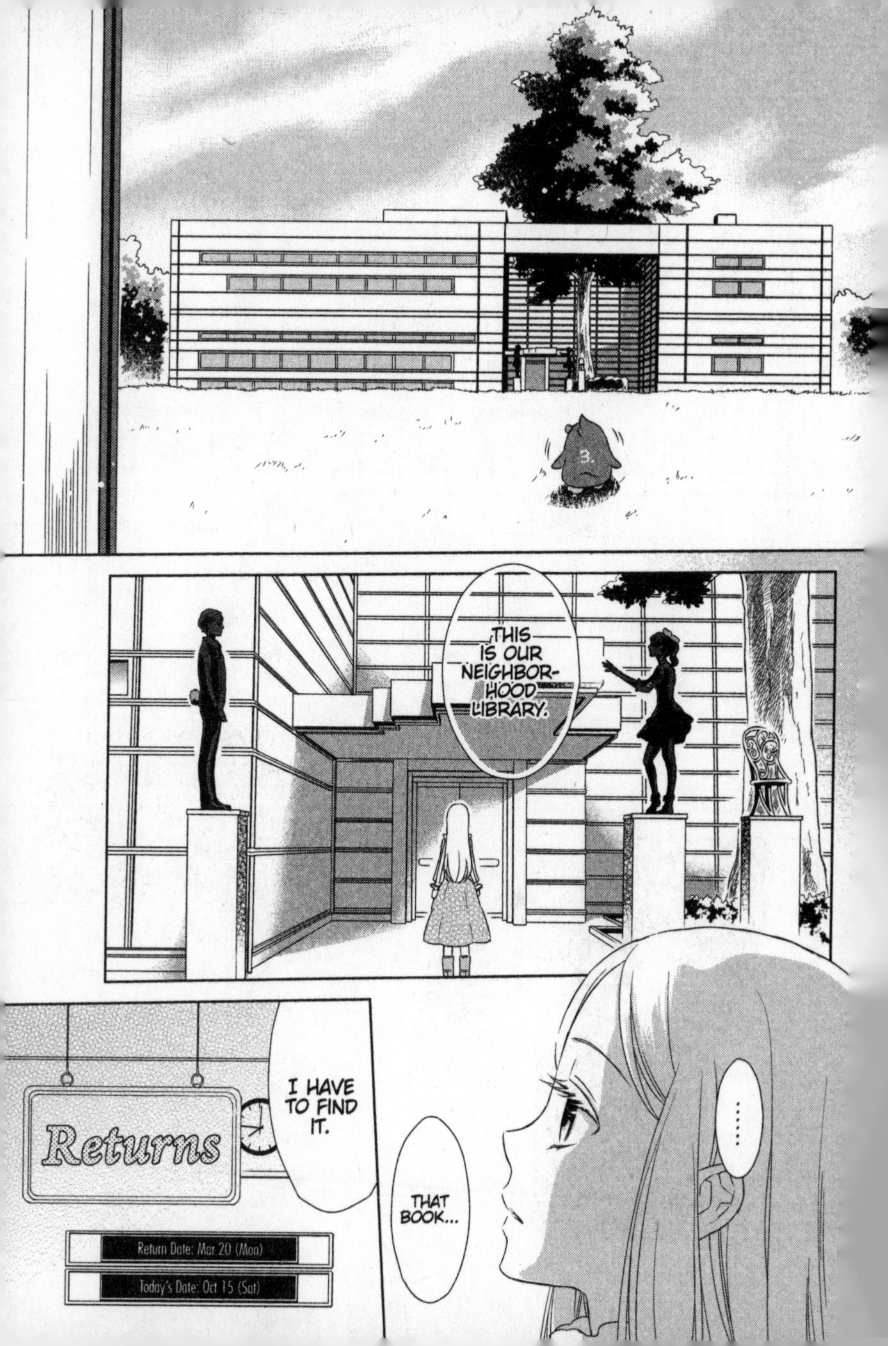
THIS IS OUR NEIGHBORHOOD LIBRARY.
......
THAT BOOK...
I HAVE TO FIND IT.
Returns
Return Date: Mar 20 (Mon)
Today's Date: Oct 15 (Sat)

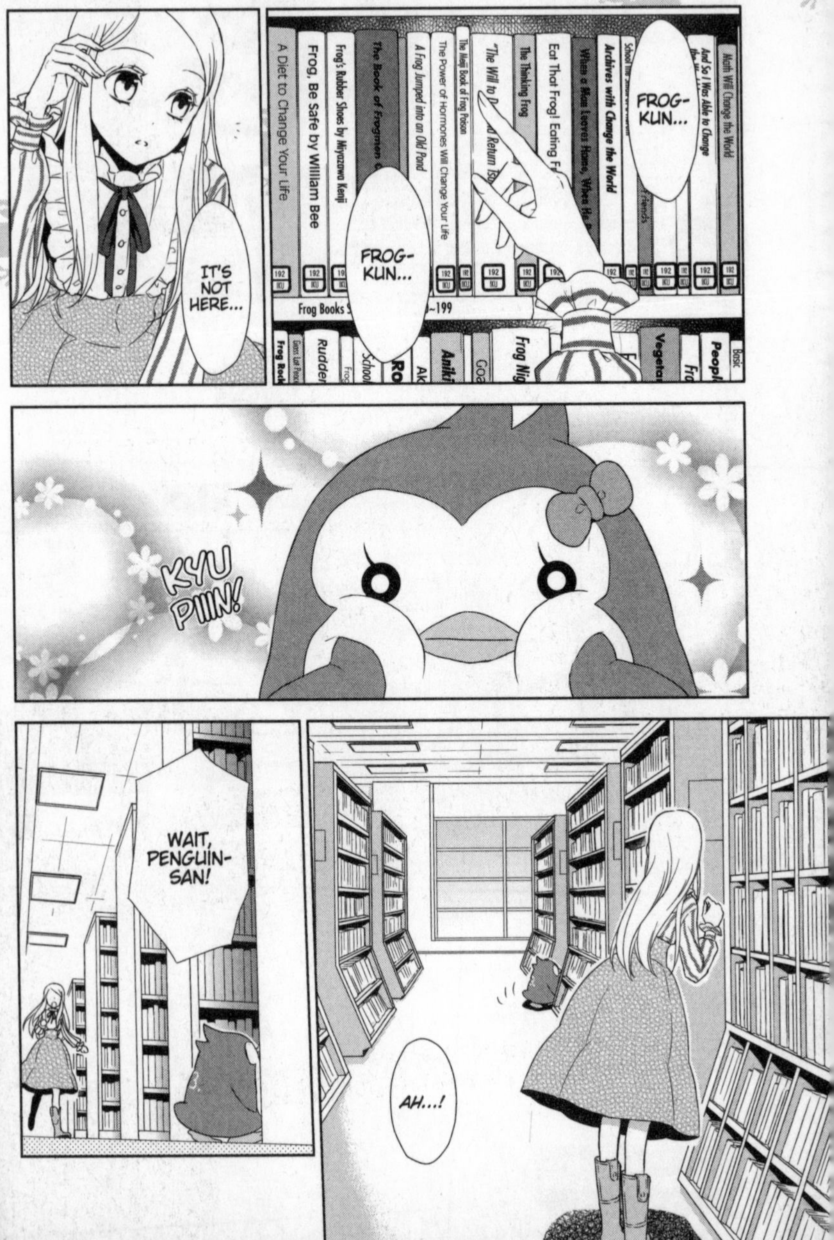
FROG-KUN...
FROG-KUN...
A Diet to Change Your Life
Frog, Be Safe by William Bee
Frog's Rubber Shoes by Miyazawa Kenji
A Frog Jumped into an Old Pond
The Power of Hormones Will Change Your Life
The Ninja Book of Frog Poison
The Thinking Frog
Archives with Change the World
Math Will Change the World
IT'S NOT HERE...
KYU PIIIN!
AH...!
WAIT, PENGUIN-SAN!

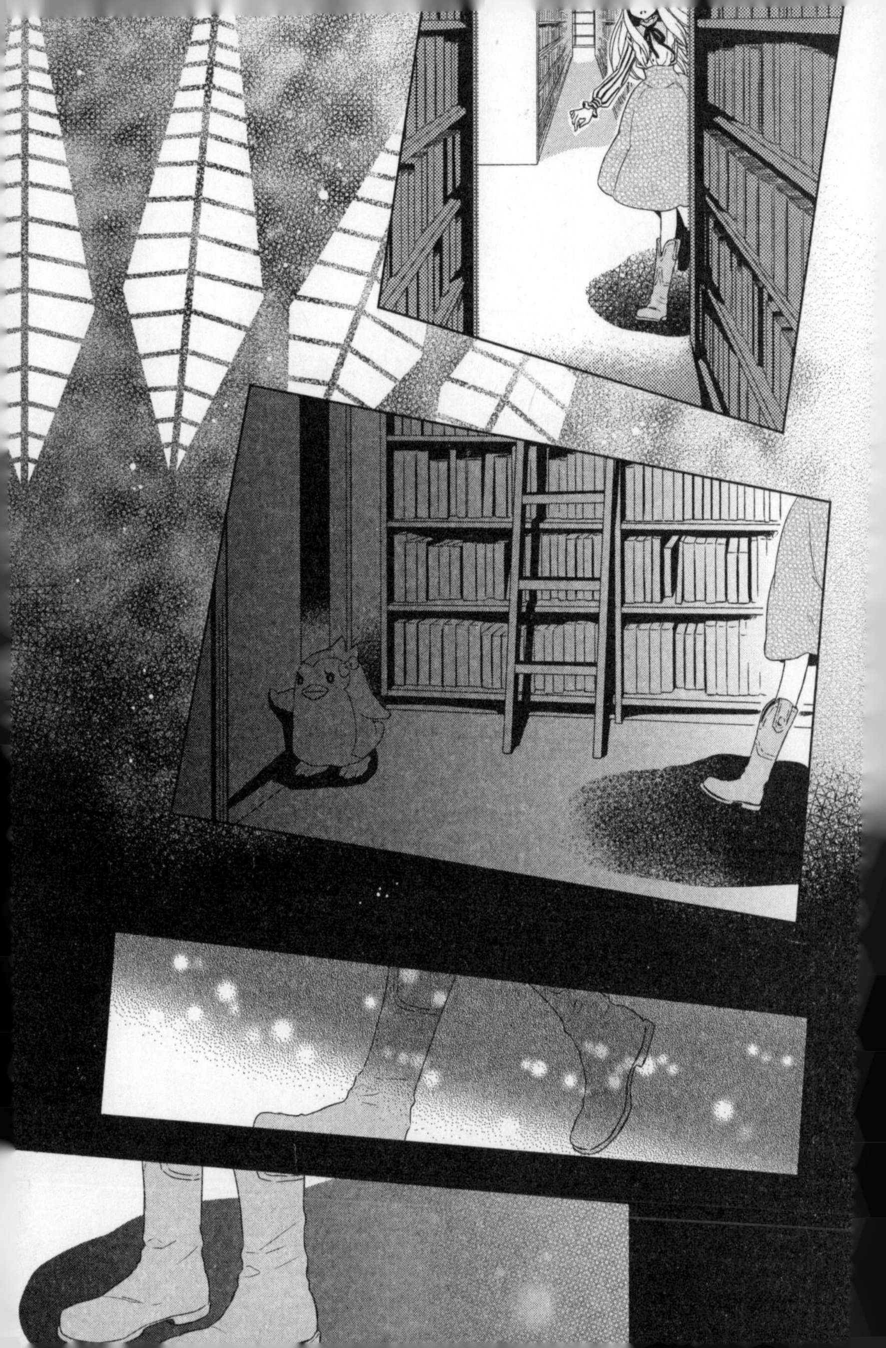

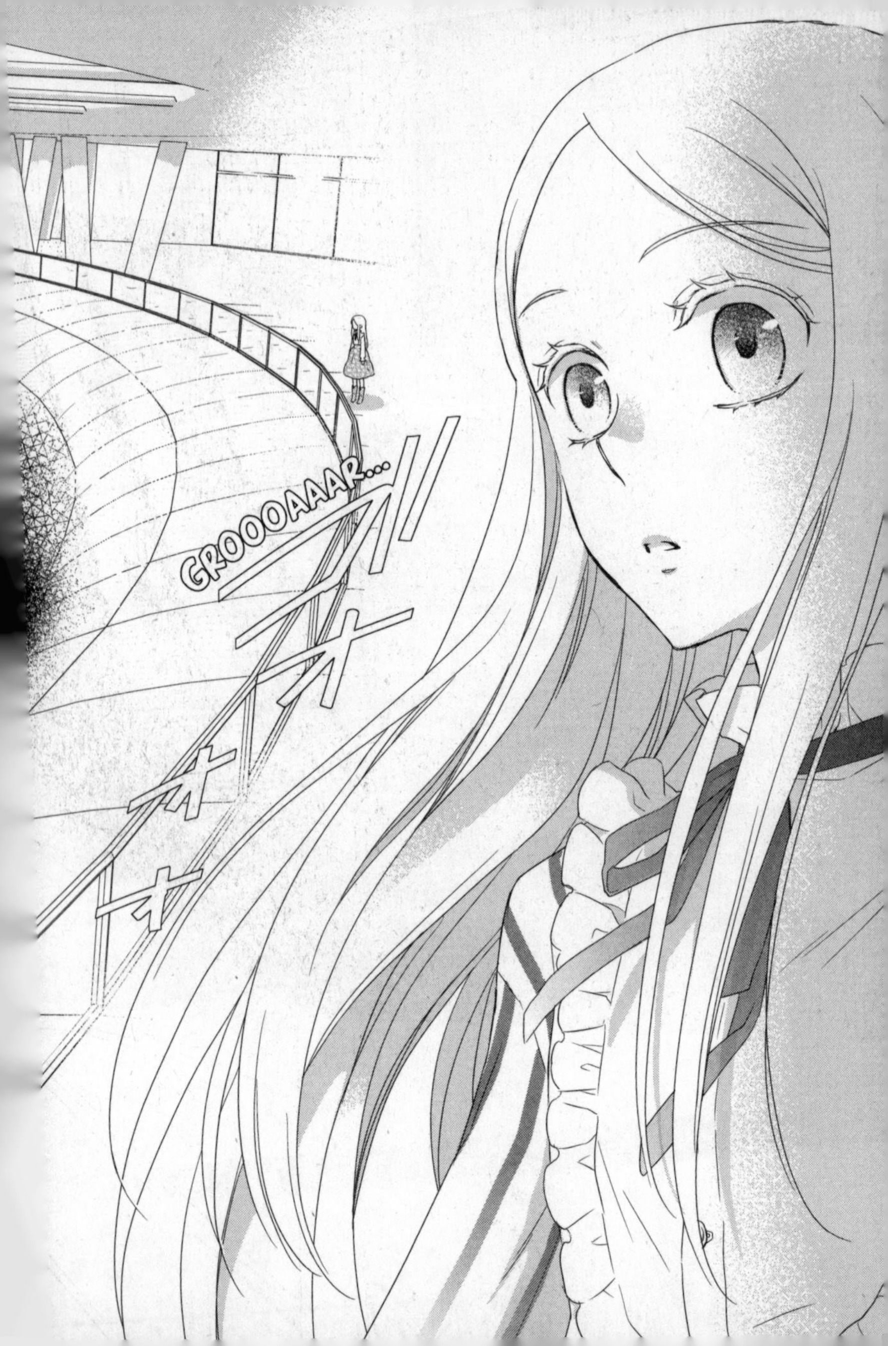
GROOOAAAR...

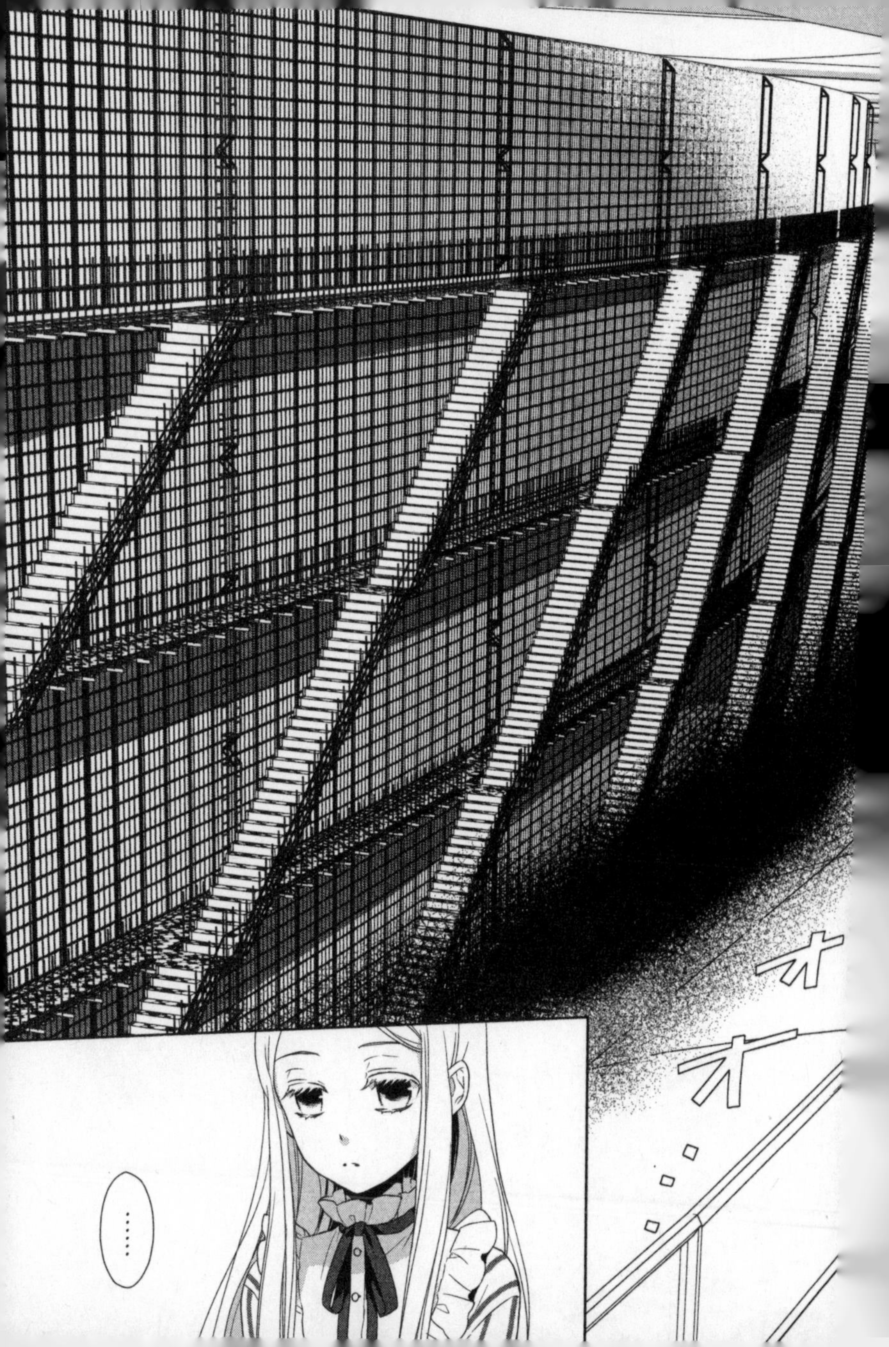
オオー……
……

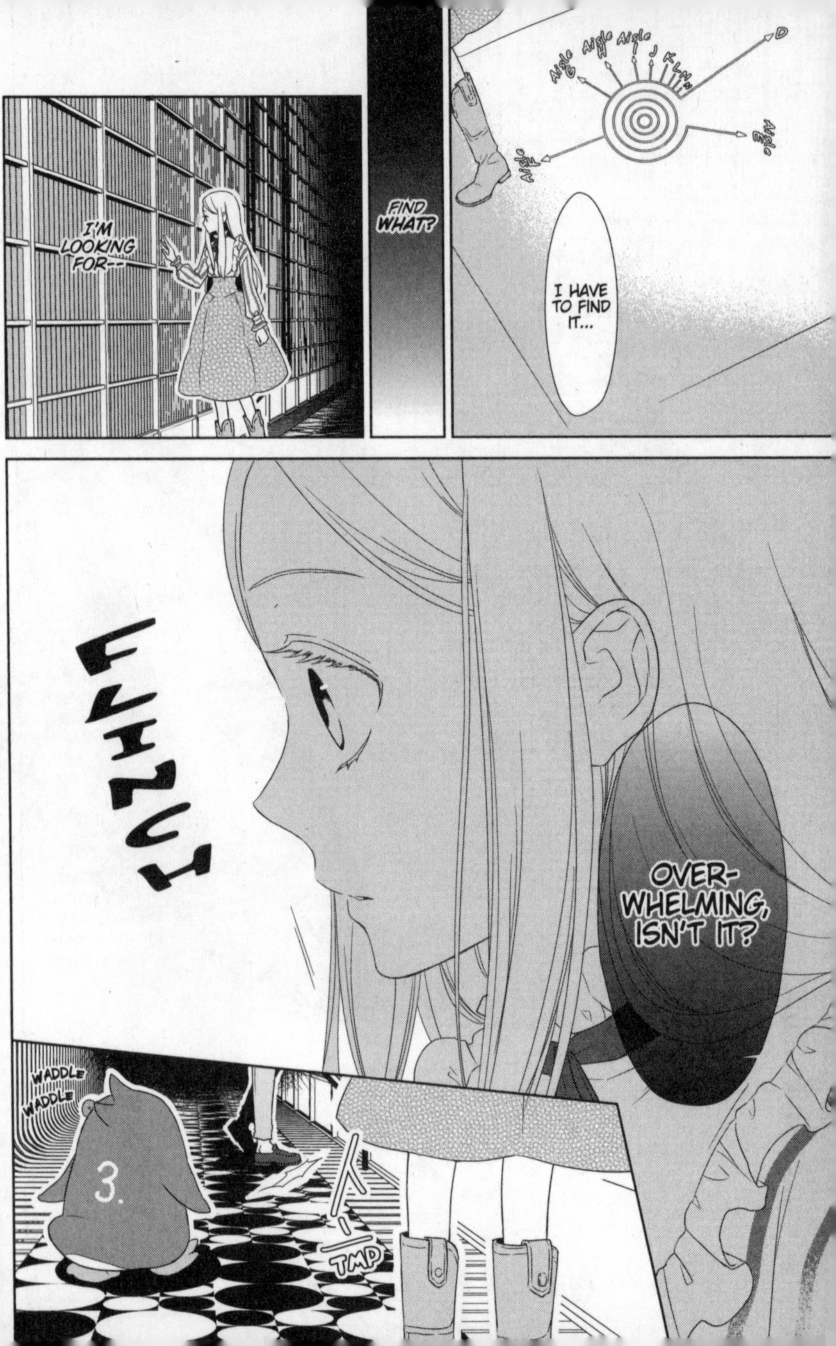

Aisle G
Aisle H
Aisle I
J
K
L
D
Aisle E
Aisle F
I HAVE TO FIND IT...
FIND WHAT?
I'M LOOKING FOR--
OVER-WHELMING, ISN'T IT?
FLINCH
TMP
WADDLE WADDLE
3.

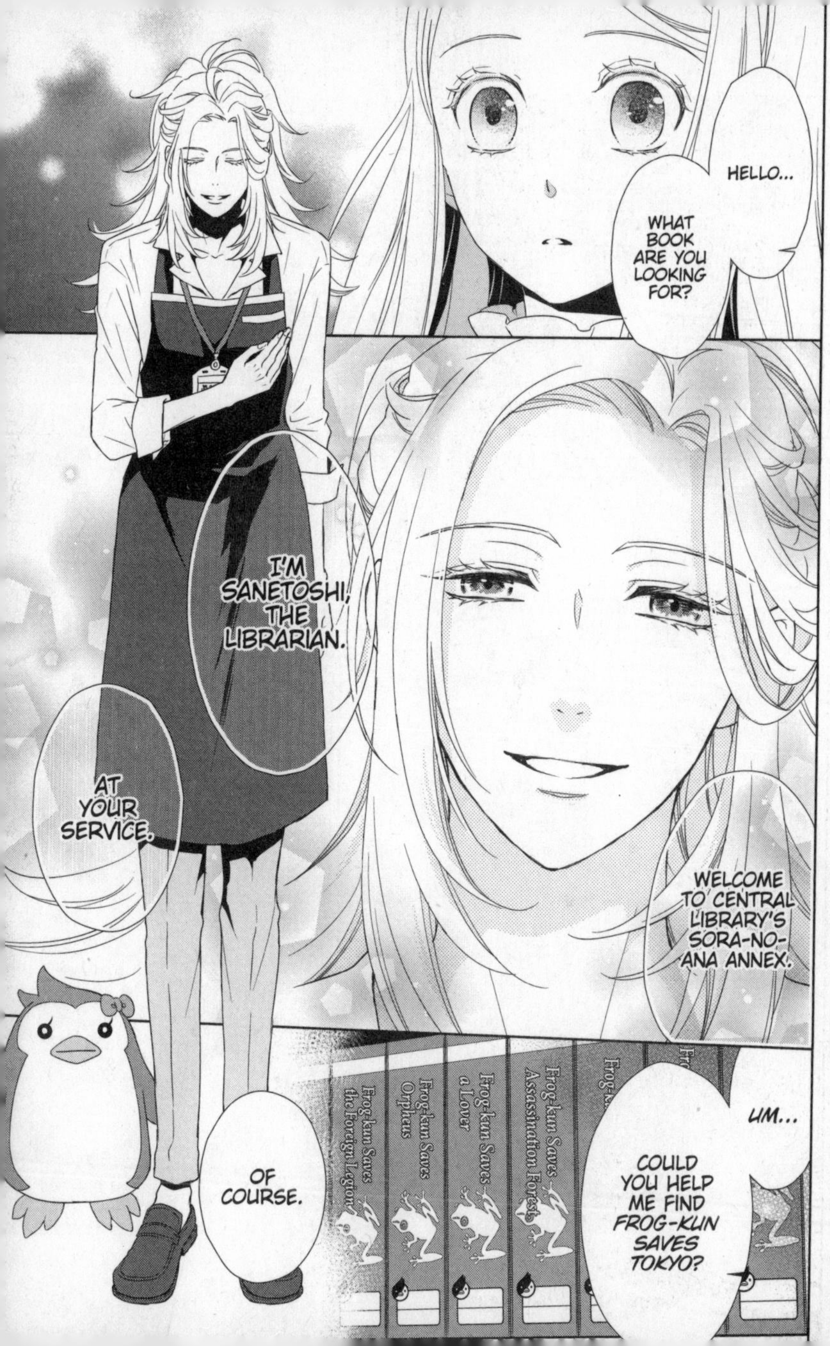
HELLO...
WHAT BOOK ARE YOU LOOKING FOR?
WELCOME TO CENTRAL LIBRARY'S SORA-NO-ANA ANNEX.
UM...
COULD YOU HELP ME FIND FROG-KUN SAVES TOKYO?
Frog-kun Saves Assassination Forest
Frog-kun Saves a Lover
Frog-kun Saves Orpheus
Frog-kun Saves the Foreign Legion
I'M SANETOSHI, THE LIBRARIAN.
AT YOUR SERVICE.
OF COURSE.

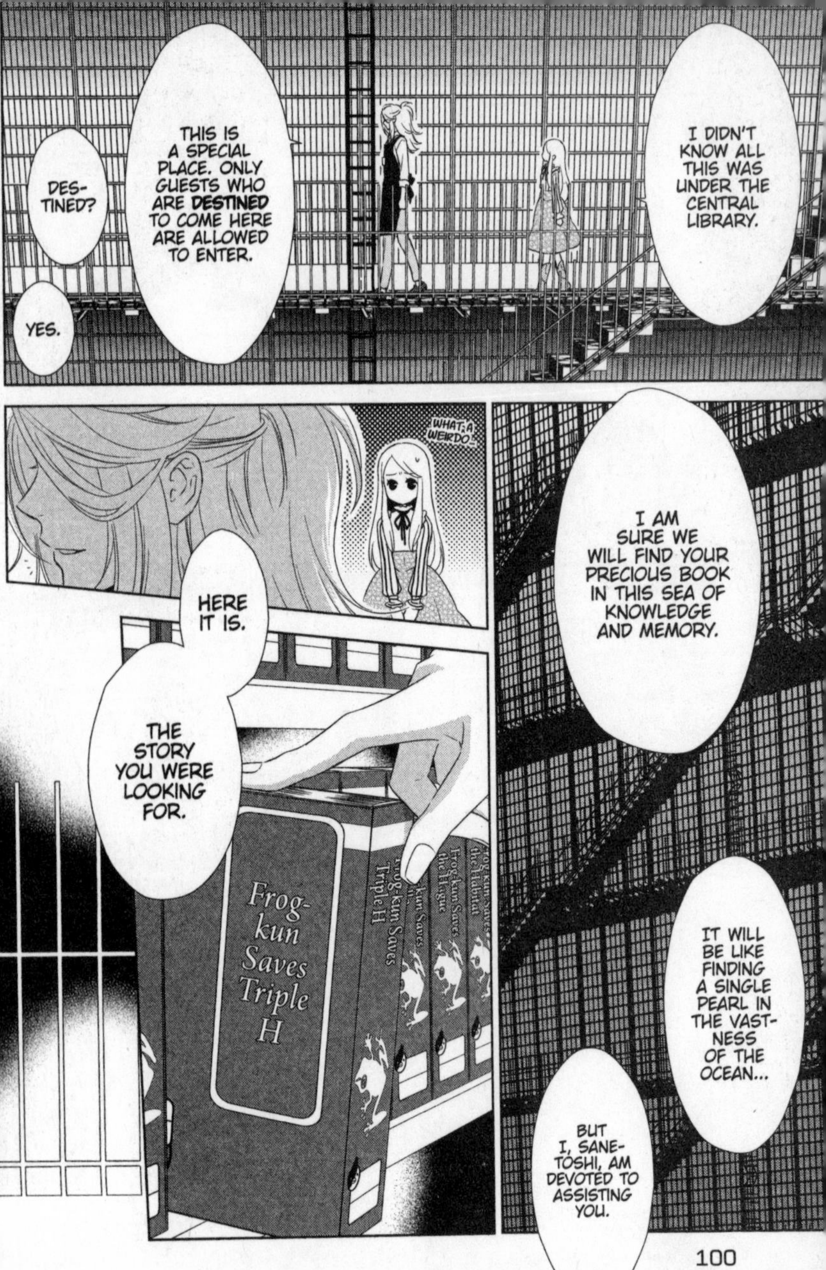
I DIDN'T KNOW ALL THIS WAS UNDER THE CENTRAL LIBRARY.
THIS IS A SPECIAL PLACE. ONLY GUESTS WHO ARE **DESTINED** TO COME HERE ARE ALLOWED TO ENTER.
DES-TINED?
YES.
I AM SURE WE WILL FIND YOUR PRECIOUS BOOK IN THIS SEA OF KNOWLEDGE AND MEMORY.
IT WILL BE LIKE FINDING A SINGLE PEARL IN THE VAST-NESS OF THE OCEAN...
BUT I, SANE-TOSHI, AM DEVOTED TO ASSISTING YOU.
WHAT A WEIRDO...
HERE IT IS.
THE STORY YOU WERE LOOKING FOR.
Frog-kun Saves Triple H
Frog-kun Saves Triple H
Frog-kun Saves the Habitat

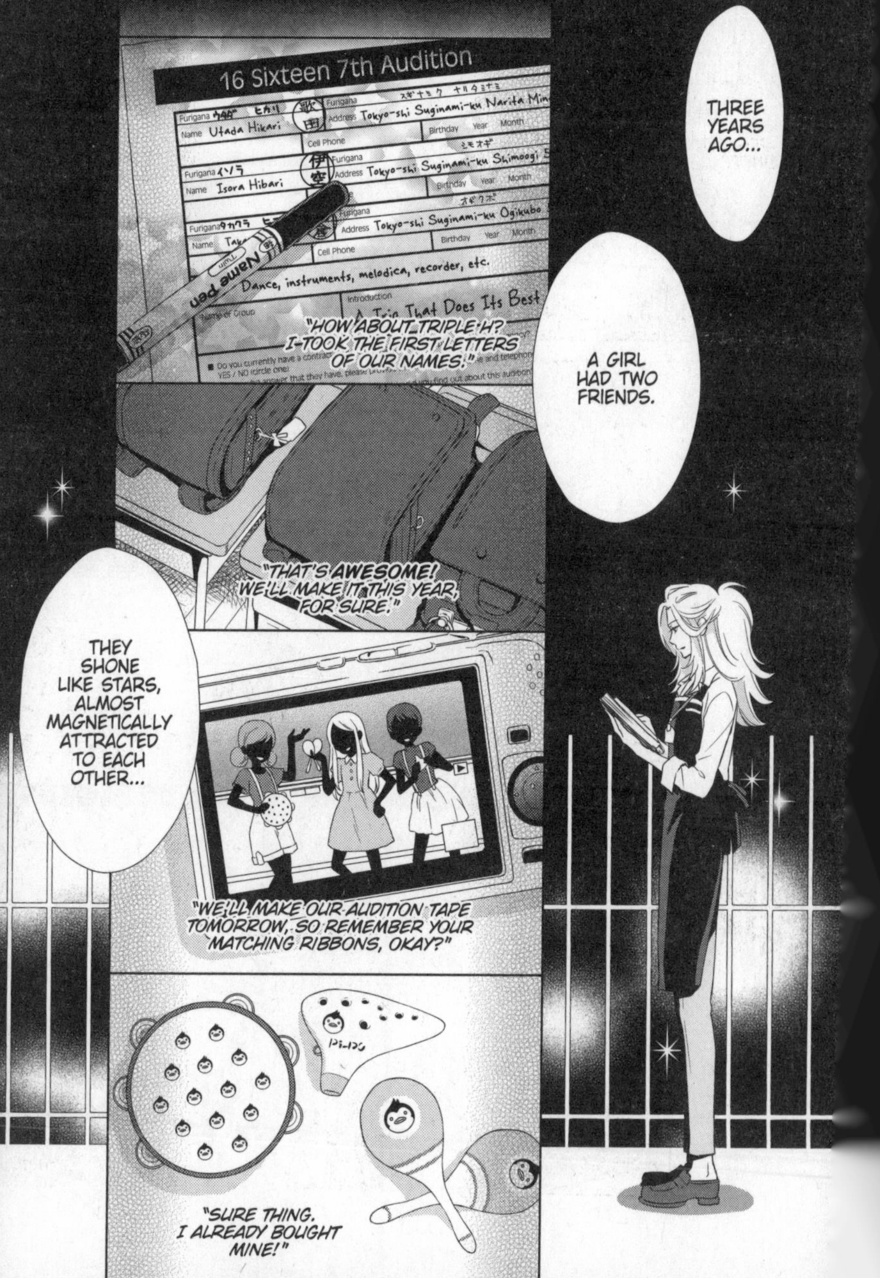
THREE YEARS AGO...
A GIRL HAD TWO FRIENDS.
16 Sixteen 7th Audition
Furigana ウタダ ヒカリ
Name Utada Hikari
Address Tokyo-shi Suginami-ku Narita Min
Birthday Year Month
Cell Phone
Furigana イソラ
Name Isora Hibari
Address Tokyo-shi Suginami-ku Shimoogi
Address Tokyo-shi Suginami-ku Ogikubo
Name pen
Dance, instruments, melodica, recorder, etc.
Introduction
A Trio That Does Its Best
"HOW ABOUT TRIPLE H? I TOOK THE FIRST LETTERS OF OUR NAMES."
"THAT'S AWESOME! WE'LL MAKE IT THIS YEAR, FOR SURE."
THEY SHONE LIKE STARS, ALMOST MAGNETICALLY ATTRACTED TO EACH OTHER...
"WE'LL MAKE OUR AUDITION TAPE TOMORROW, SO REMEMBER YOUR MATCHING RIBBONS, OKAY?"
"SURE THING. I ALREADY BOUGHT MINE!"

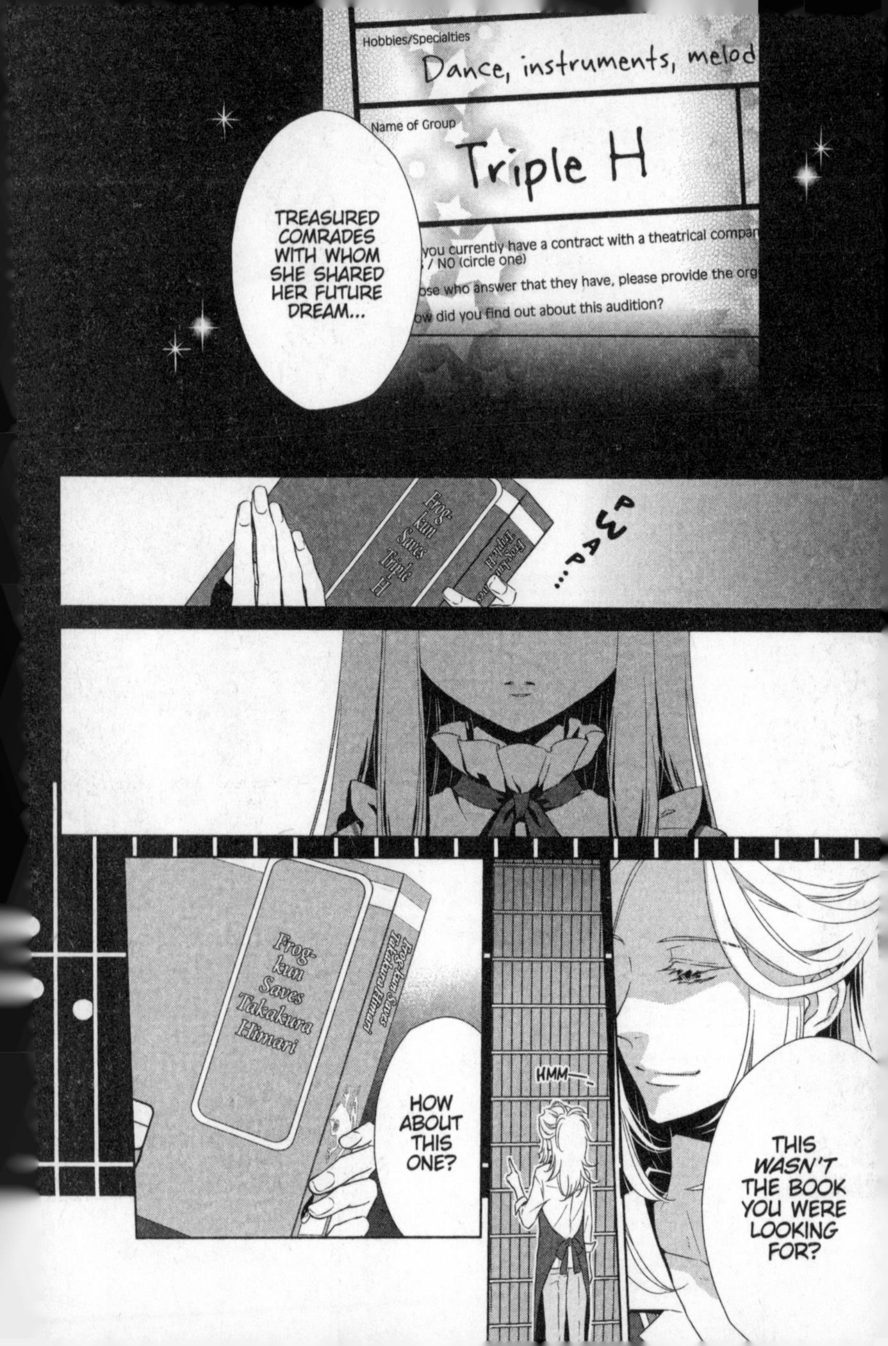
Hobbies/Specialties
Dance, instruments, melod
Name of Group
Triple H
you currently have a contract with a theatrical compan
/ NO (circle one)
ose who answer that they have, please provide the org
ow did you find out about this audition?
TREASURED COMRADES WITH WHOM SHE SHARED HER FUTURE DREAM...
Frog-kun Saves Triple H
Frog-kun Saves Triple H
PWAP...
THIS *WASN'T* THE BOOK YOU WERE LOOKING FOR?
HMM—
HOW ABOUT THIS ONE?
Frog-kun Saves Takakura Himari
Frog-kun Saves Takakura Himari

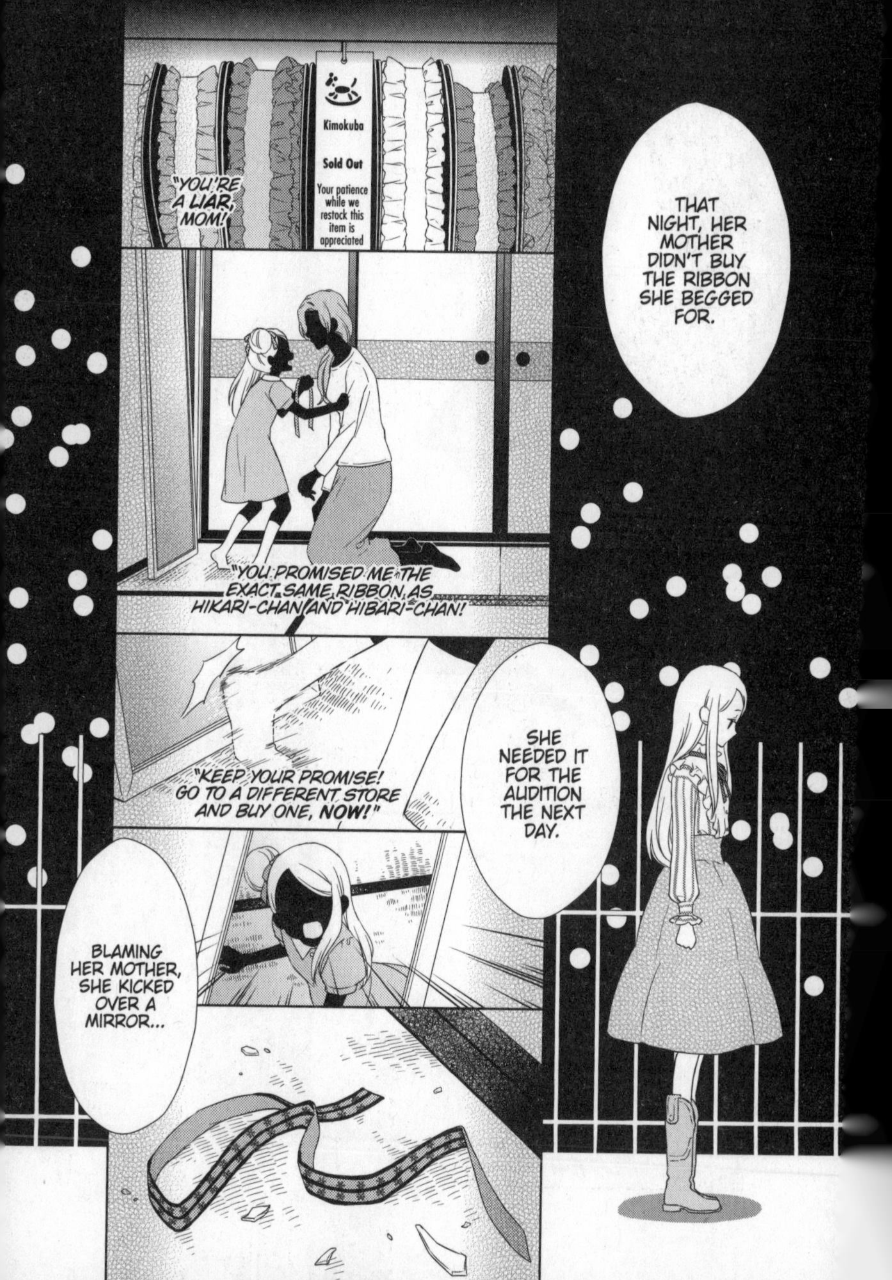
THAT NIGHT, HER MOTHER DIDN'T BUY THE RIBBON SHE BEGGED FOR.
SHE NEEDED IT FOR THE AUDITION THE NEXT DAY.
Kimokuba
Sold Out
Your patience while we restock this item is appreciated
"YOU'RE A LIAR, MOM!
"YOU PROMISED ME THE EXACT SAME RIBBON AS HIKARI-CHAN AND HIBARI-CHAN!
"KEEP YOUR PROMISE! GO TO A DIFFERENT STORE AND BUY ONE, NOW!"
BLAMING HER MOTHER, SHE KICKED OVER A MIRROR...

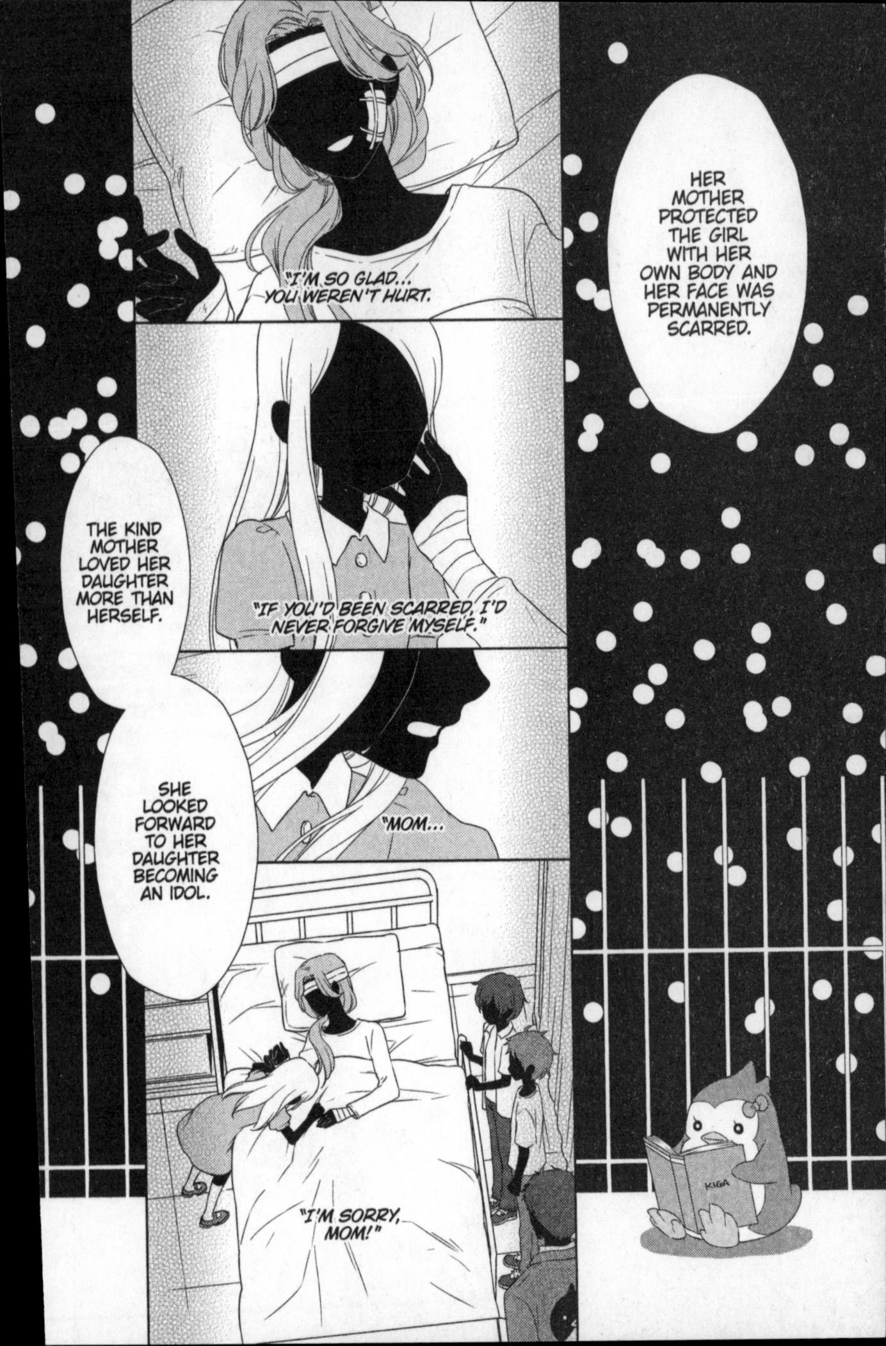
HER MOTHER PROTECTED THE GIRL WITH HER OWN BODY AND HER FACE WAS PERMANENTLY SCARRED.
"I'M SO GLAD... YOU WEREN'T HURT.
THE KIND MOTHER LOVED HER DAUGHTER MORE THAN HERSELF.
"IF YOU'D BEEN SCARRED, I'D NEVER FORGIVE MYSELF."
"MOM...
SHE LOOKED FORWARD TO HER DAUGHTER BECOMING AN IDOL.
"I'M SORRY, MOM!"
KIGA

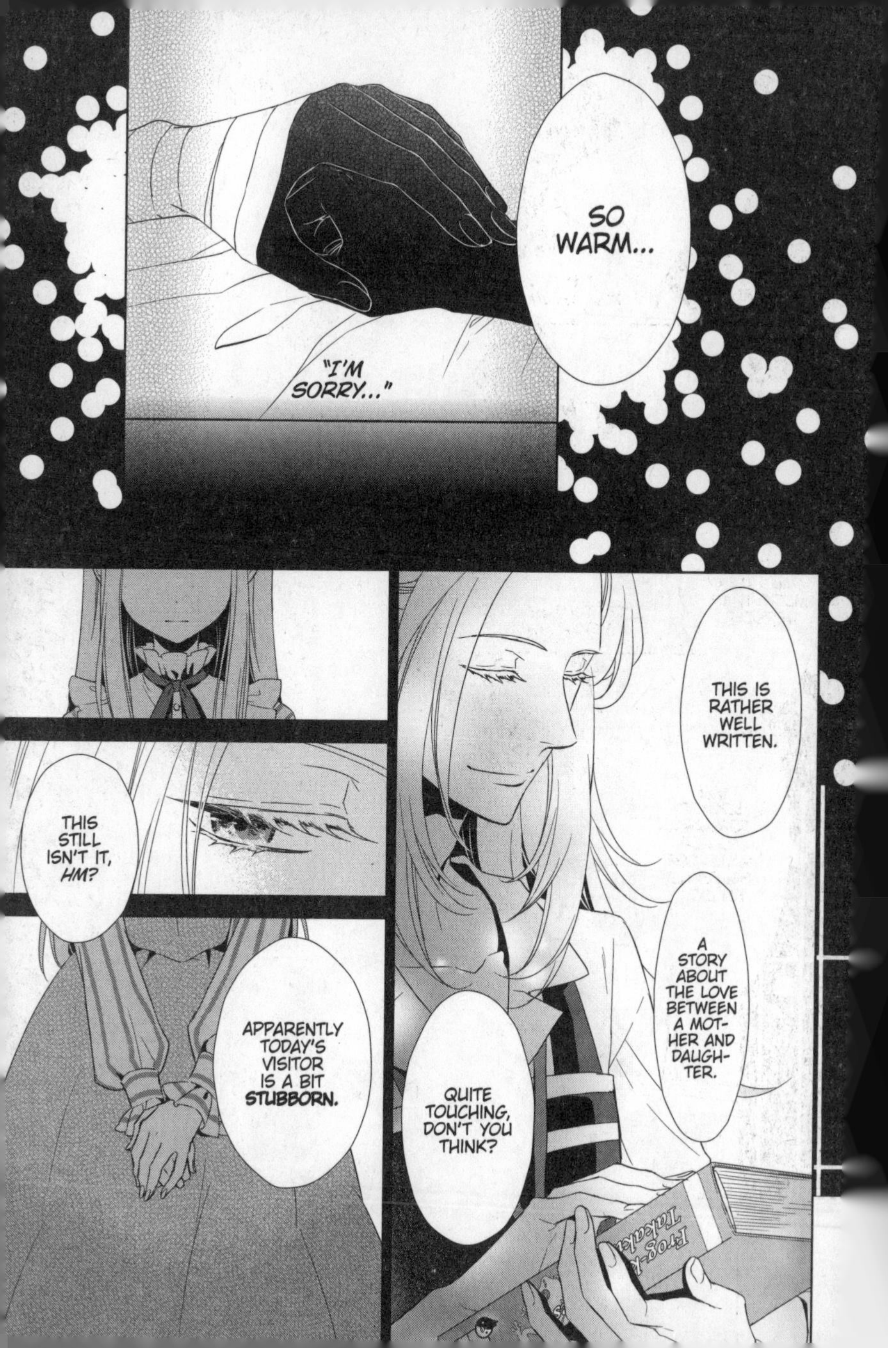
SO WARM...
"I'M SORRY..."
THIS IS RATHER WELL WRITTEN.
A STORY ABOUT THE LOVE BETWEEN A MOTHER AND DAUGHTER.
QUITE TOUCHING, DON'T YOU THINK?
THIS STILL ISN'T IT, *HM?*
APPARENTLY TODAY'S VISITOR IS A BIT **STUBBORN.**

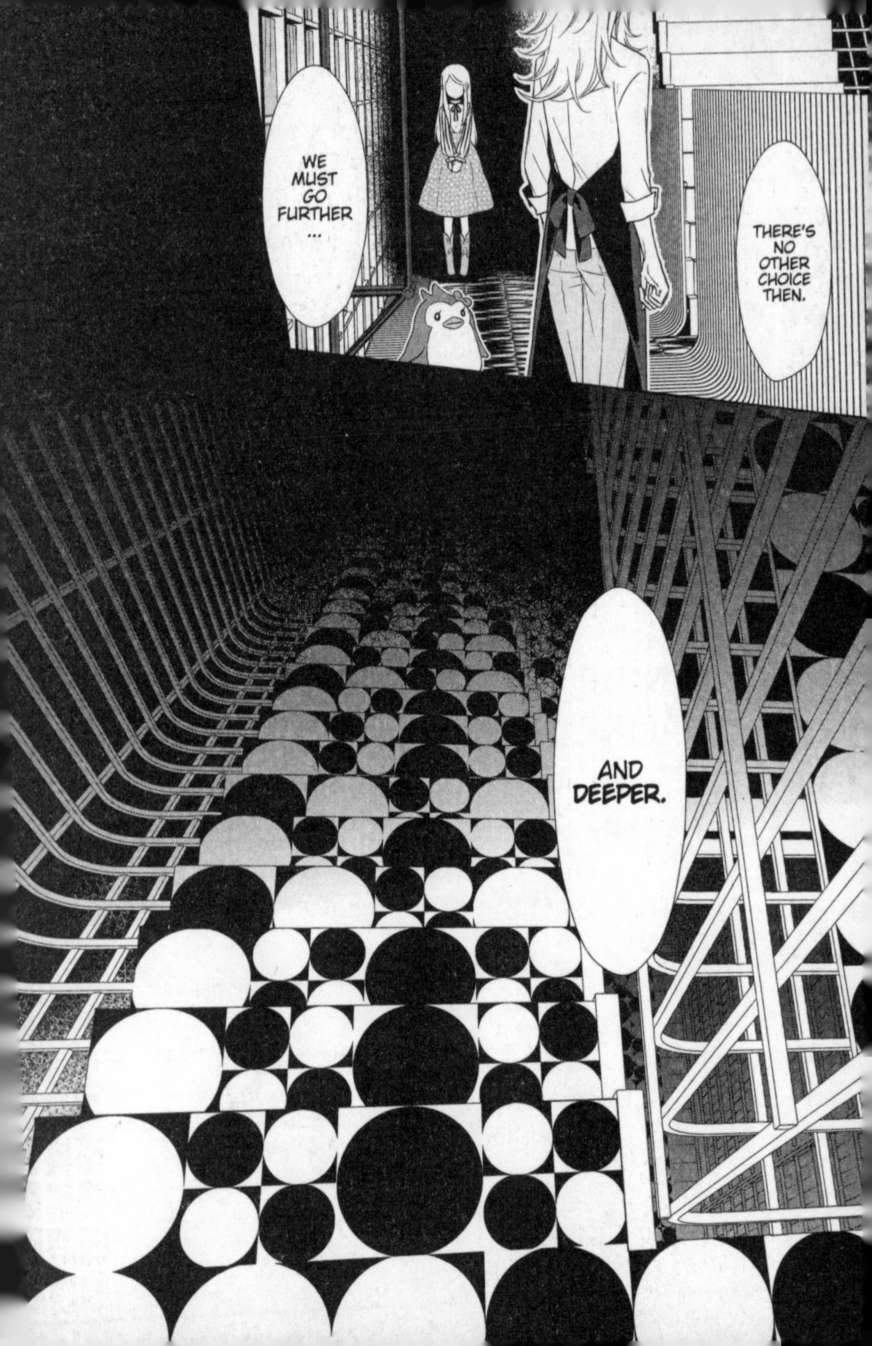
THERE'S NO OTHER CHOICE THEN.
WE MUST GO FURTHER ...
AND DEEPER.

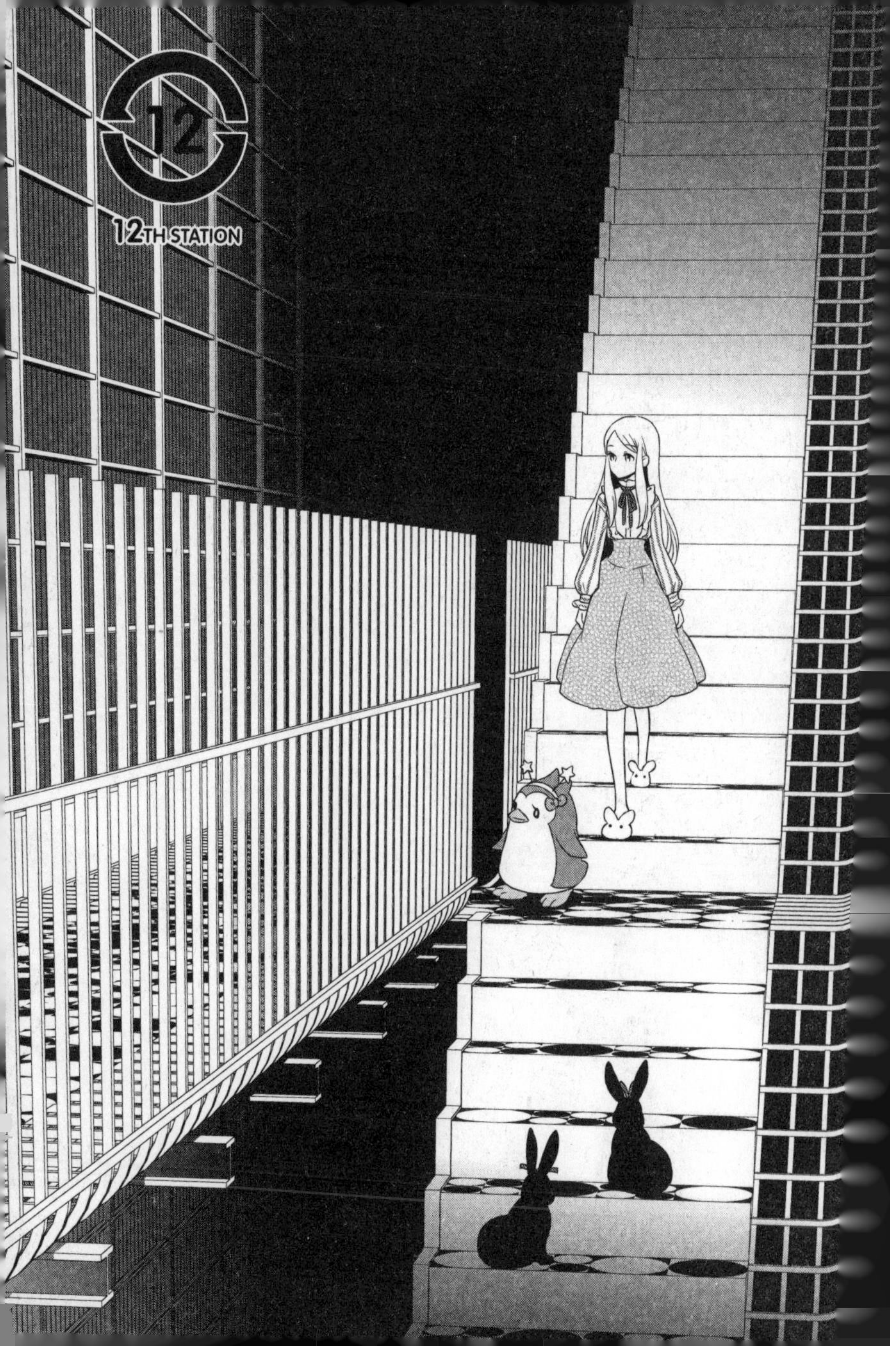
12
12TH STATION

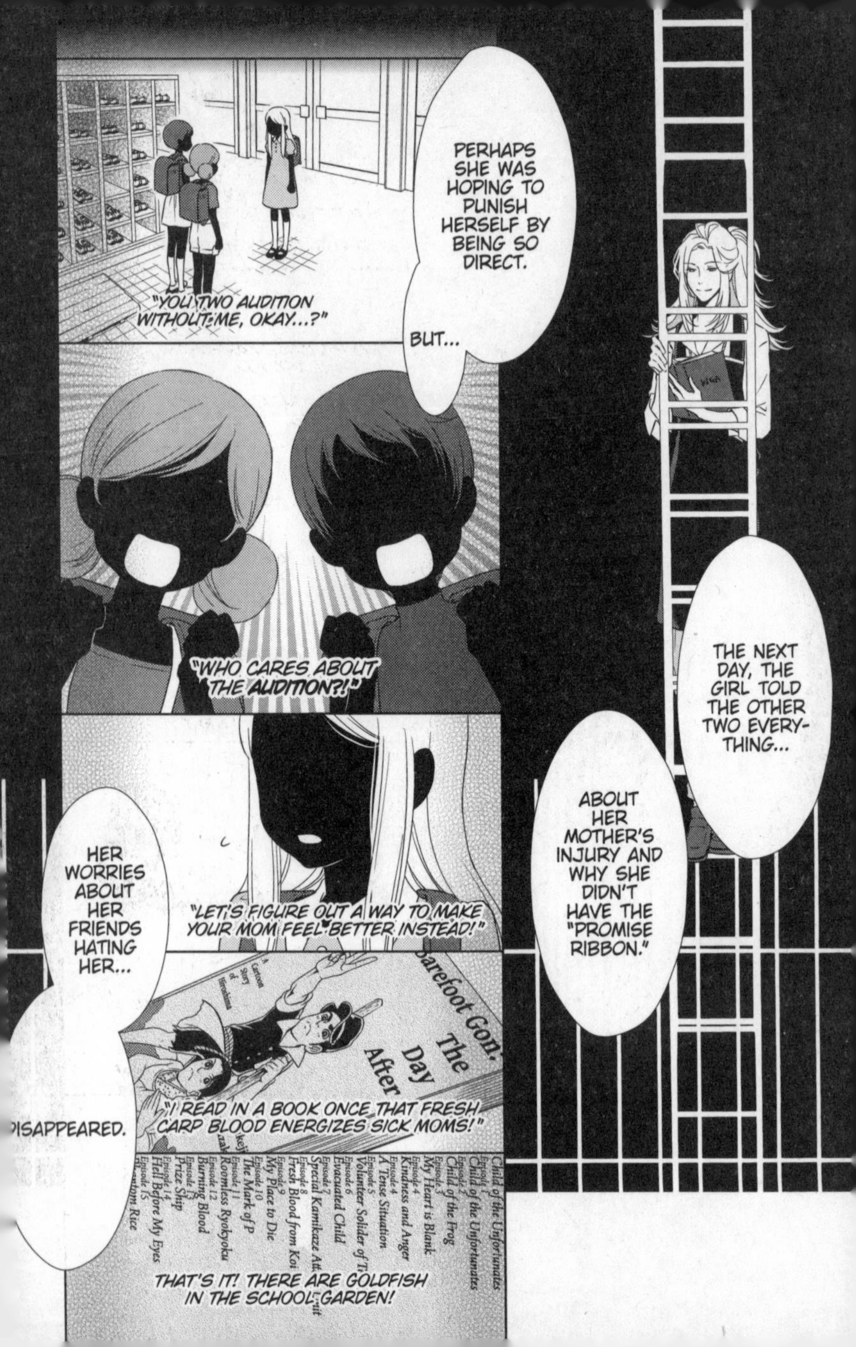
THE NEXT DAY, THE GIRL TOLD THE OTHER TWO EVERY-THING...
ABOUT HER MOTHER'S INJURY AND WHY SHE DIDN'T HAVE THE "PROMISE RIBBON."
"YOU TWO AUDITION WITHOUT ME, OKAY...?"
PERHAPS SHE WAS HOPING TO PUNISH HERSELF BY BEING SO DIRECT.
BUT...
"WHO CARES ABOUT THE AUDITION?!"
"LET'S FIGURE OUT A WAY TO MAKE YOUR MOM FEEL BETTER INSTEAD!"
HER WORRIES ABOUT HER FRIENDS HATING HER...
DISAPPEARED.
A Cartoon Story of Hiroshima
Barefoot Gon: The Day After
"I READ IN A BOOK ONCE THAT FRESH CARP BLOOD ENERGIZES SICK MOMS!"
Episode 1 Child of the Unfortunates
Episode 2 Child of the Frog
Episode 3 My Heart is Blank
Episode 4 Kindness and Anger
Episode 5 A Tense Situation
Episode 6 Evacuated Child
Episode 7 Special Kamikaze Att
Episode 8 Fresh Blood from Koi
Episode 9 My Place to Die
Episode 10 The Mark of P
Episode 11 Roomless Ryokyoku
Episode 12 Burning Blood
Prize Ship
Episode 14 Hell Before My Eyes
Episode 15
THAT'S IT! THERE ARE GOLDFISH IN THE SCHOOL GARDEN!

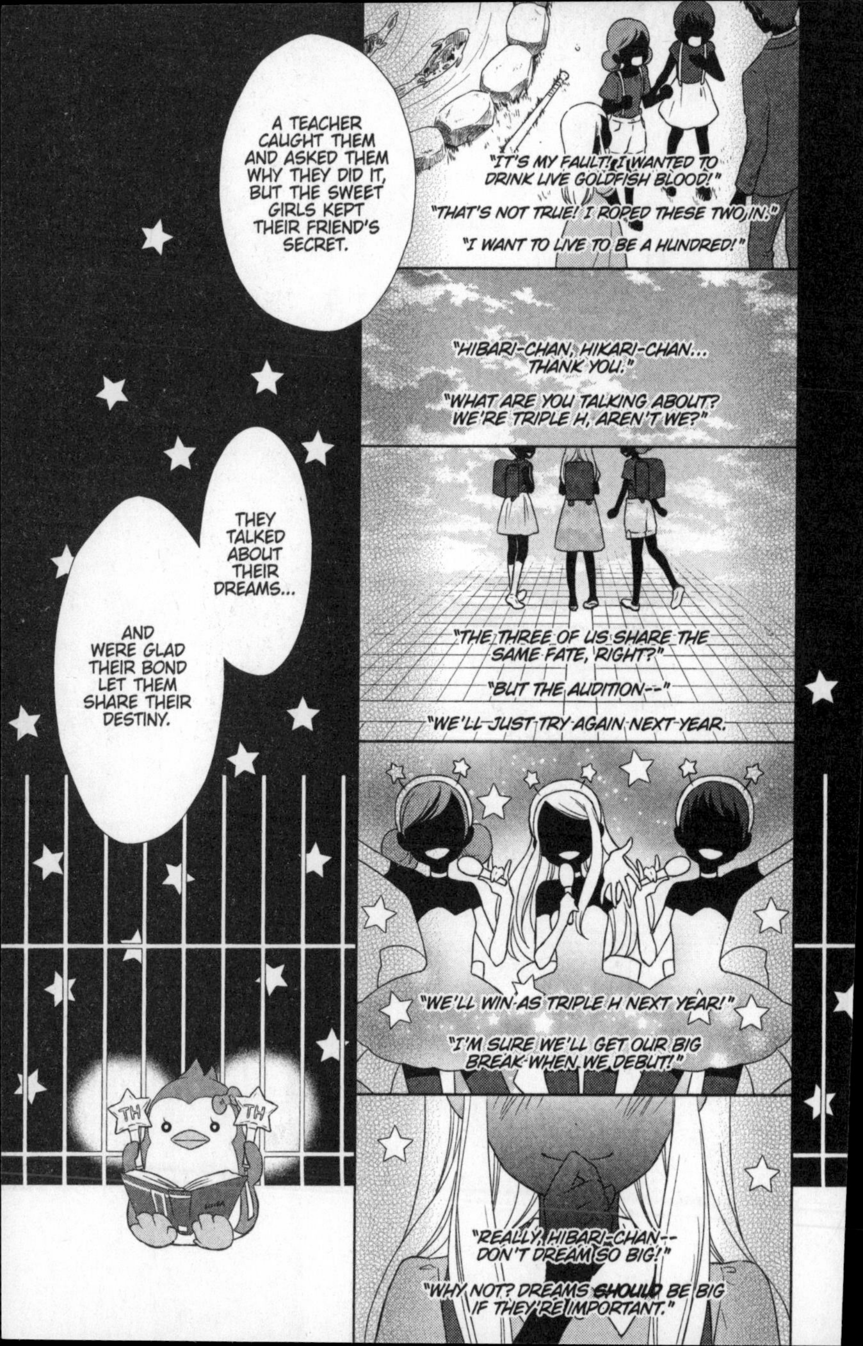
"IT'S MY FAULT! I WANTED TO DRINK LIVE GOLDFISH BLOOD!"
"THAT'S NOT TRUE! I ROPED THESE TWO IN."
"I WANT TO LIVE TO BE A HUNDRED!"
"HIBARI-CHAN, HIKARI-CHAN... THANK YOU."
"WHAT ARE YOU TALKING ABOUT? WE'RE TRIPLE H, AREN'T WE?"
"THE THREE OF US SHARE THE SAME FATE, RIGHT?"
"BUT THE AUDITION--"
"WE'LL JUST TRY AGAIN NEXT YEAR.
"WE'LL WIN AS TRIPLE H NEXT YEAR!"
"I'M SURE WE'LL GET OUR BIG BREAK WHEN WE DEBUT!"
"REALLY, HIBARI-CHAN-- DON'T DREAM SO BIG!"
"WHY NOT? DREAMS SHOULD BE BIG IF THEY'RE IMPORTANT."
A TEACHER CAUGHT THEM AND ASKED THEM WHY THEY DID IT, BUT THE SWEET GIRLS KEPT THEIR FRIEND'S SECRET.
THEY TALKED ABOUT THEIR DREAMS...
AND WERE GLAD THEIR BOND LET THEM SHARE THEIR DESTINY.
TH
TH

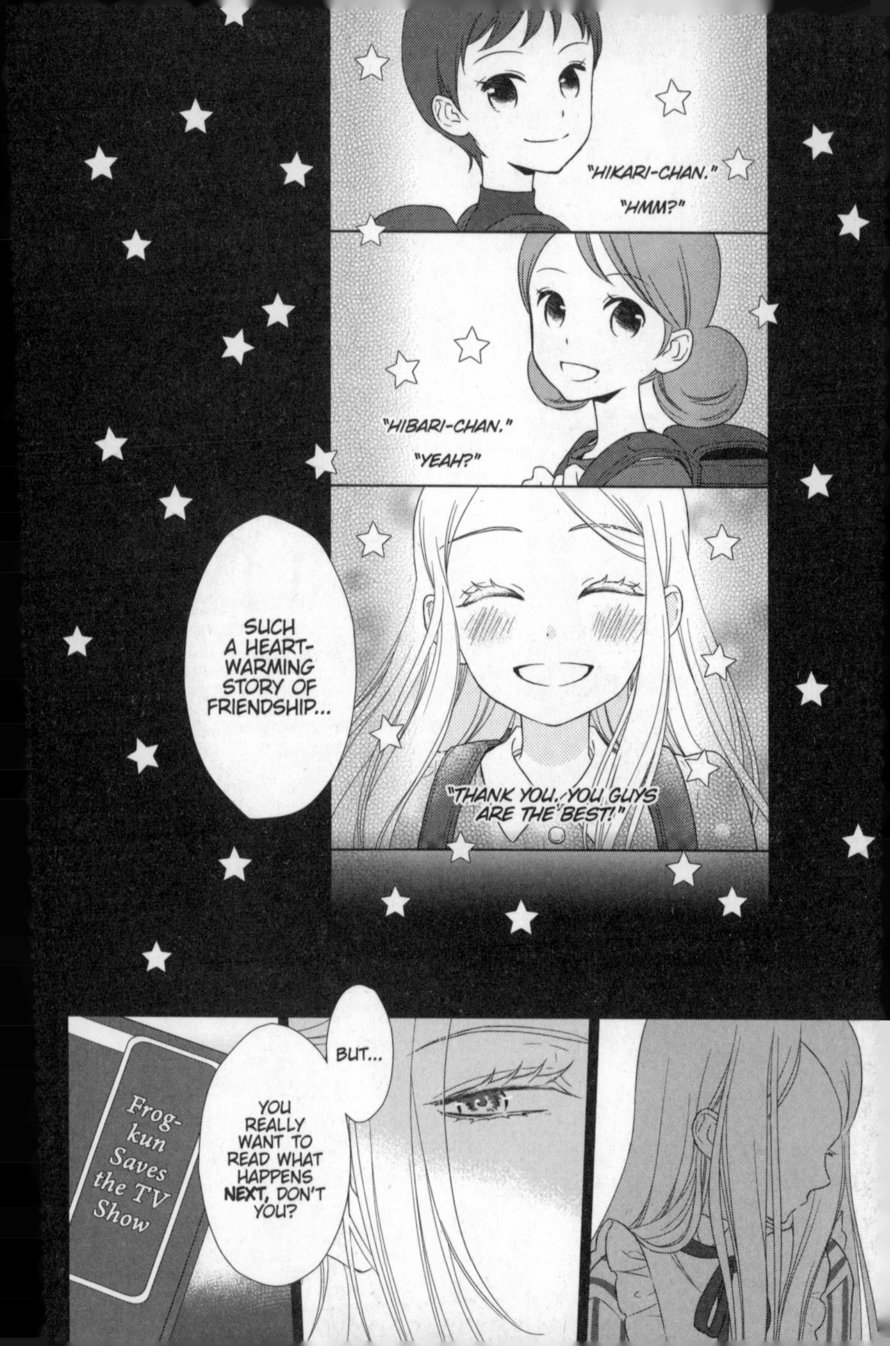

"HIKARI-CHAN."
"HMM?"
"HIBARI-CHAN."
"YEAH?"
"THANK YOU. YOU GUYS ARE THE BEST!"
SUCH A HEART-WARMING STORY OF FRIENDSHIP...
BUT...
YOU REALLY WANT TO READ WHAT HAPPENS **NEXT**, DON'T YOU?
Frog-kun Saves the TV Show

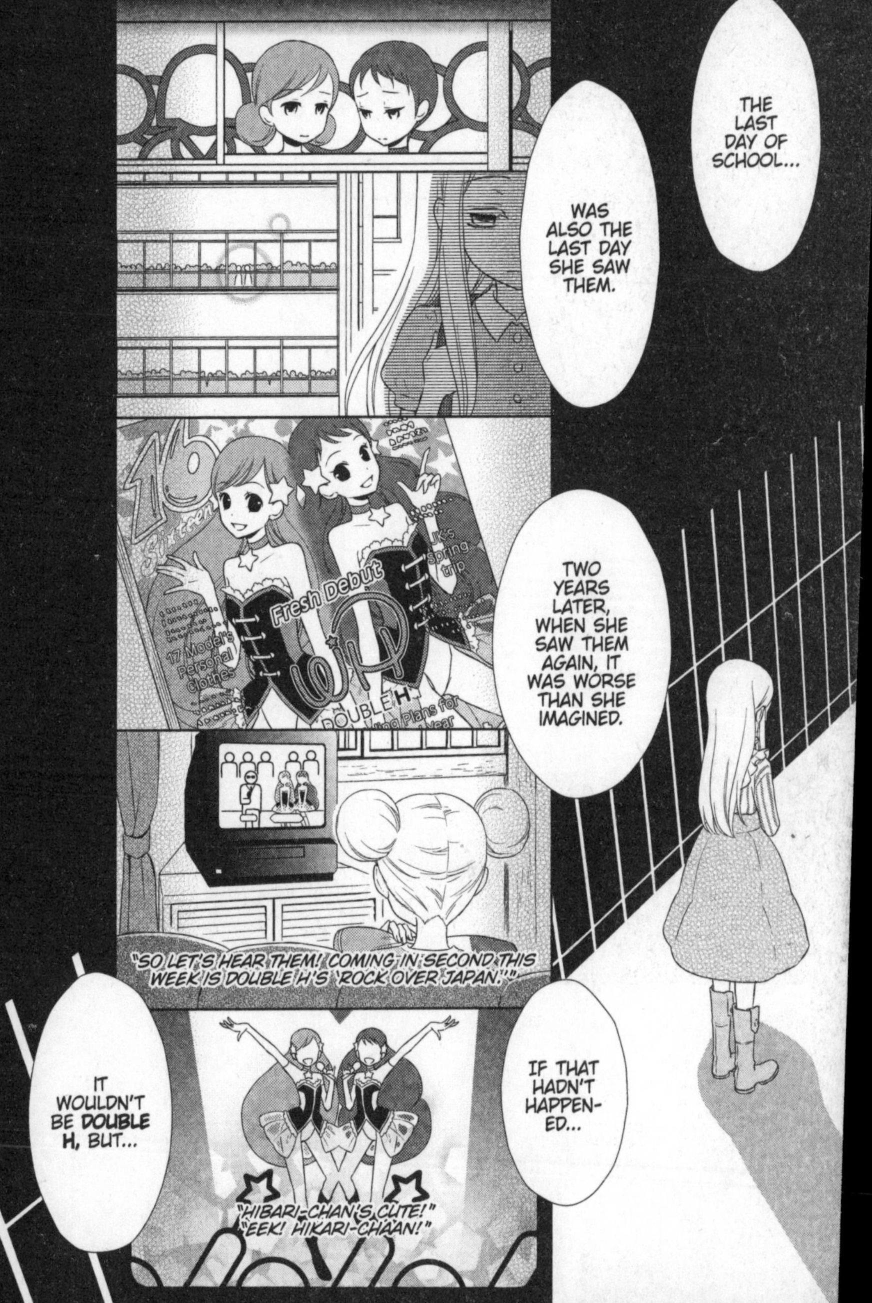
THE LAST DAY OF SCHOOL...
WAS ALSO THE LAST DAY SHE SAW THEM.
Sixteen
JK'S Spring trip
Fresh Debut
17 Model's Personal Clothes
DOUBLE H
TWO YEARS LATER, WHEN SHE SAW THEM AGAIN, IT WAS WORSE THAN SHE IMAGINED.
"SO LET'S HEAR THEM! COMING IN SECOND THIS WEEK IS DOUBLE H'S 'ROCK OVER JAPAN.'"
IF THAT HADN'T HAPPEN-ED...
IT WOULDN'T BE DOUBLE H, BUT...
"HIBARI-CHAN'S CUTE!"
"EEK! HIKARI-CHAAN!"

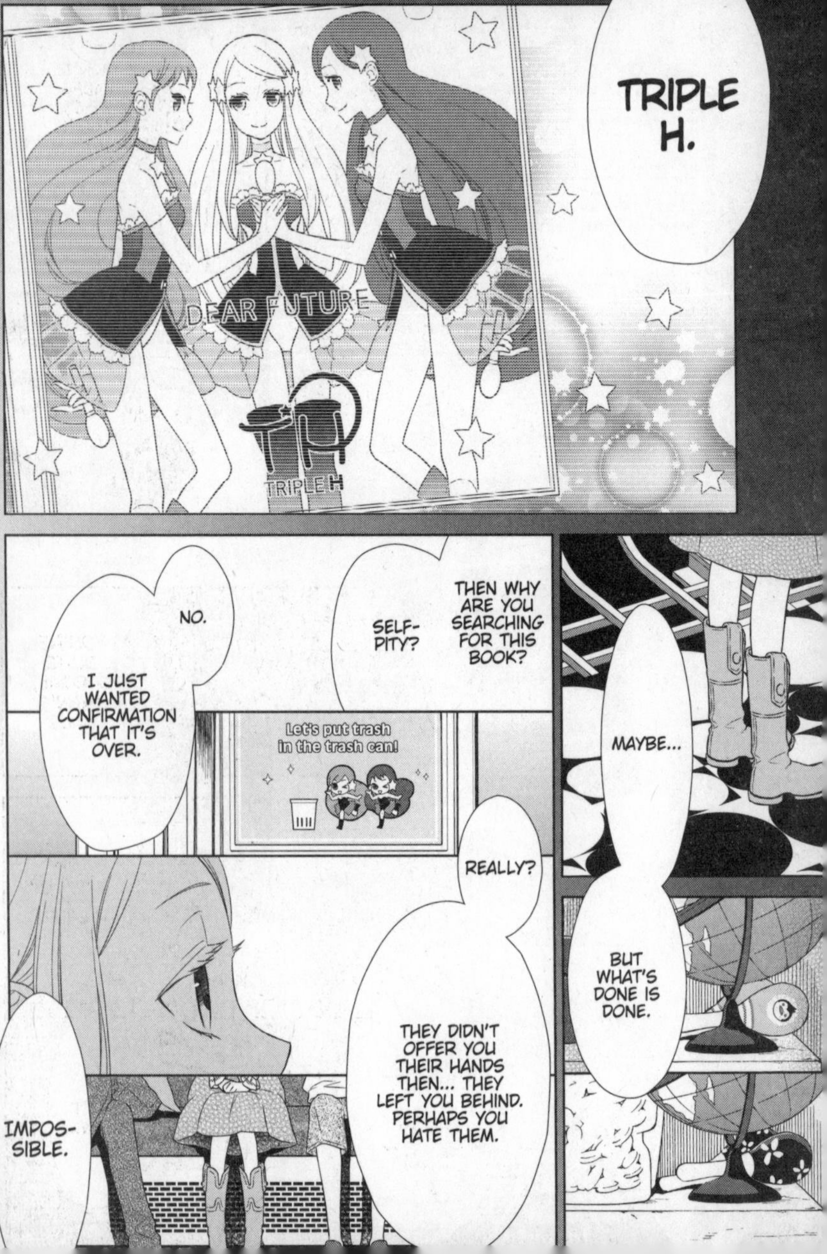
TRIPLE H.
DEAR FUTURE
TRIPLE H
MAYBE...
BUT WHAT'S DONE IS DONE.
THEN WHY ARE YOU SEARCHING FOR THIS BOOK?
SELF-PITY?
NO.
I JUST WANTED CONFIRMATION THAT IT'S OVER.
Let's put trash in the trash can!
REALLY?
THEY DIDN'T OFFER YOU THEIR HANDS THEN... THEY LEFT YOU BEHIND. PERHAPS YOU HATE THEM.
IMPOS-SIBLE.

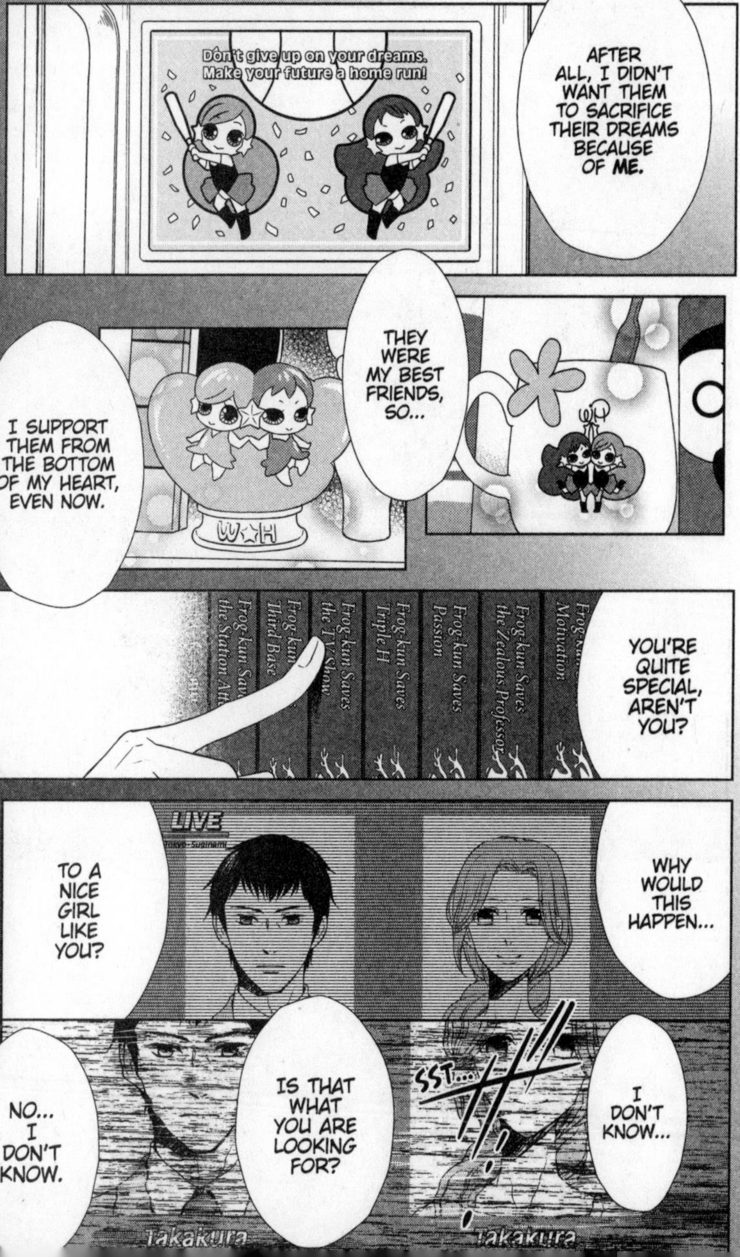
AFTER ALL, I DIDN'T WANT THEM TO SACRIFICE THEIR DREAMS BECAUSE OF ME.
Don't give up on your dreams. Make your future a home run!
THEY WERE MY BEST FRIENDS, SO...
I SUPPORT THEM FROM THE BOTTOM OF MY HEART, EVEN NOW.
W☆H
YOU'RE QUITE SPECIAL, AREN'T YOU?
Motivation
Frog-kun Saves the Zealous Professor
Frog-kun Saves Passion
Frog-kun Saves Triple H
Frog-kun Saves the TV Show
Third Base
WHY WOULD THIS HAPPEN...
TO A NICE GIRL LIKE YOU?
LIVE
Tokyo · Suginami
I DON'T KNOW...
SST...
IS THAT WHAT YOU ARE LOOKING FOR?
NO... I DON'T KNOW.
Takakura
Takakura

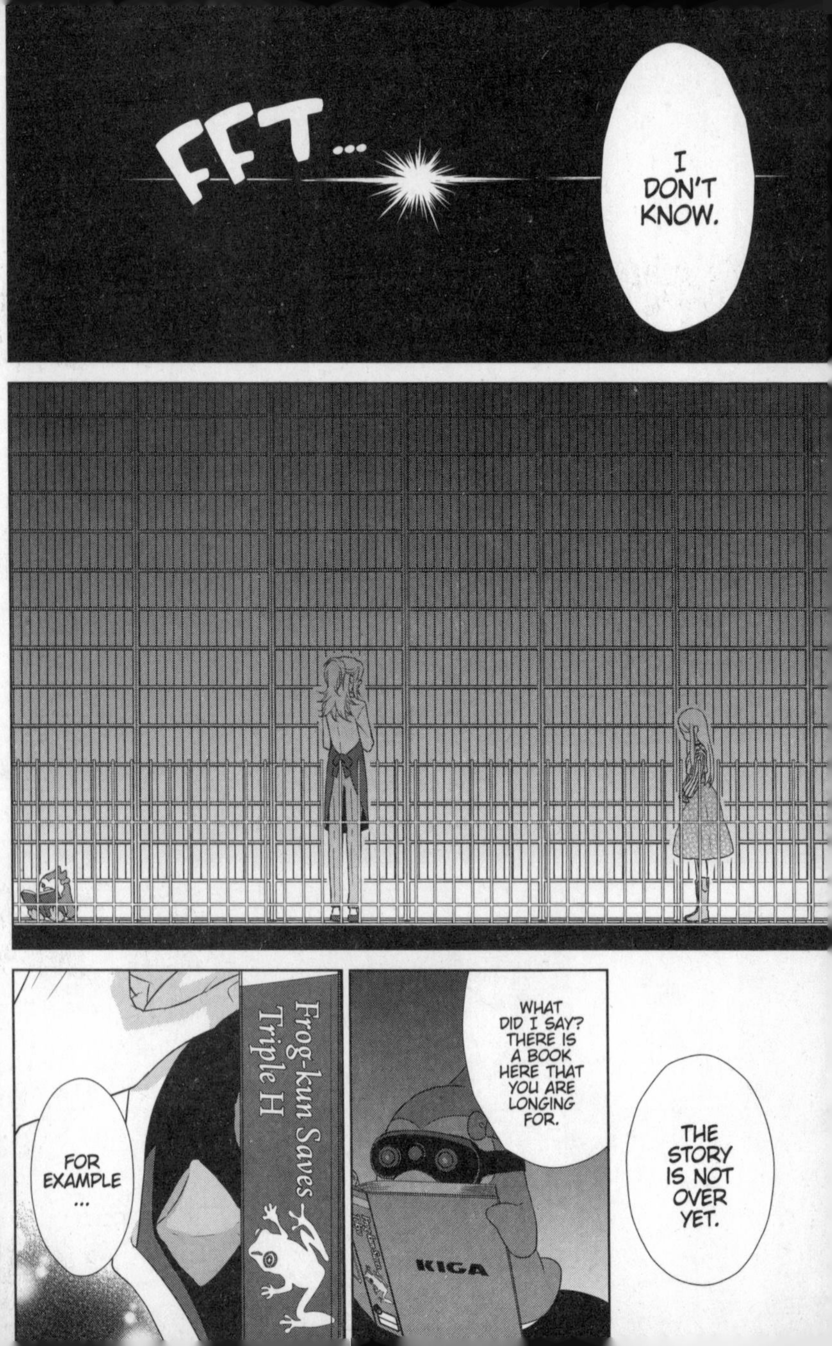
I DON'T KNOW.
FFT...
THE STORY IS NOT OVER YET.
WHAT DID I SAY? THERE IS A BOOK HERE THAT YOU ARE LONGING FOR.
KIGA
Frog-kun Saves Triple H
FOR EXAMPLE ...

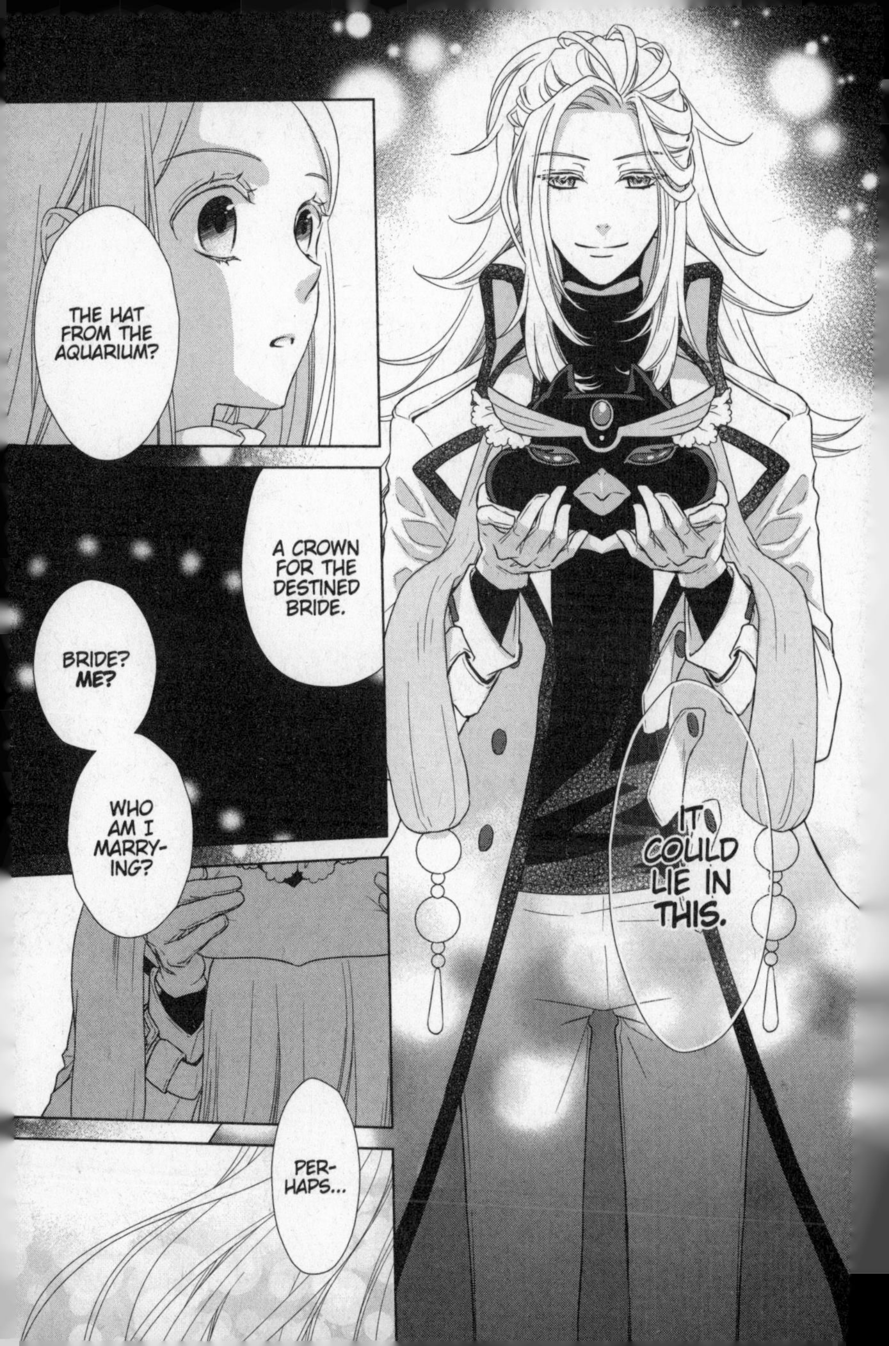
IT COULD LIE IN THIS.
THE HAT FROM THE AQUARIUM?
A CROWN FOR THE DESTINED BRIDE.
BRIDE? ME?
WHO AM I MARRY-ING?
PER-HAPS...

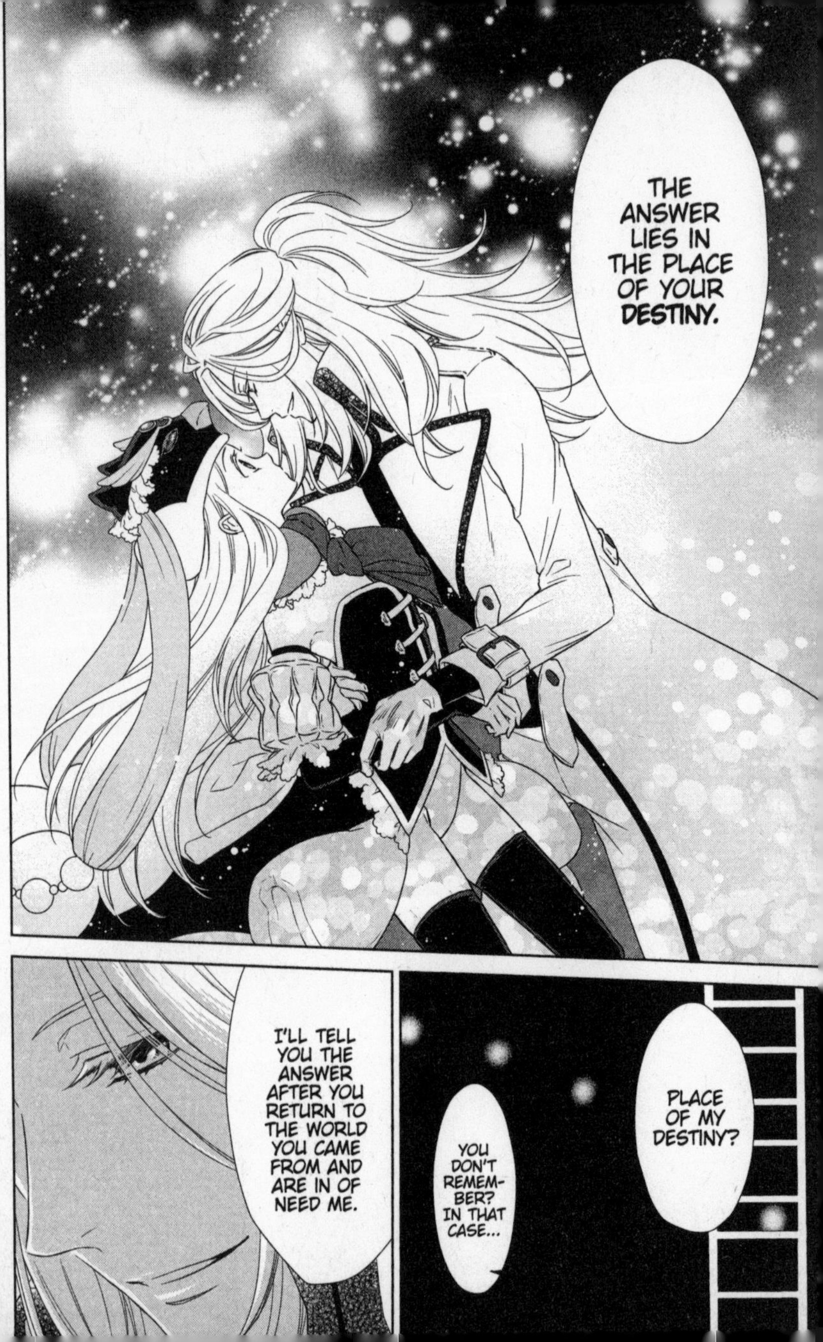
THE ANSWER LIES IN THE PLACE OF YOUR DESTINY.
PLACE OF MY DESTINY?
YOU DON'T REMEM-BER? IN THAT CASE...
I'LL TELL YOU THE ANSWER AFTER YOU RETURN TO THE WORLD YOU CAME FROM AND ARE IN OF NEED ME.

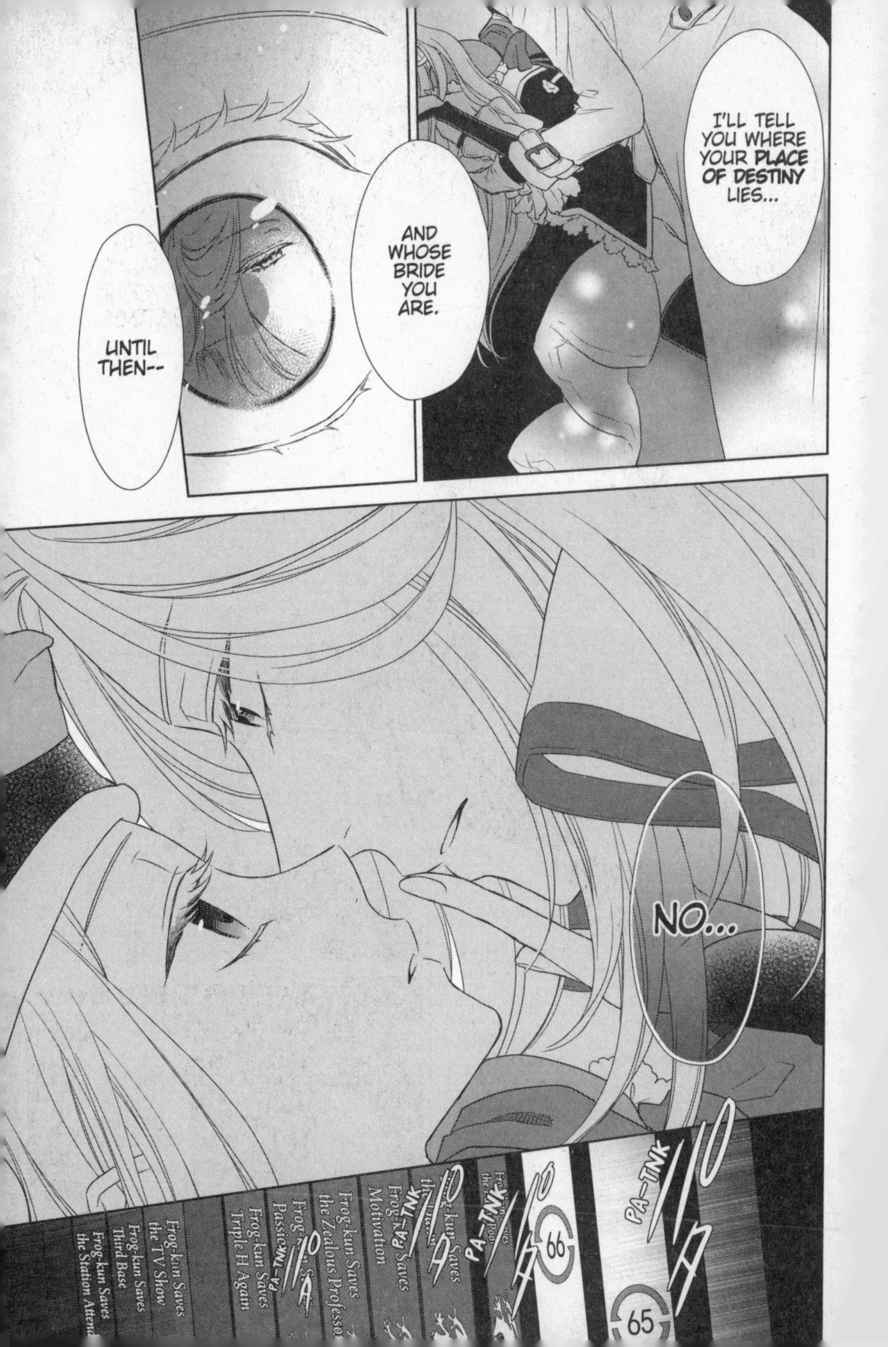
I'LL TELL YOU WHERE YOUR PLACE OF DESTINY LIES...
AND WHOSE BRIDE YOU ARE.
UNTIL THEN--
NO...
PA-TNK
65
66
PA-TNK
PA-TNK
Frog-kun Saves Motivation
Frog-kun Saves Triple H Again
Frog-kun Saves the TV Show
Frog-kun Saves Third Base

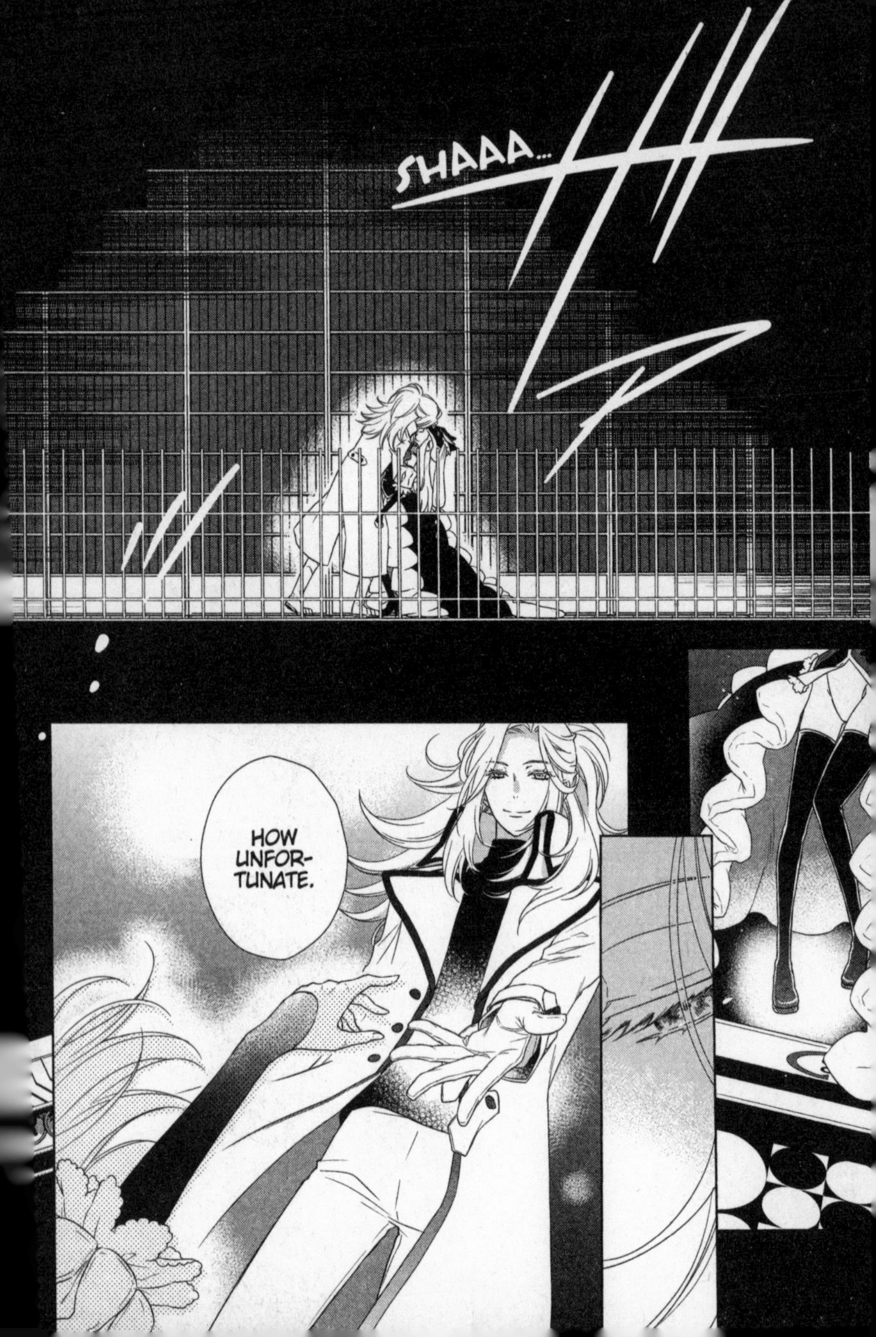
SHAAA...
HOW UNFORTUNATE.

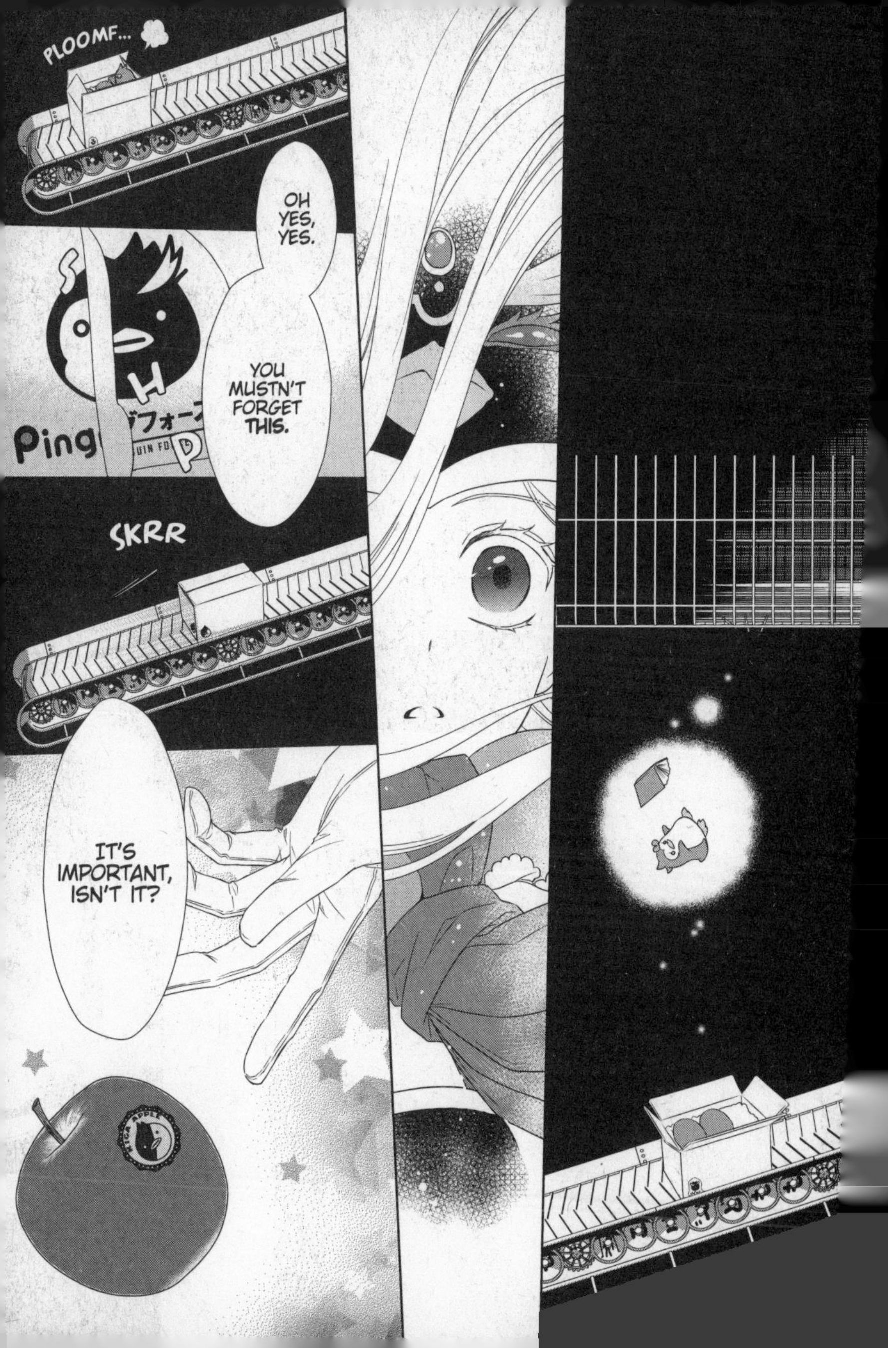
PLOOMF...
OH YES, YES.
YOU MUSTN'T FORGET THIS.
SKRR
IT'S IMPORTANT, ISN'T IT?

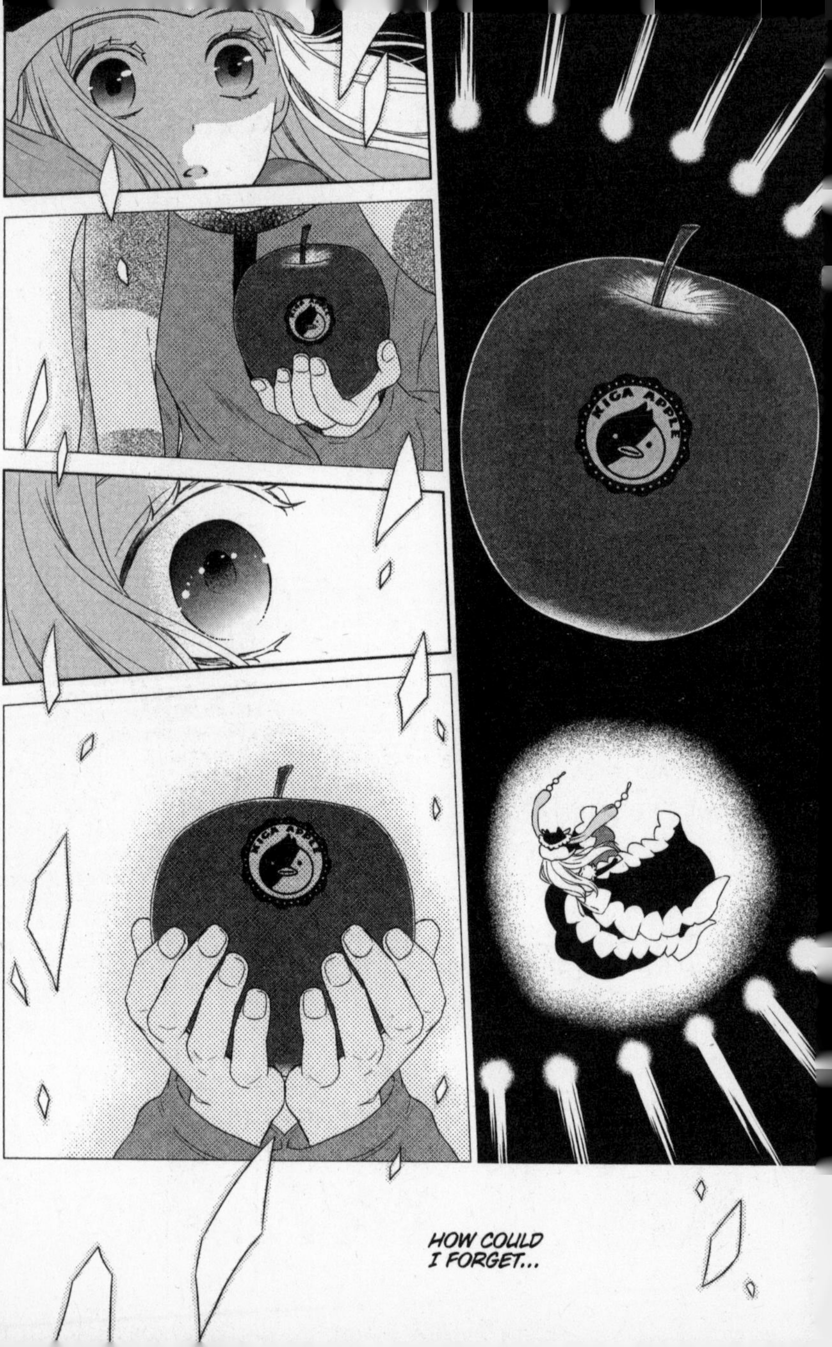
KIGA APPLE
HOW COULD I FORGET...

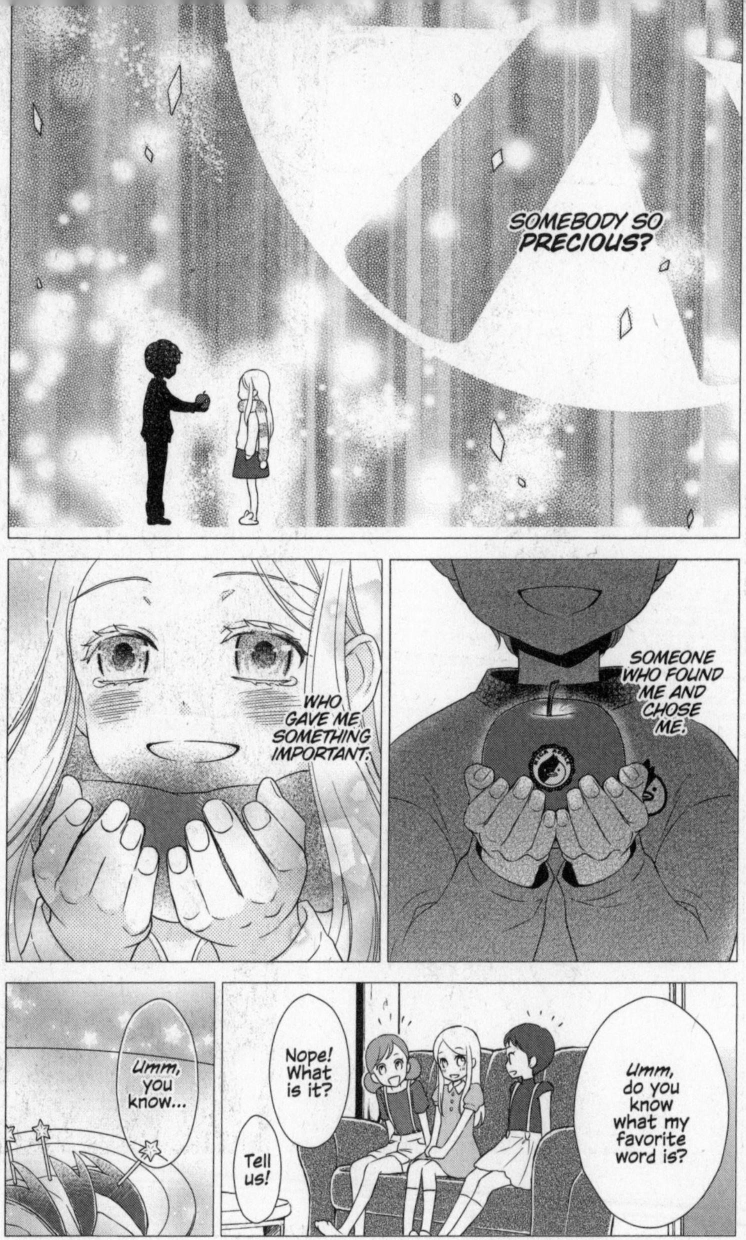
SOMEBODY SO PRECIOUS?
SOMEONE WHO FOUND ME AND CHOSE ME.
WHO GAVE ME SOMETHING IMPORTANT.
Umm, do you know what my favorite word is?
Nope! What is it?
Tell us!
Umm, you know...

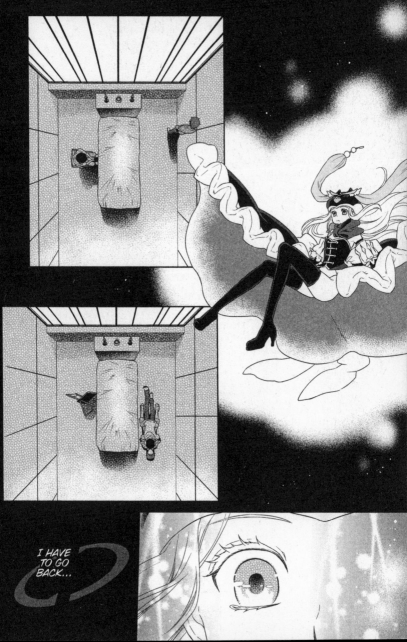

I HAVE
TO GO
BACK...

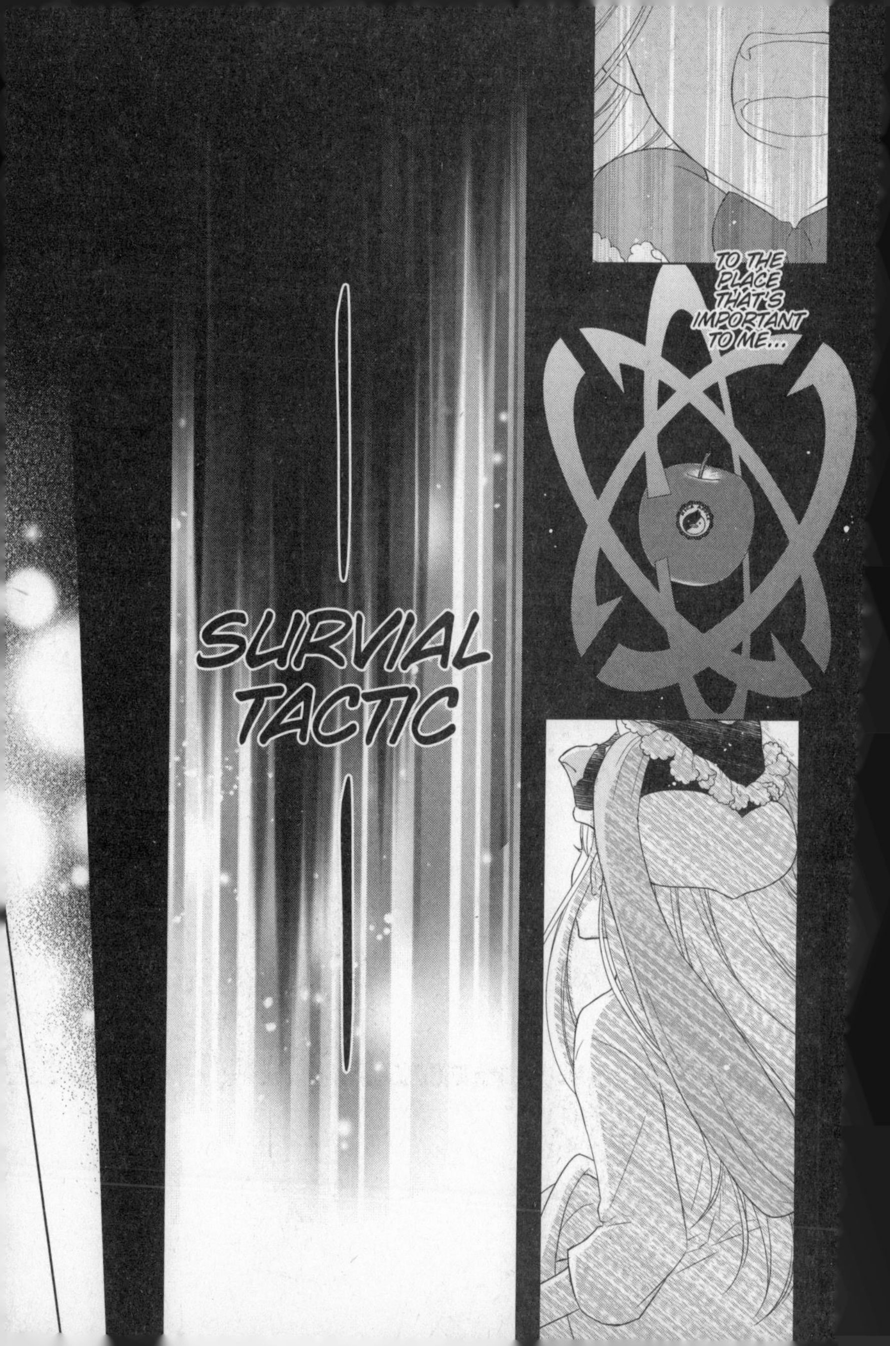
TO THE PLACE THAT'S IMPORTANT TO ME...
SURVIAL TACTIC

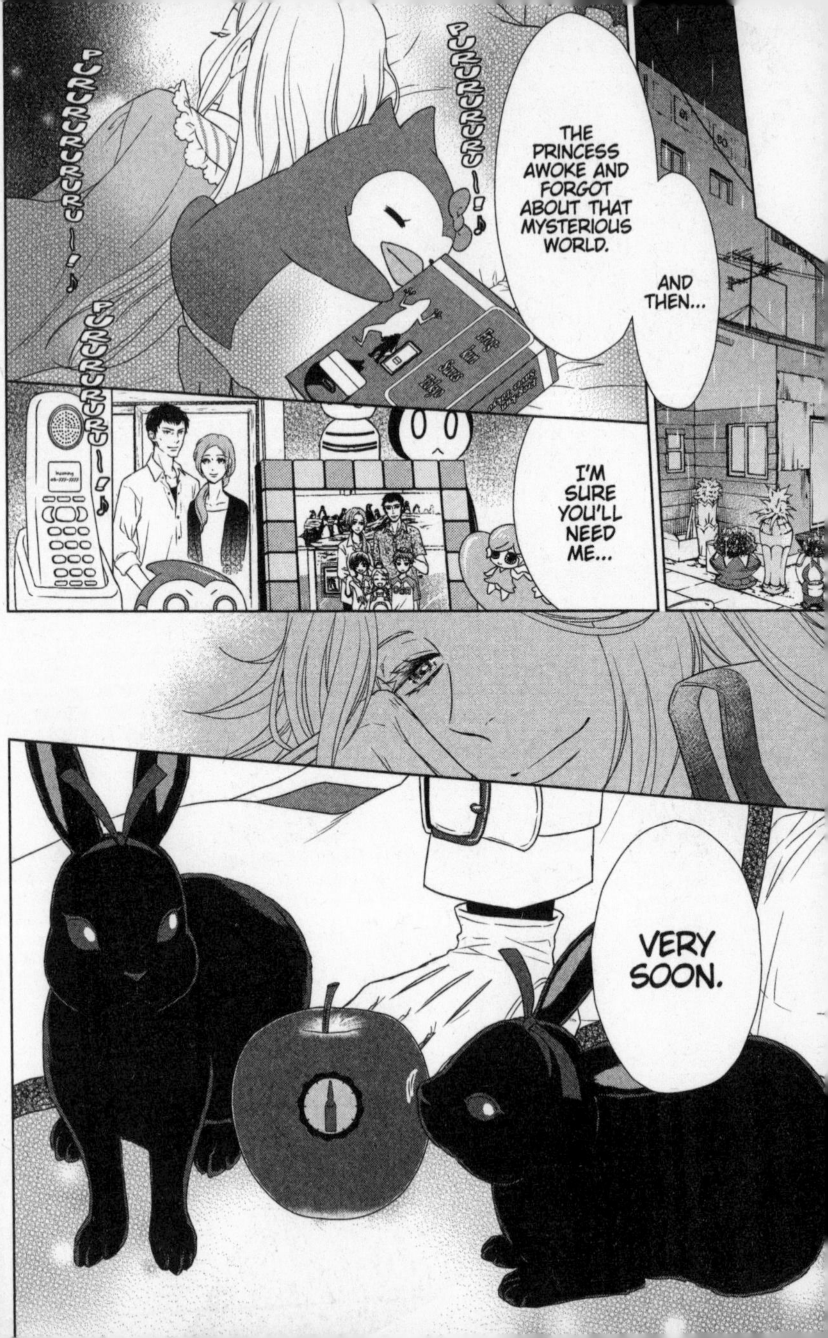
THE PRINCESS AWOKE AND FORGOT ABOUT THAT MYSTERIOUS WORLD.
AND THEN...
PURURURURU~!♪
PURURURURURU~!♪
I'M SURE YOU'LL NEED ME...
PURURURURU~!♪
VERY SOON.

13

13TH STATION

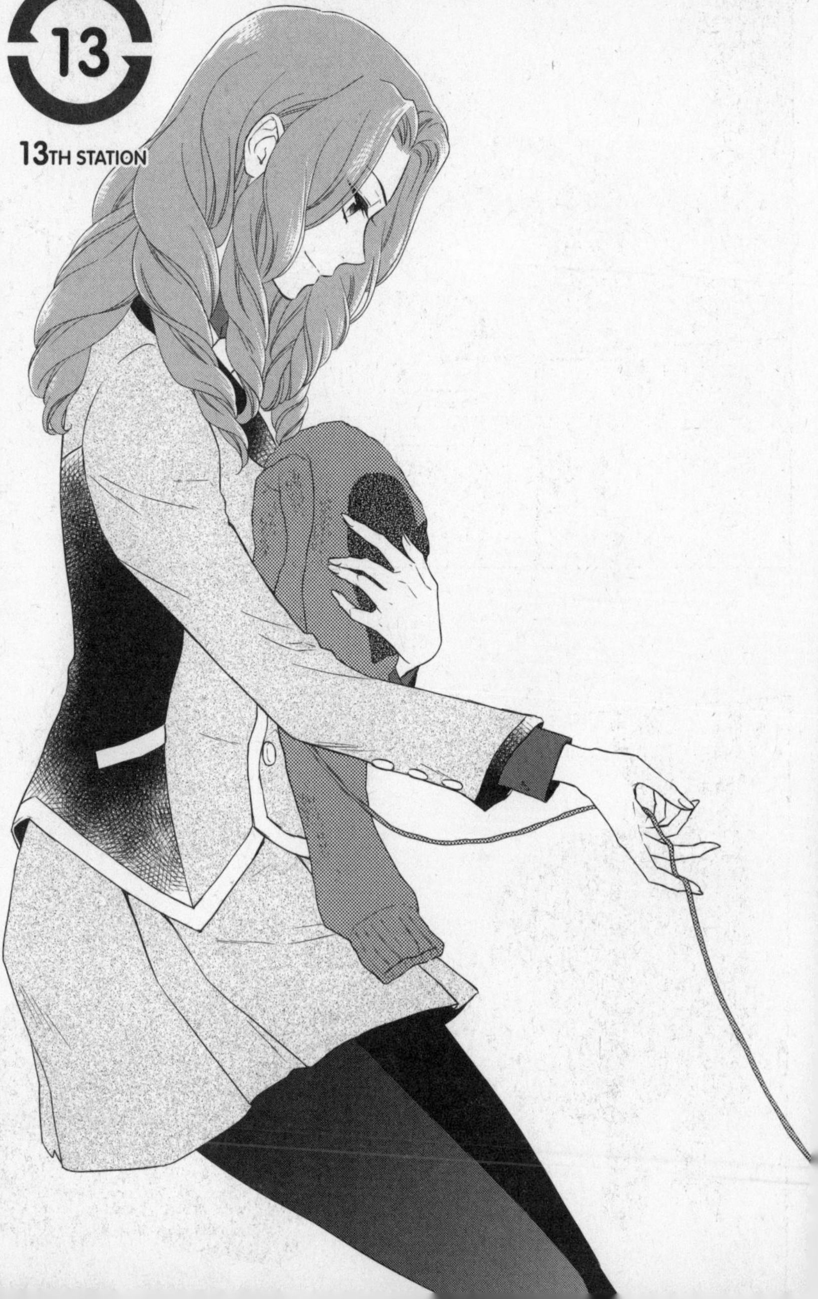

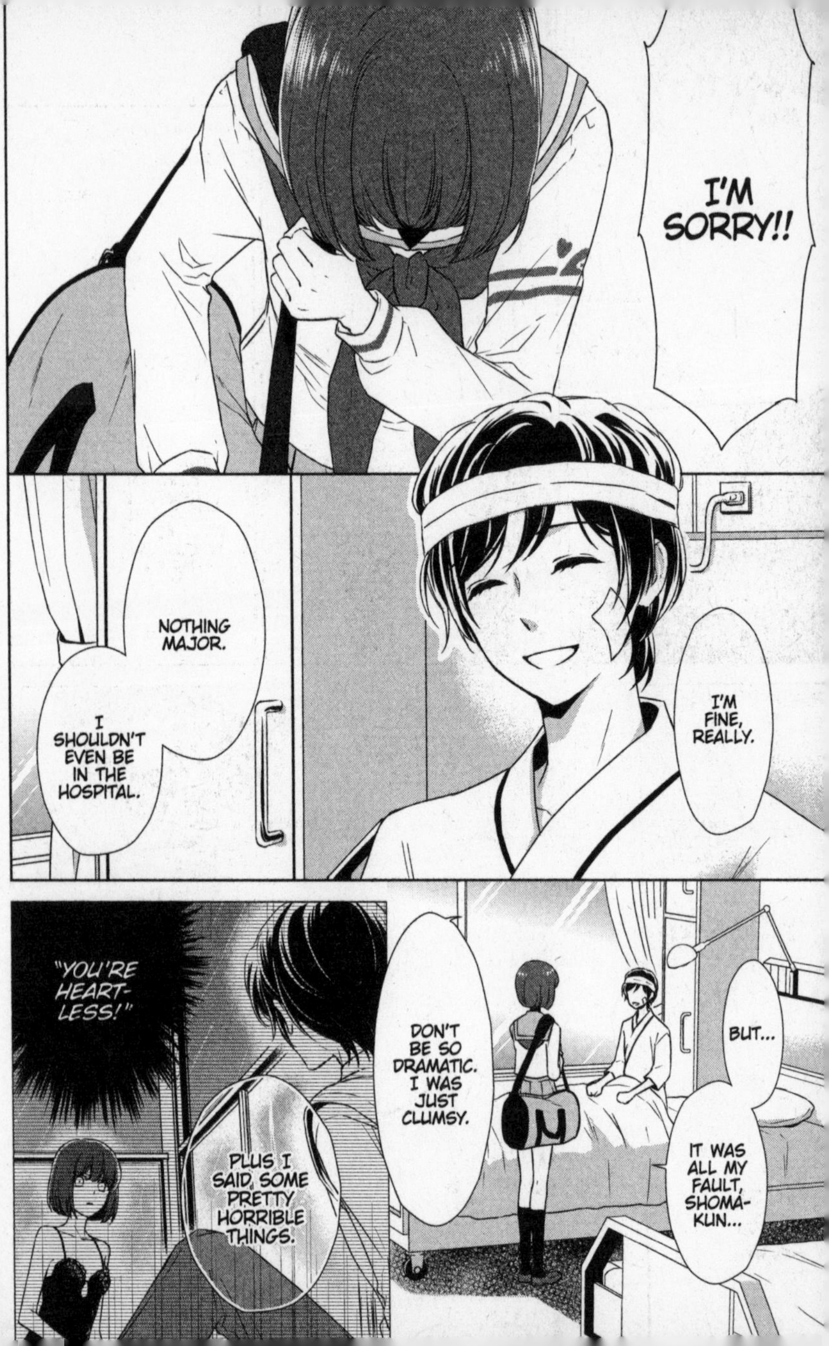
I'M SORRY!!
I'M FINE, REALLY.
NOTHING MAJOR.
I SHOULDN'T EVEN BE IN THE HOSPITAL.
BUT...
IT WAS ALL MY FAULT, SHOMA-KUN...
DON'T BE SO DRAMATIC. I WAS JUST CLUMSY.
PLUS I SAID SOME PRETTY HORRIBLE THINGS.
"YOU'RE HEARTLESS!"

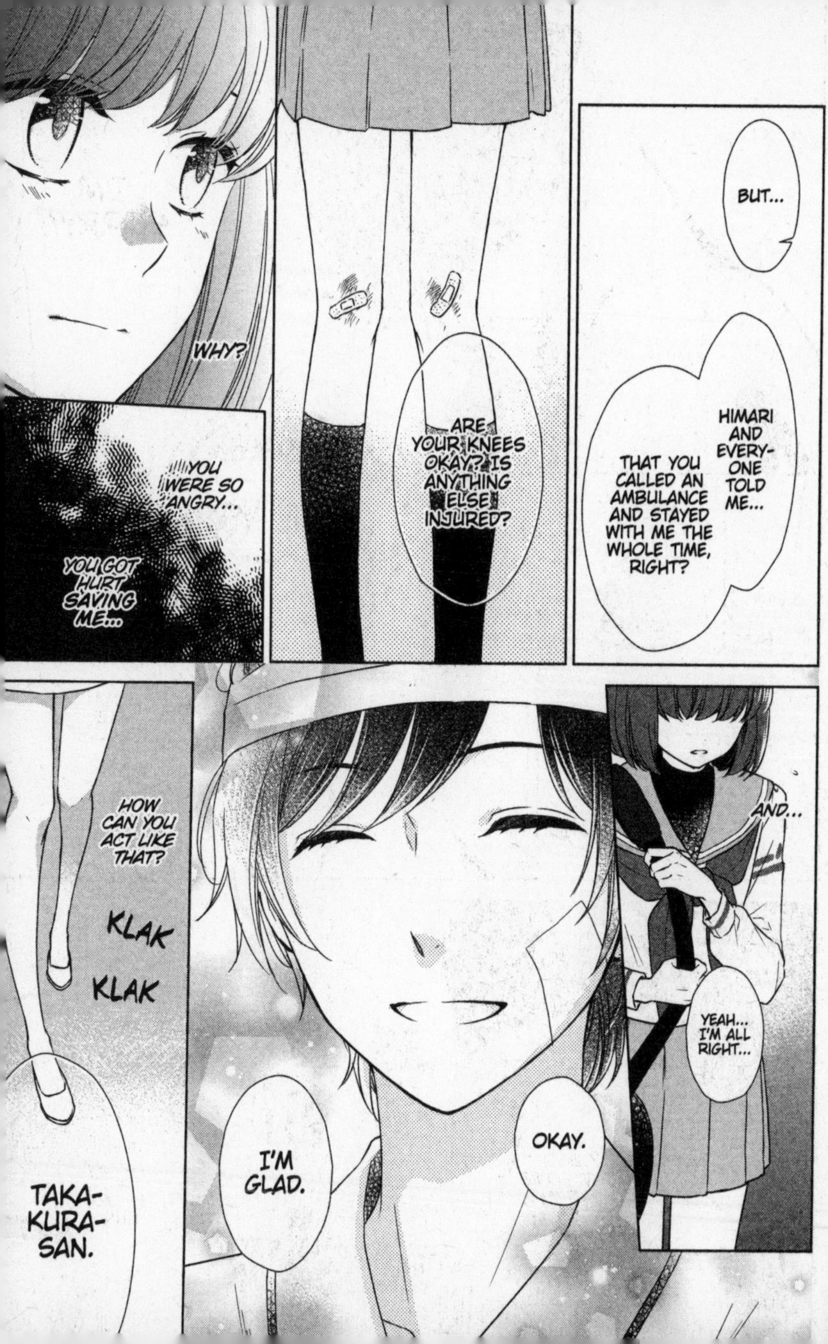

BUT...
HIMARI AND EVERY-ONE TOLD ME...
THAT YOU CALLED AN AMBULANCE AND STAYED WITH ME THE WHOLE TIME, RIGHT?
ARE YOUR KNEES OKAY? IS ANYTHING ELSE INJURED?
WHY?
YOU WERE SO ANGRY...
YOU GOT HURT SAVING ME...
AND...
YEAH... I'M ALL RIGHT...
OKAY.
I'M GLAD.
HOW CAN YOU ACT LIKE THAT?
KLAK
KLAK
TAKA-KURA-SAN.

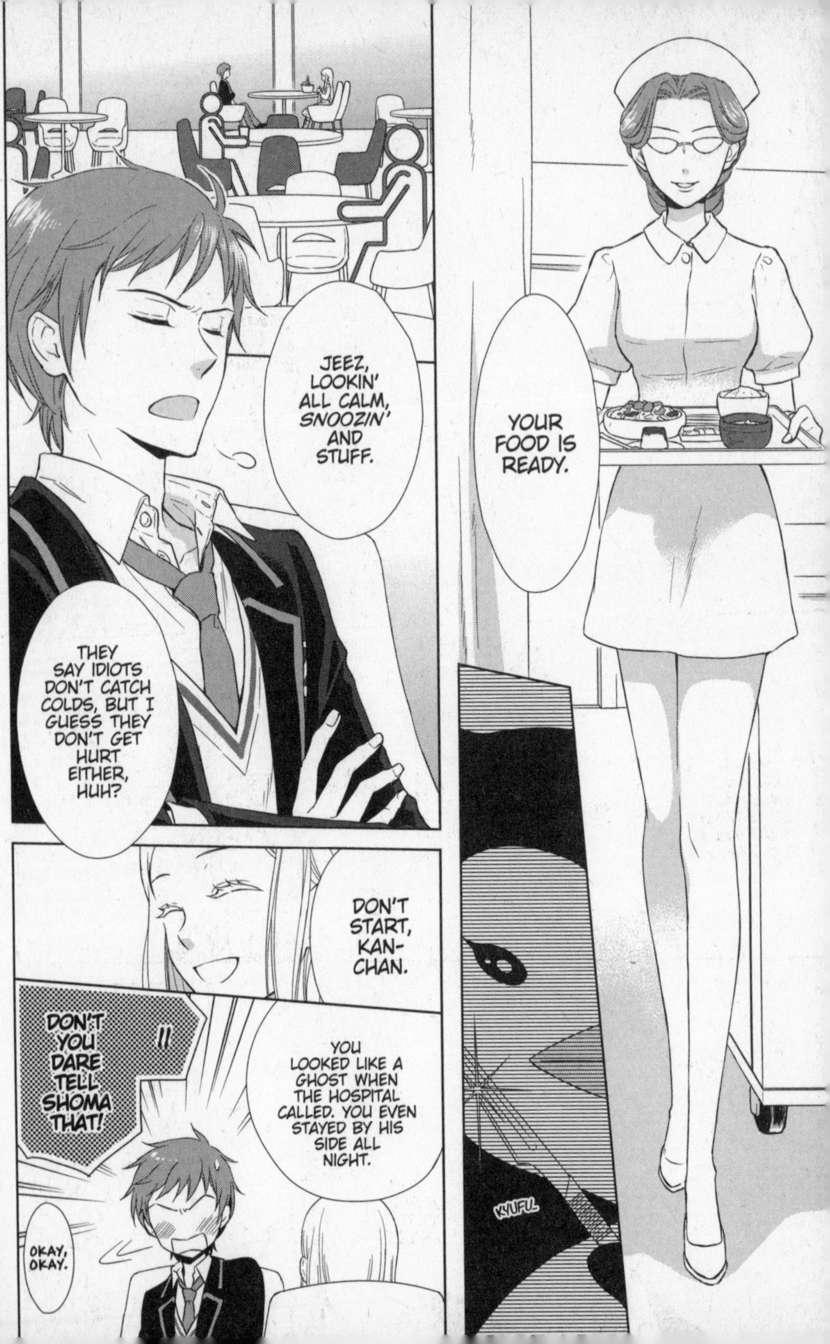
YOUR FOOD IS READY.
KYUFU
JEEZ, LOOKIN' ALL CALM, SNOOZIN' AND STUFF.
THEY SAY IDIOTS DON'T CATCH COLDS, BUT I GUESS THEY DON'T GET HURT EITHER, HUH?
DON'T START, KAN-CHAN.
YOU LOOKED LIKE A GHOST WHEN THE HOSPITAL CALLED. YOU EVEN STAYED BY HIS SIDE ALL NIGHT.
DON'T YOU DARE TELL SHOMA THAT!
!!
OKAY, OKAY.

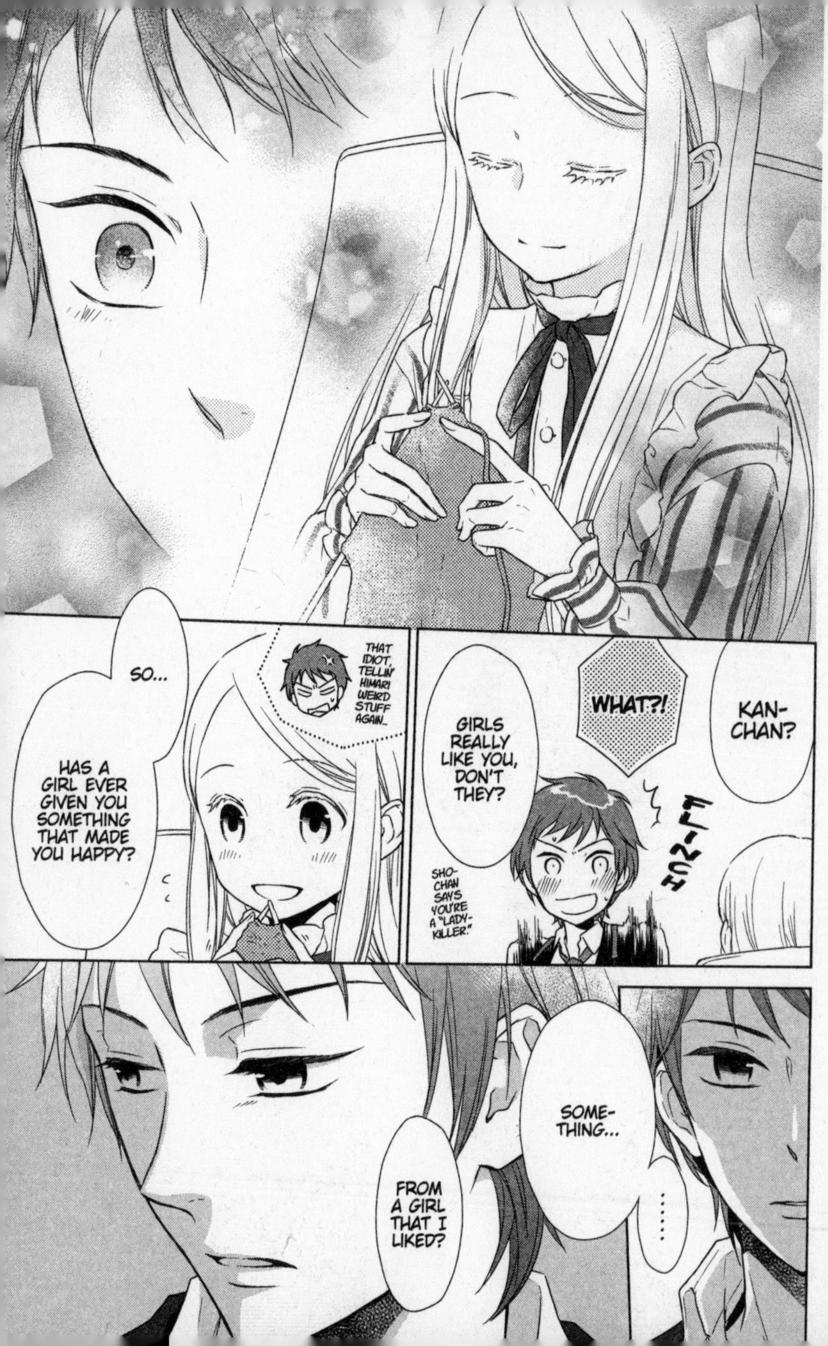
KAN-CHAN?
WHAT?!
FLINCH
GIRLS REALLY LIKE YOU, DON'T THEY?
SHO-CHAN SAYS YOU'RE A "LADY-KILLER."
THAT IDIOT, TELLIN' HIMARI WEIRD STUFF AGAIN...
SO...
HAS A GIRL EVER GIVEN YOU SOMETHING THAT MADE YOU HAPPY?
......
SOME-THING...
FROM A GIRL THAT I LIKED?

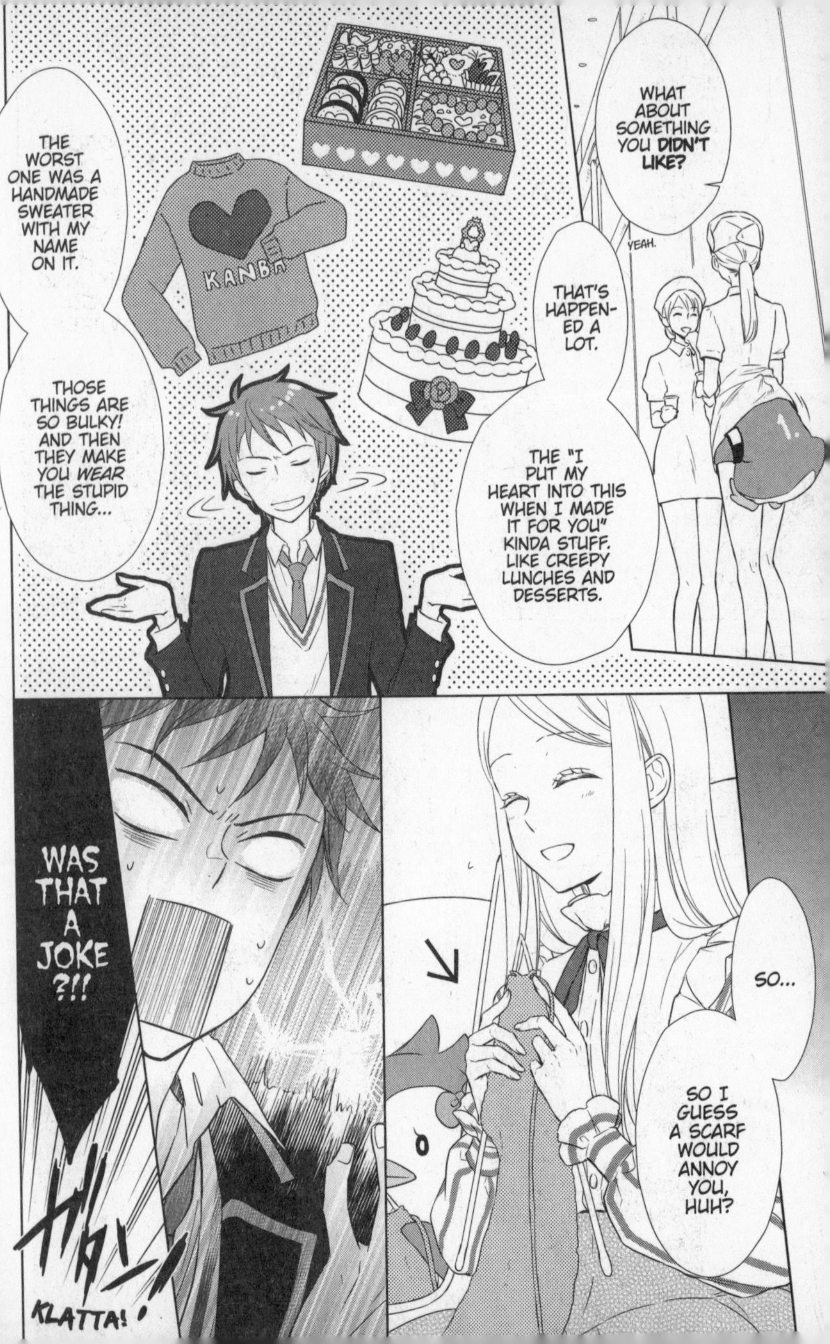
WHAT ABOUT SOMETHING YOU **DIDN'T LIKE?**
YEAH.
THAT'S HAPPEN-ED A LOT.
THE "I PUT MY HEART INTO THIS WHEN I MADE IT FOR YOU" KINDA STUFF. LIKE CREEPY LUNCHES AND DESSERTS.
THE WORST ONE WAS A HANDMADE SWEATER WITH MY NAME ON IT.
KANBA
THOSE THINGS ARE SO BULKY! AND THEN THEY MAKE YOU *WEAR* THE STUPID THING...
SO...
SO I GUESS A SCARF WOULD ANNOY YOU, HUH?
WAS THAT A JOKE?!!
KLATTA!

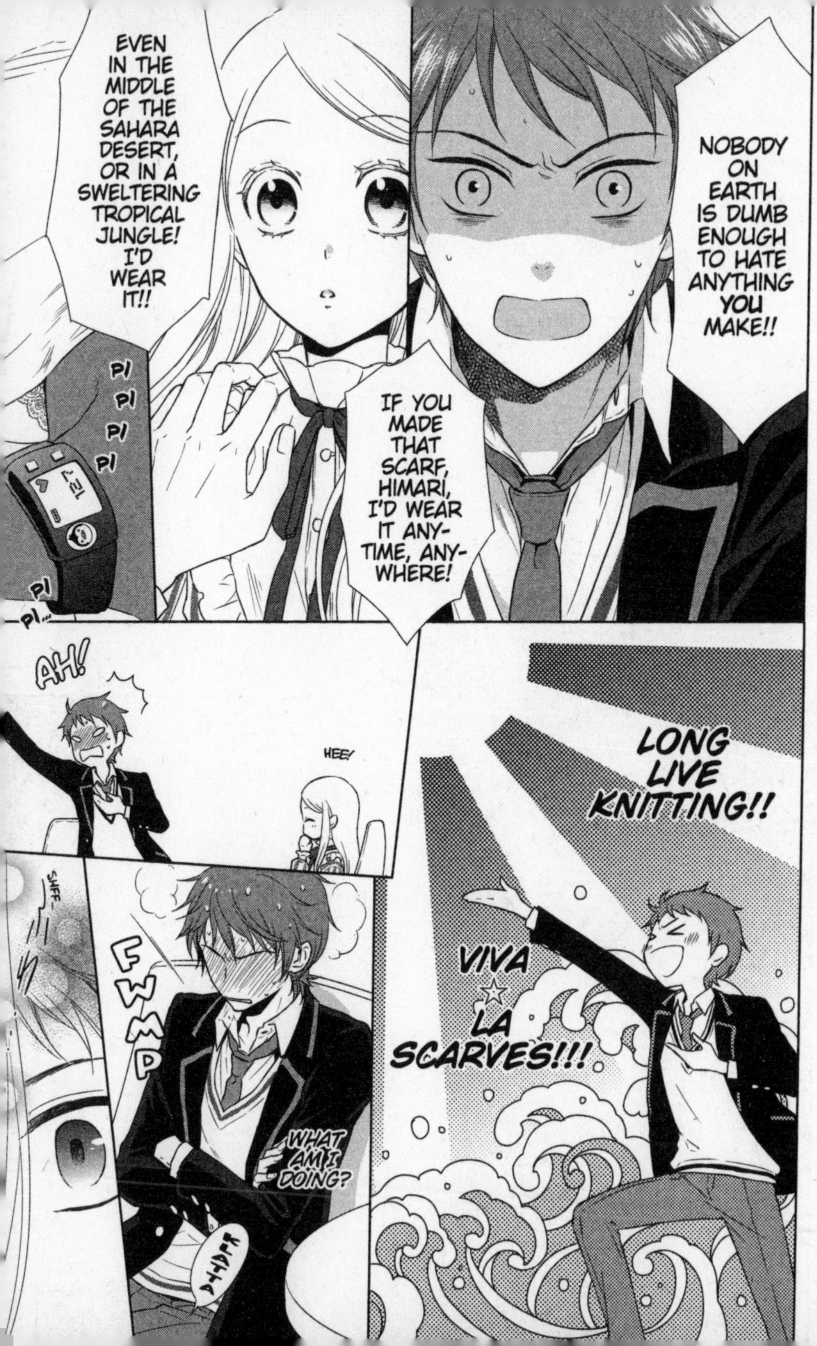
NOBODY ON EARTH IS DUMB ENOUGH TO HATE ANYTHING YOU MAKE!!
IF YOU MADE THAT SCARF, HIMARI, I'D WEAR IT ANY-TIME, ANY-WHERE!
EVEN IN THE MIDDLE OF THE SAHARA DESERT, OR IN A SWELTERING TROPICAL JUNGLE! I'D WEAR IT!!
PI PI PI PI
PI PI...
LONG LIVE KNITTING!!
VIVA ☆ LA SCARVES!!!
AH!
HEE!
SHFF...
FWMP
WHAT AM I DOING?
KLATTA

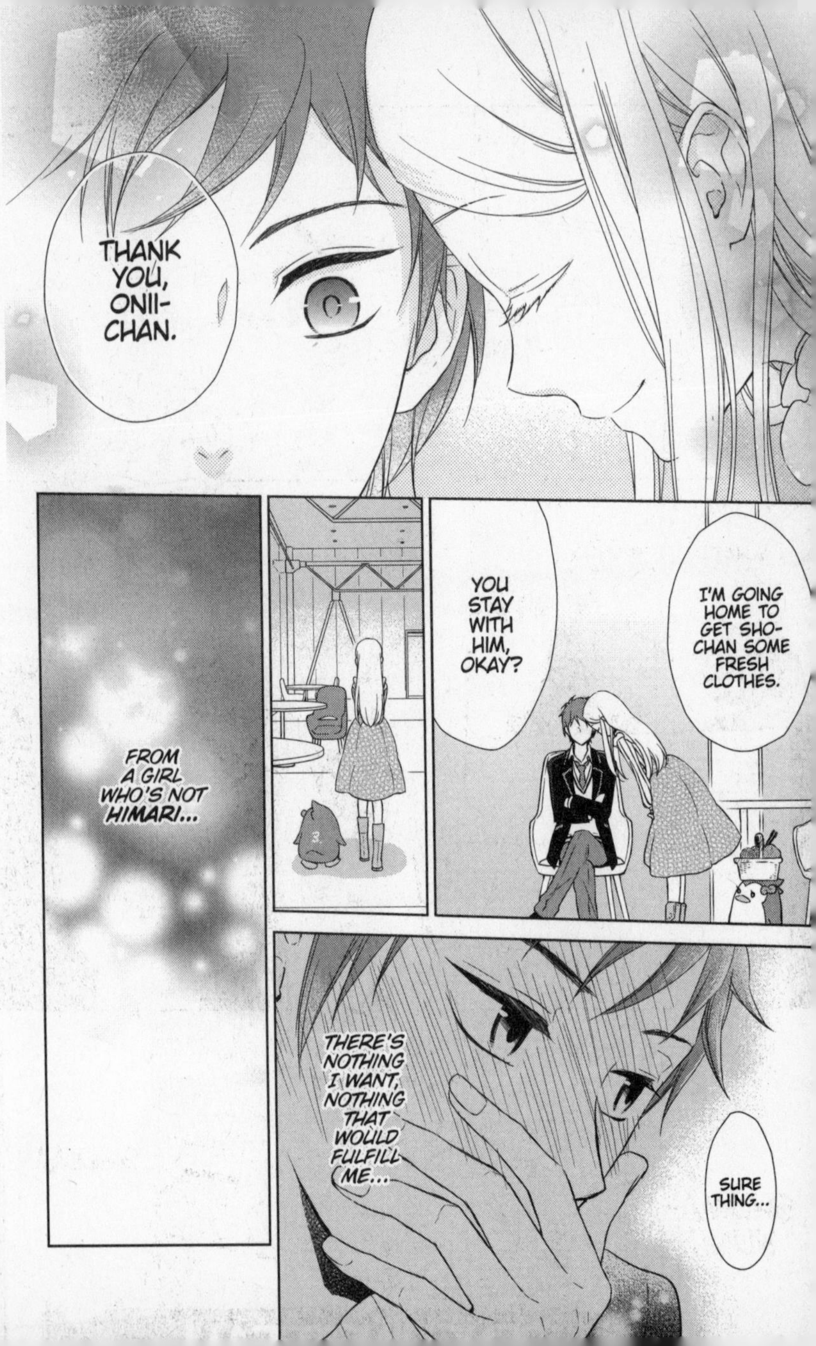
THANK YOU, ONII-CHAN.
I'M GOING HOME TO GET SHO-CHAN SOME FRESH CLOTHES.
YOU STAY WITH HIM, OKAY?
SURE THING...
THERE'S NOTHING I WANT, NOTHING THAT WOULD FULFILL ME...
FROM A GIRL WHO'S NOT HIMARI...

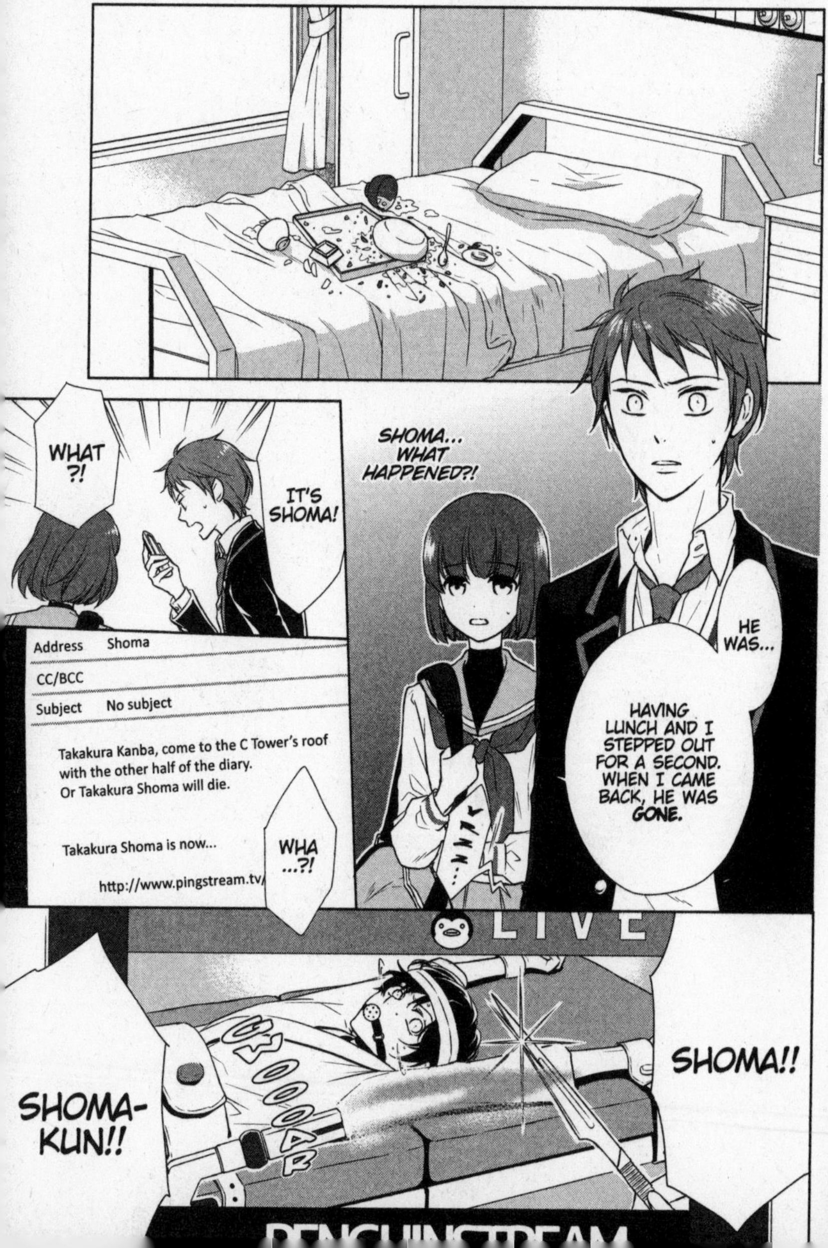
SHOMA... WHAT HAPPENED?!
HE WAS...
HAVING LUNCH AND I STEPPED OUT FOR A SECOND. WHEN I CAME BACK, HE WAS **GONE.**
IT'S SHOMA!
WHAT ?!
Address Shoma
CC/BCC
Subject No subject
Takakura Kanba, come to the C Tower's roof with the other half of the diary.
Or Takakura Shoma will die.
Takakura Shoma is now...
http://www.pingstream.tv/
WHA ...?!
LIVE
SHOMA!!
GWOOOOAR
SHOMA-KUN!!

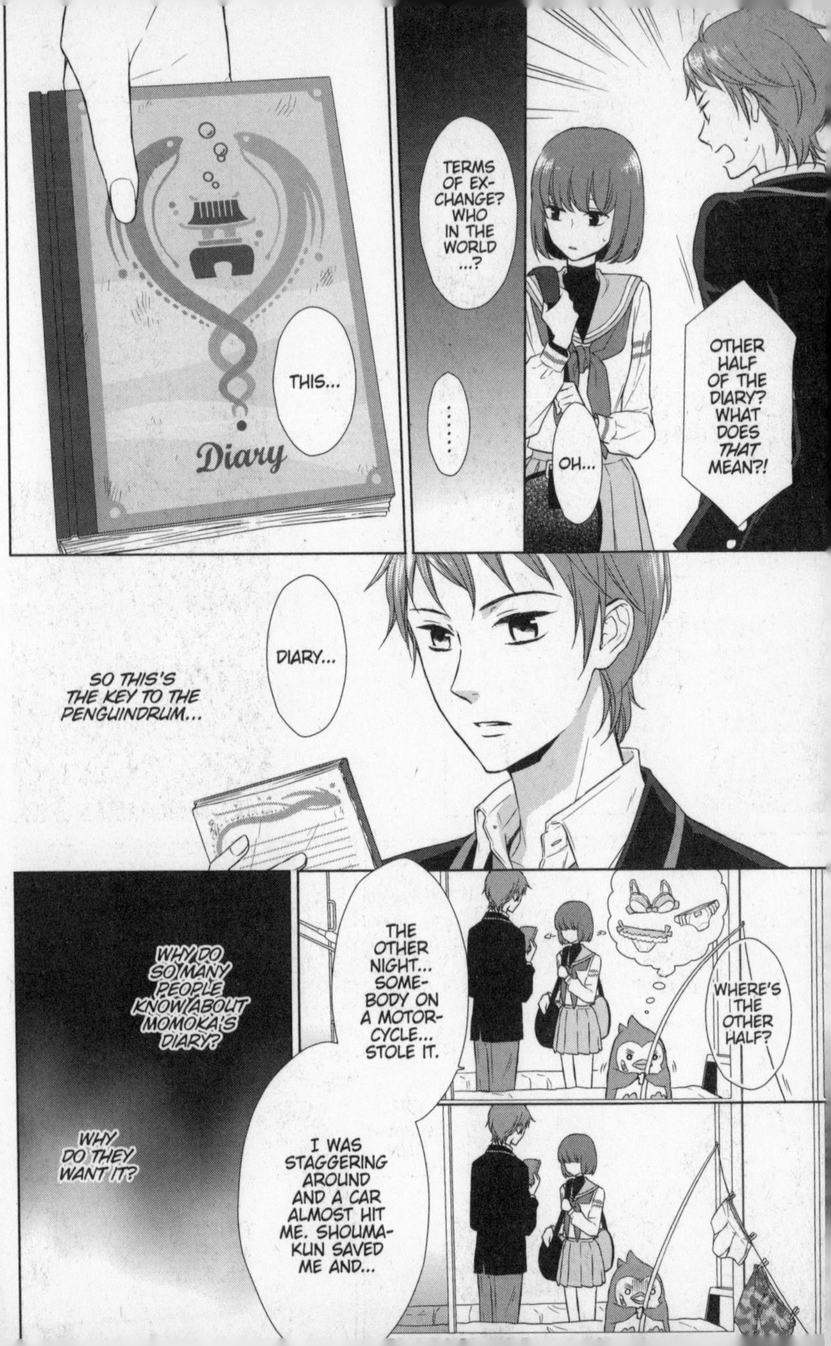
OTHER HALF OF THE DIARY? WHAT DOES *THAT* MEAN?!
TERMS OF EX-CHANGE? WHO IN THE WORLD ...?
OH...
......
THIS...
Diary
DIARY...
SO THIS'S THE KEY TO THE PENGUINDRUM...
WHERE'S THE OTHER HALF?
THE OTHER NIGHT... SOME-BODY ON A MOTOR-CYCLE... STOLE IT.
I WAS STAGGERING AROUND AND A CAR ALMOST HIT ME. SHOUMA-KUN SAVED ME AND...
WHY DO SO MANY PEOPLE KNOW ABOUT MOMOKA'S DIARY?
WHY DO THEY WANT IT?

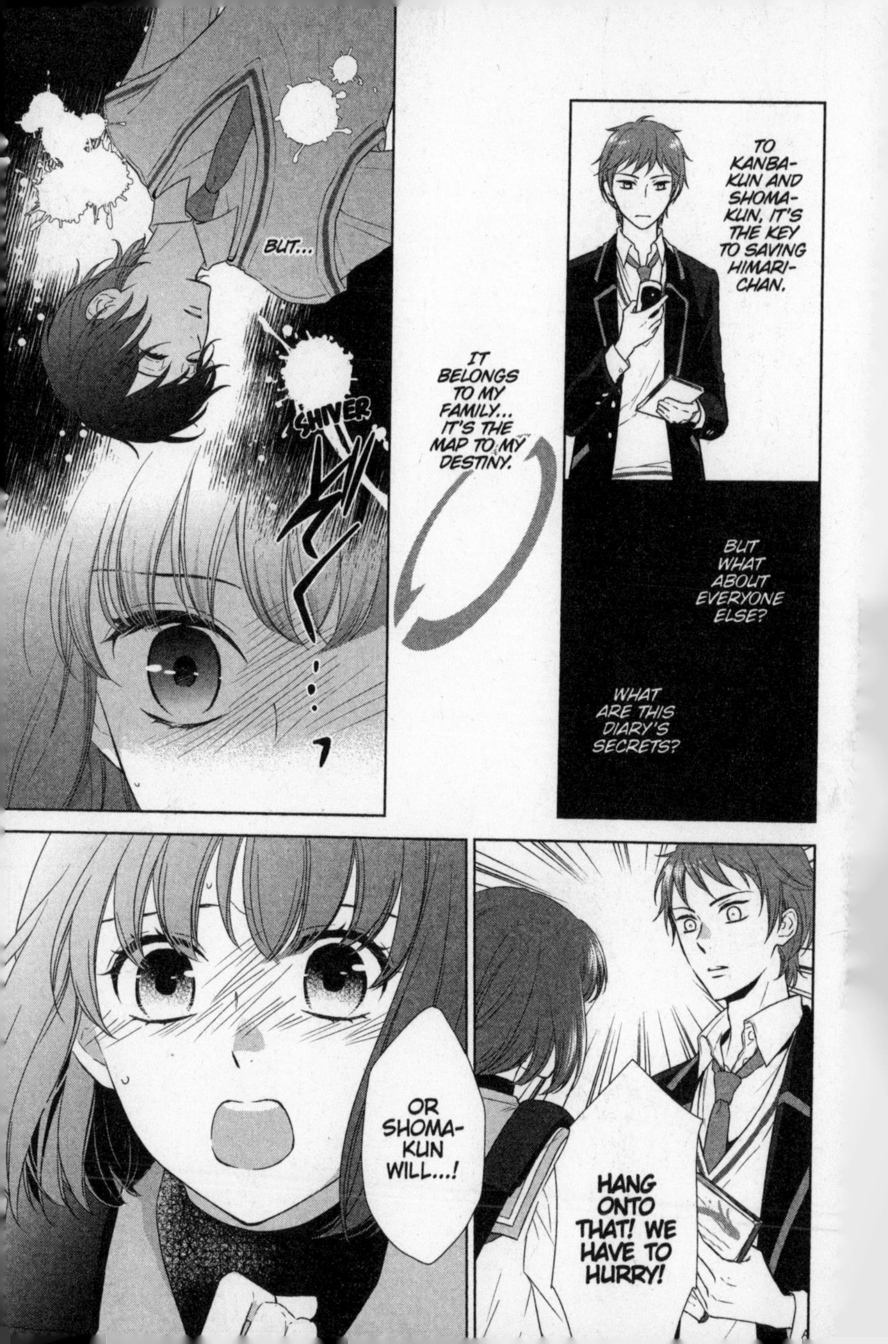
TO KANBA-KUN AND SHOMA-KUN, IT'S THE KEY TO SAVING HIMARI-CHAN.
BUT WHAT ABOUT EVERYONE ELSE?
WHAT ARE THIS DIARY'S SECRETS?
IT BELONGS TO MY FAMILY... IT'S THE MAP TO MY DESTINY.
BUT...
SHIVER
HANG ONTO THAT! WE HAVE TO HURRY!
OR SHOMA-KUN WILL...!

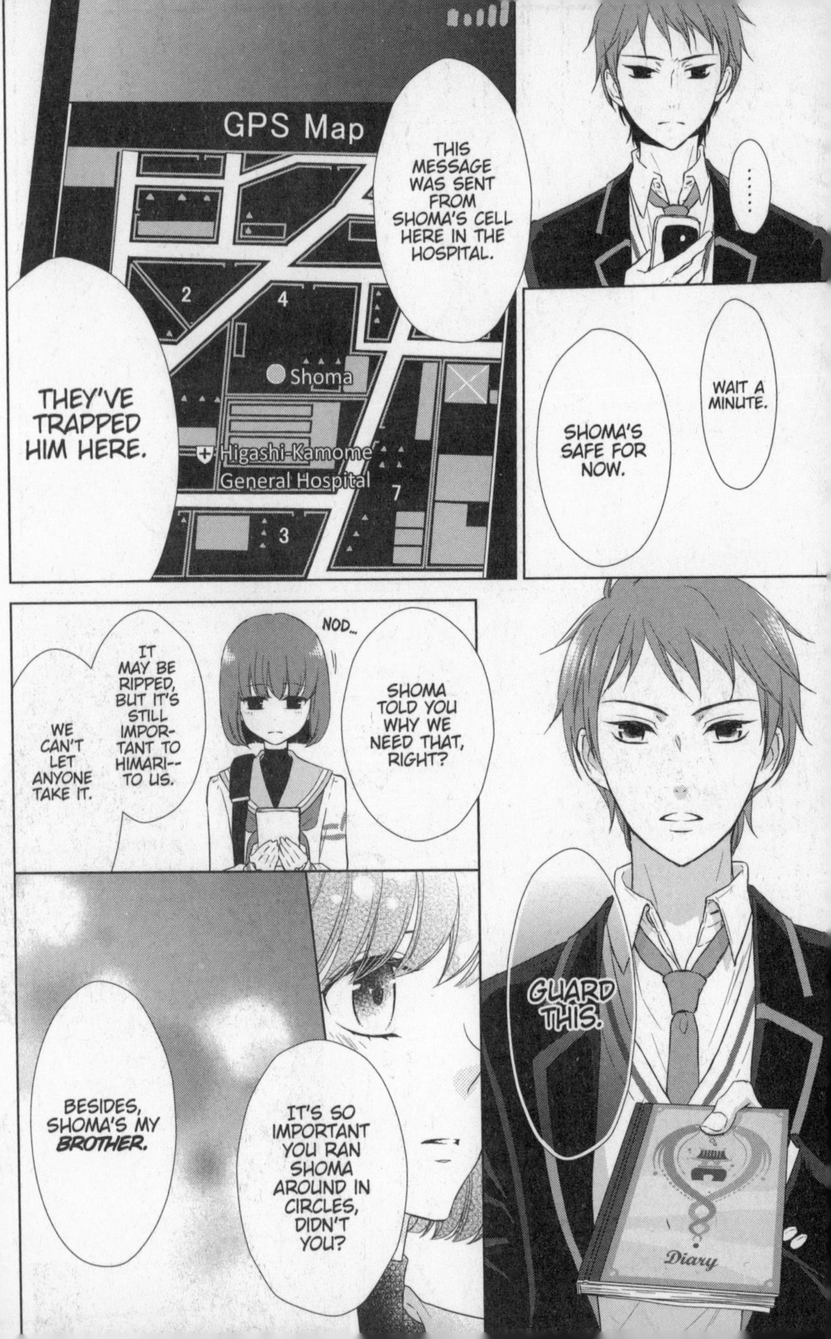

THIS MESSAGE WAS SENT FROM SHOMA'S CELL HERE IN THE HOSPITAL.
......
WAIT A MINUTE.
SHOMA'S SAFE FOR NOW.
GPS Map
2
4
Shoma
Higashi-Kamome General Hospital
7
3
THEY'VE TRAPPED HIM HERE.
GUARD THIS.
Diary
NOD...
SHOMA TOLD YOU WHY WE NEED THAT, RIGHT?
IT MAY BE RIPPED, BUT IT'S STILL IMPOR-TANT TO HIMARI-- TO US.
WE CAN'T LET ANYONE TAKE IT.
IT'S SO IMPORTANT YOU RAN SHOMA AROUND IN CIRCLES, DIDN'T YOU?
BESIDES, SHOMA'S MY *BROTHER*.

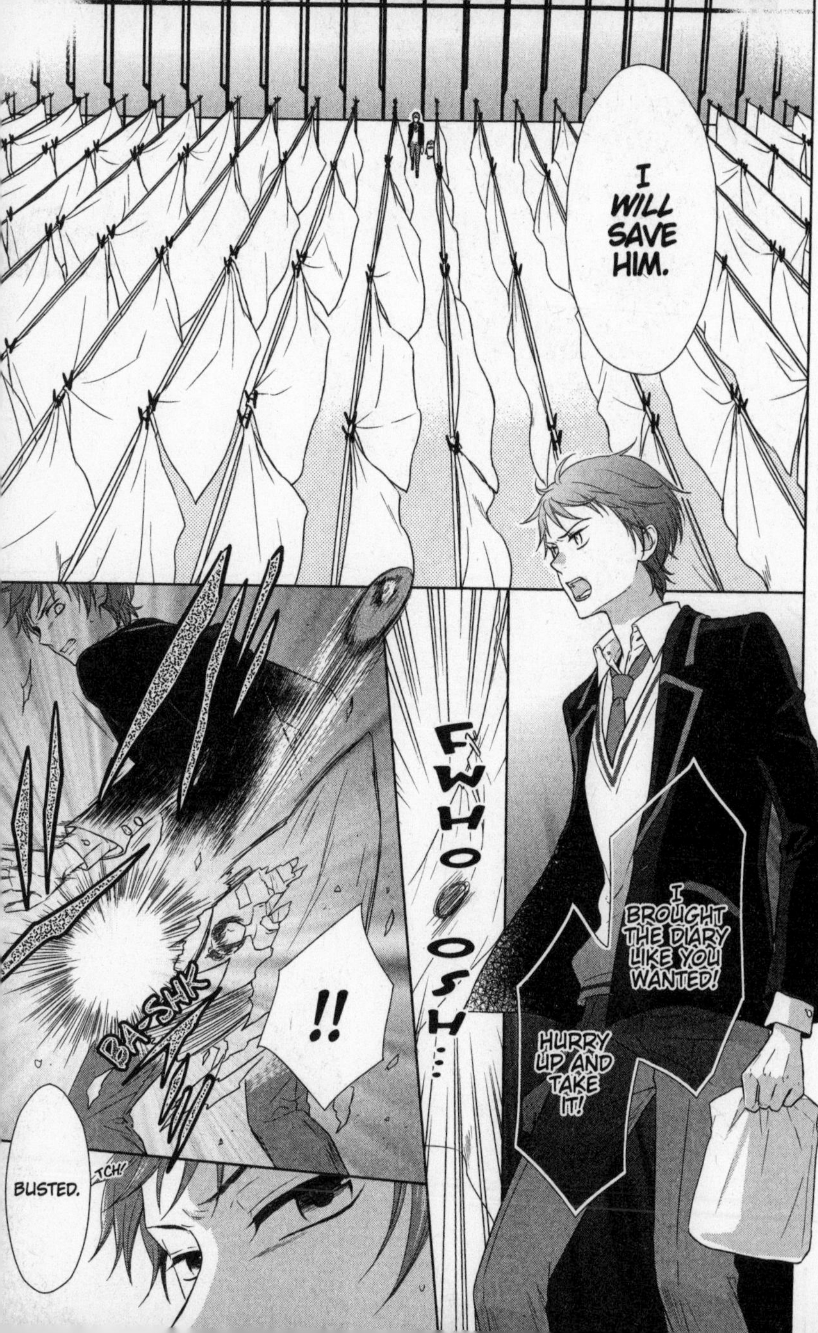
I WILL SAVE HIM.
I BROUGHT THE DIARY LIKE YOU WANTED!
HURRY UP AND TAKE IT!
FWHOOSH...
BA-SHK
!!
TCH!
BUSTED.

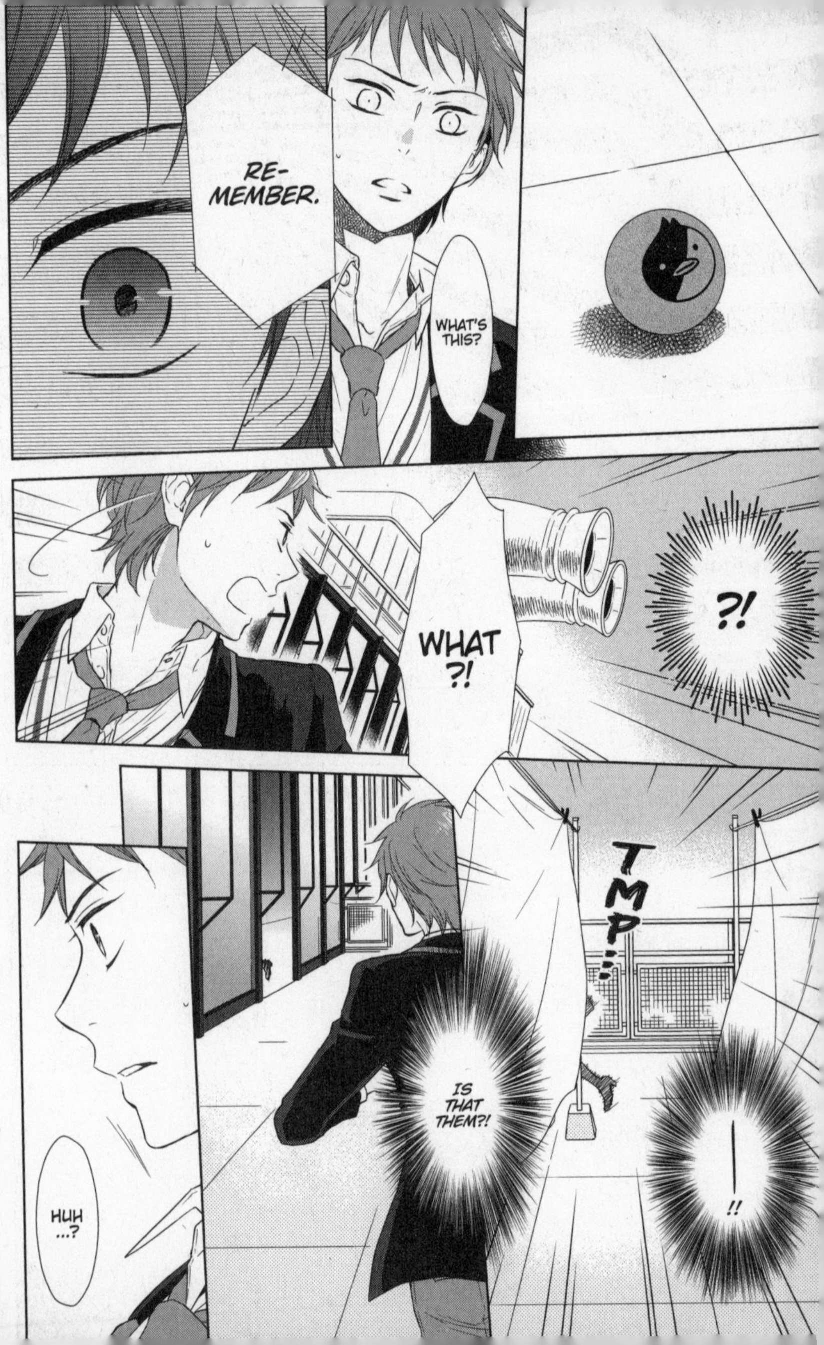

WHAT'S THIS?
RE-MEMBER.
?!
WHAT ?!
TMP...
!!
IS THAT THEM?!
HUH ...?

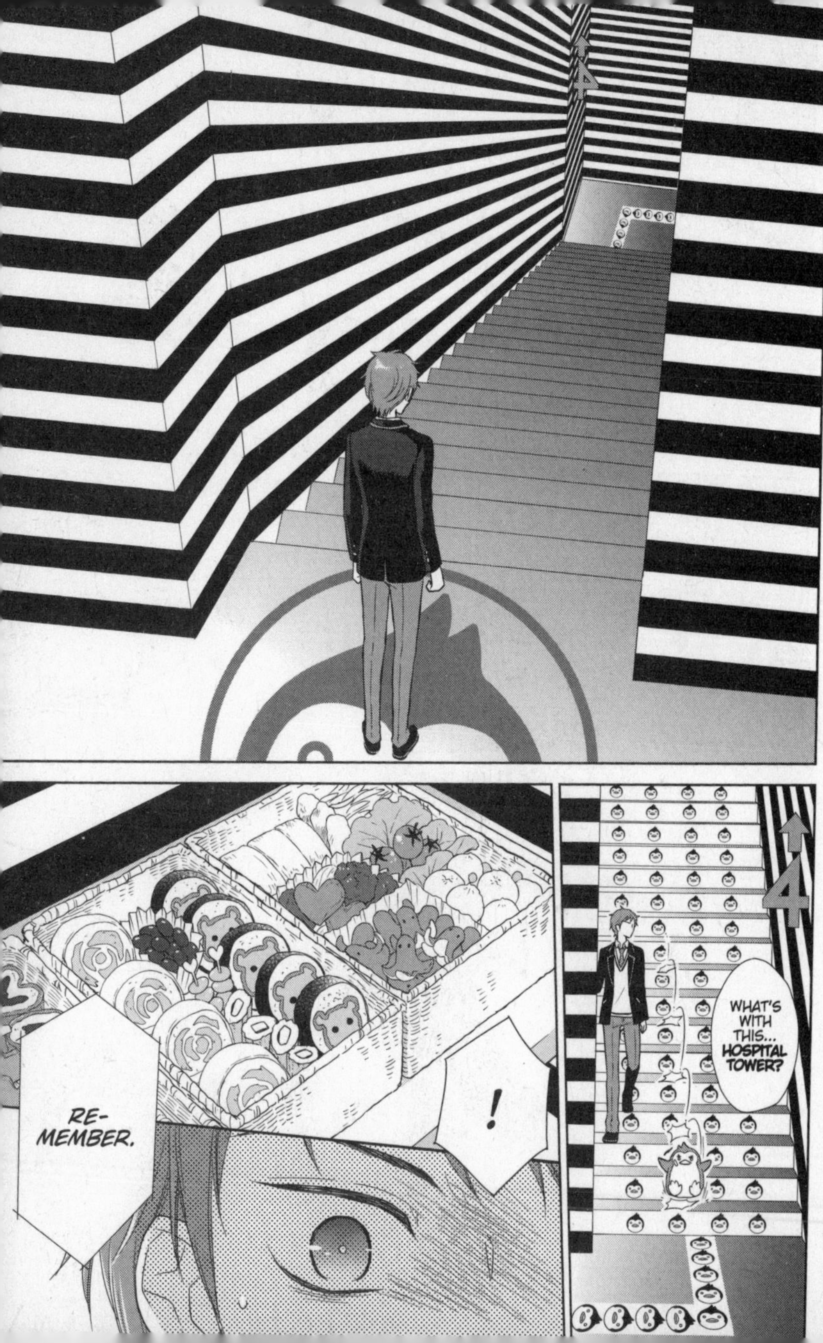
4
WHAT'S WITH THIS... **HOSPITAL TOWER?**
!
RE-MEMBER.

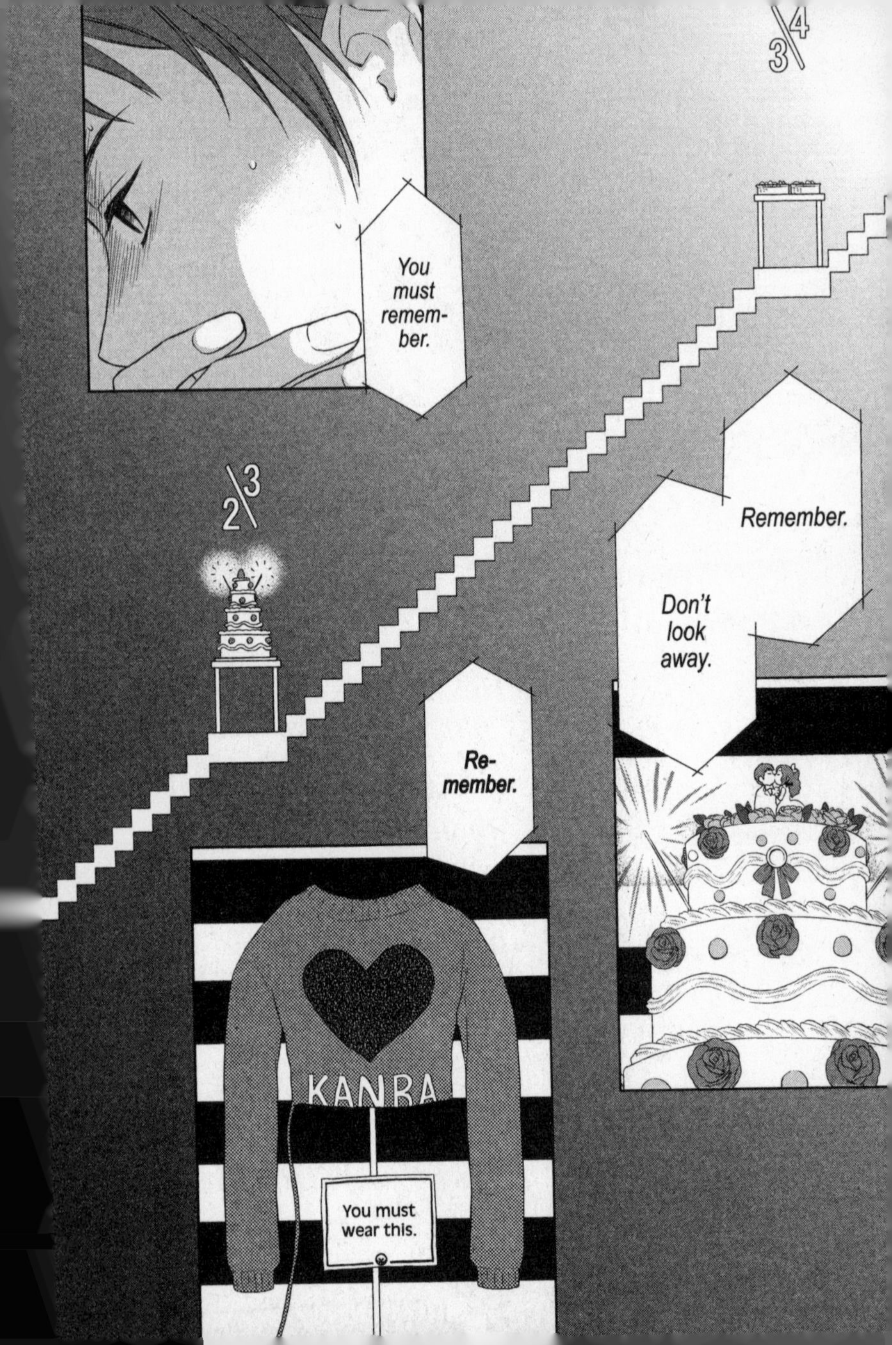
You must remember.
Remember.
Don't look away.
Re-member.
KANRA
You must wear this.

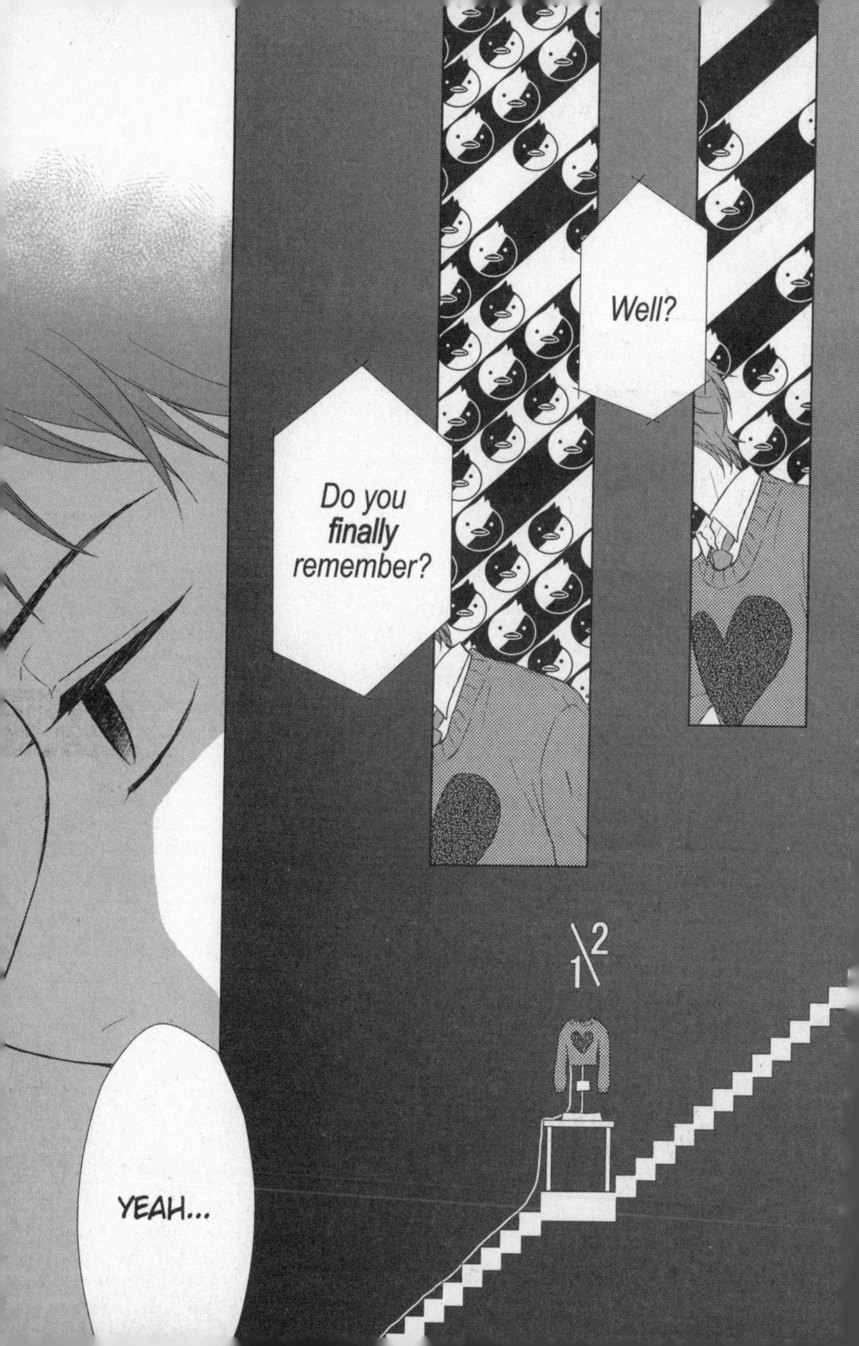
Well?
Do you finally remember?
1/2
YEAH...

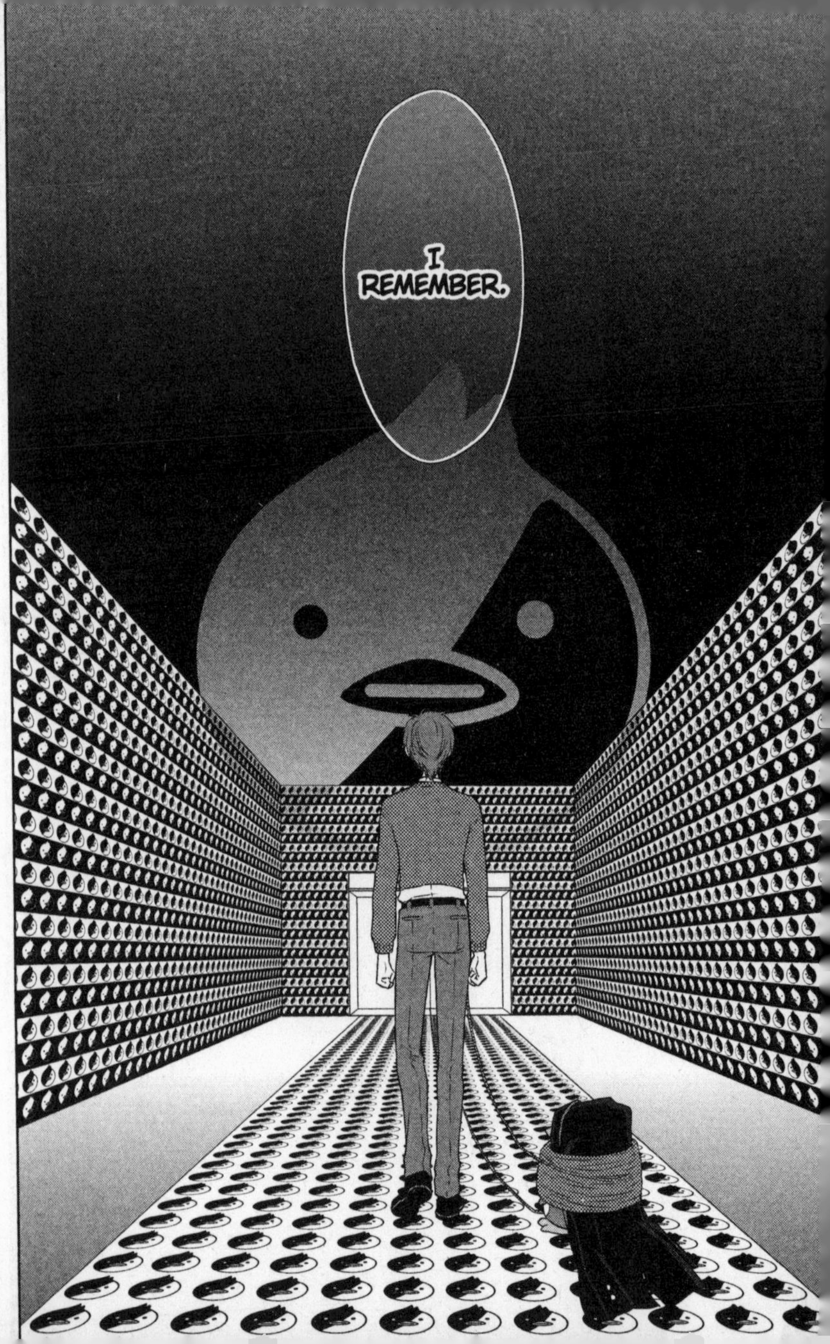
I REMEMBER.

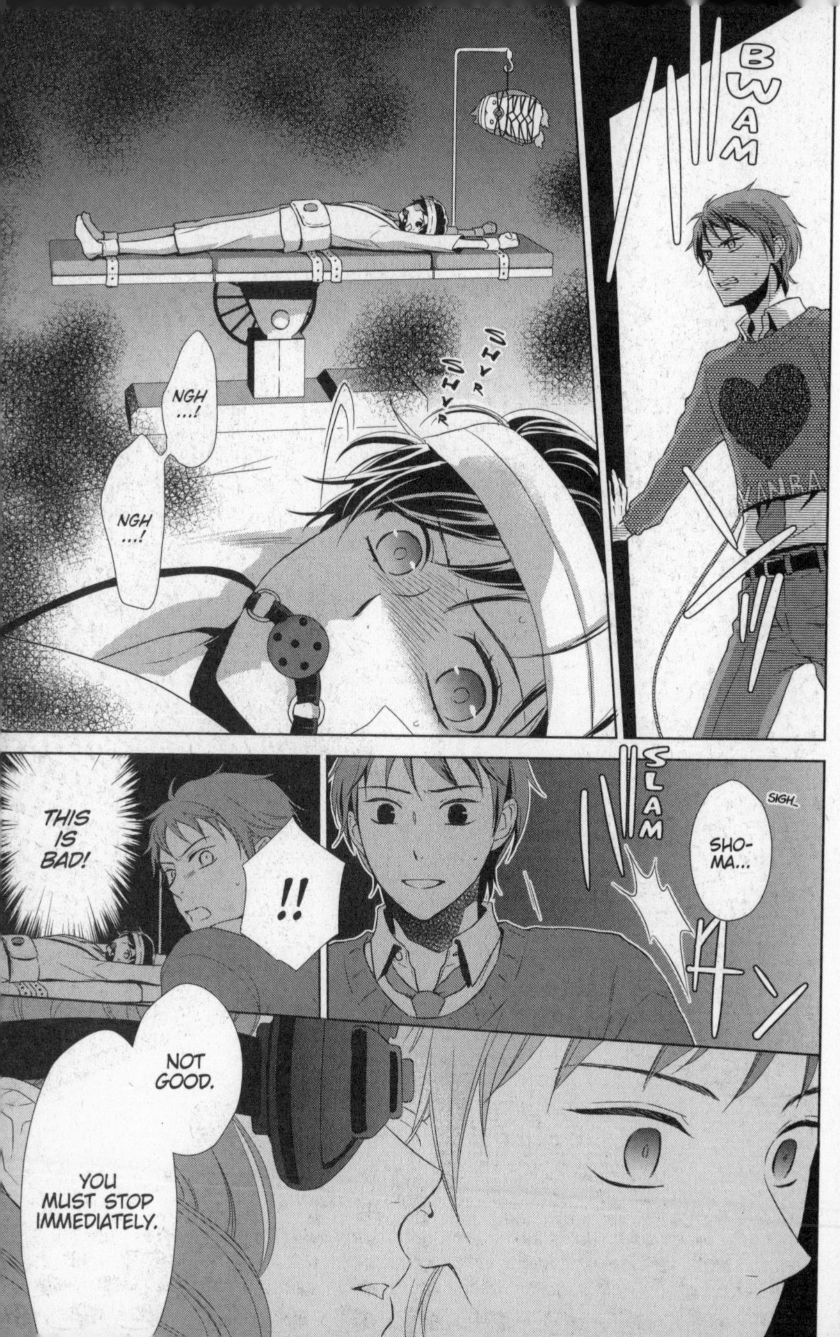
BWAM
SHVR SHVR
NGH ...!
NGH ...!
SLAM
SIGH
SHO-MA...
THIS IS BAD!
!!
NOT GOOD.
YOU MUST STOP IMMEDIATELY.

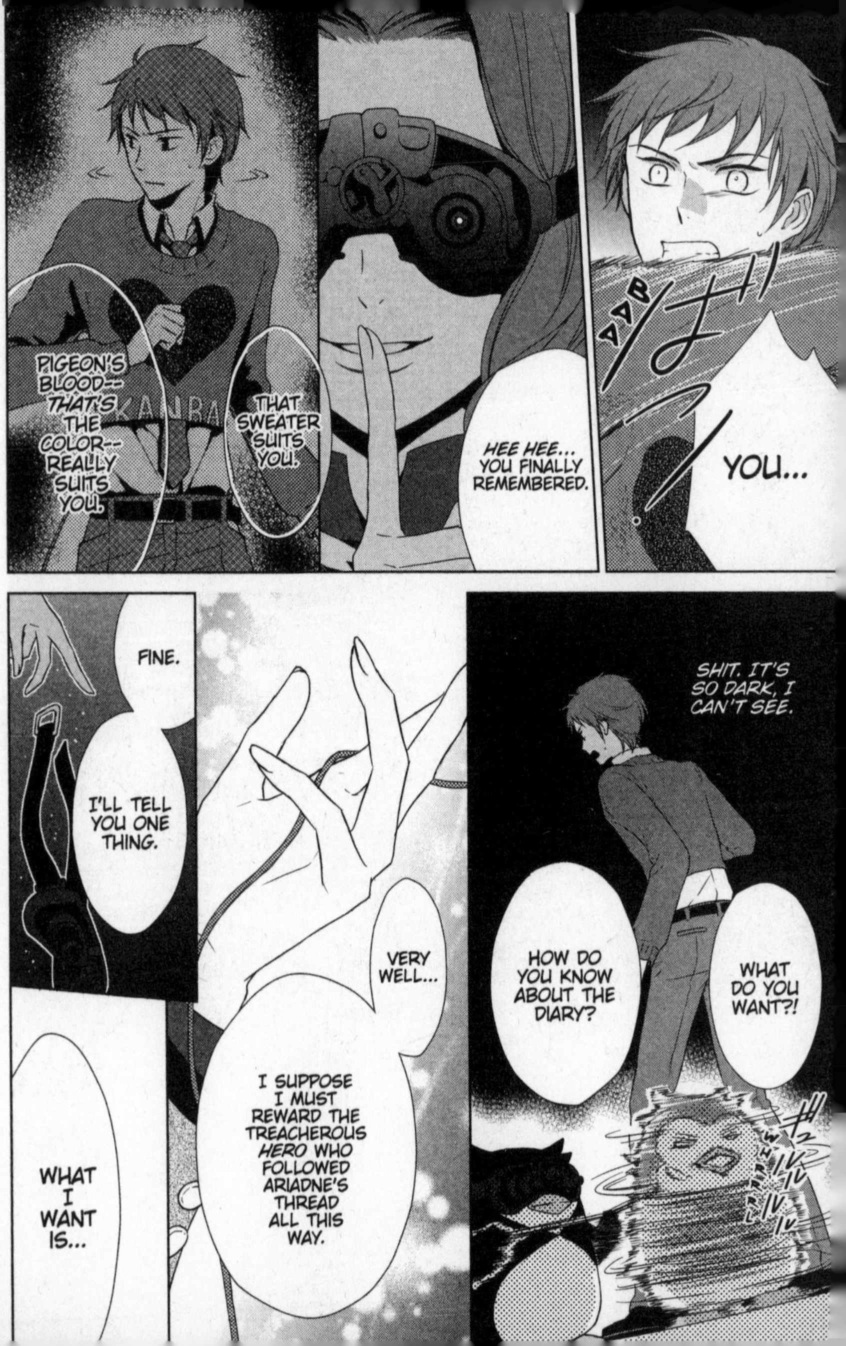
BADA
YOU...
HEE HEE... YOU FINALLY REMEMBERED.
THAT SWEATER SUITS YOU.
PIGEON'S BLOOD-- THAT'S THE COLOR-- REALLY SUITS YOU.
SHIT. IT'S SO DARK, I CAN'T SEE.
WHAT DO YOU WANT?!
HOW DO YOU KNOW ABOUT THE DIARY?
WHIRRL
VERY WELL...
I SUPPOSE I MUST REWARD THE TREACHEROUS HERO WHO FOLLOWED ARIADNE'S THREAD ALL THIS WAY.
FINE.
I'LL TELL YOU ONE THING.
WHAT I WANT IS...

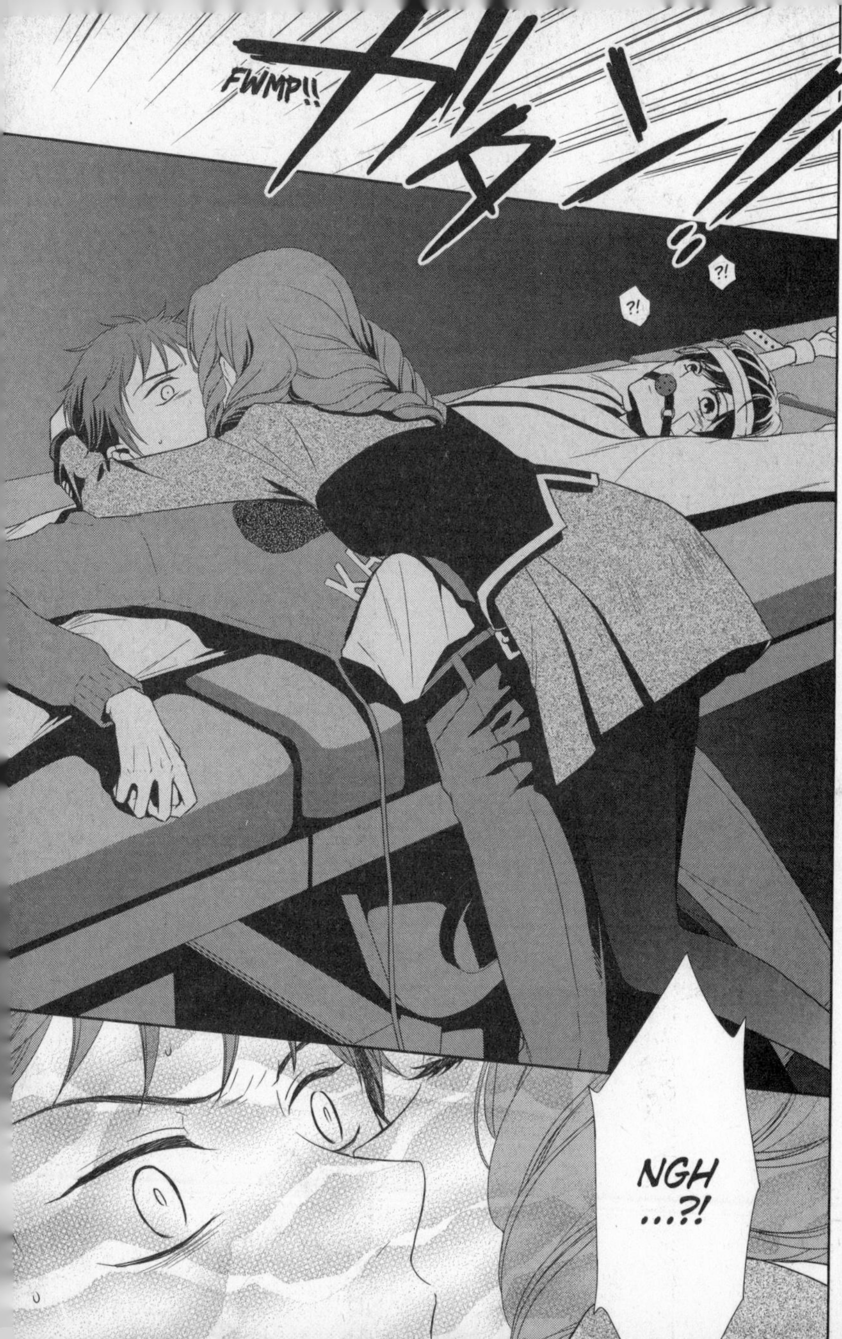
FWMP!!
?!
?!
NGH ...?!

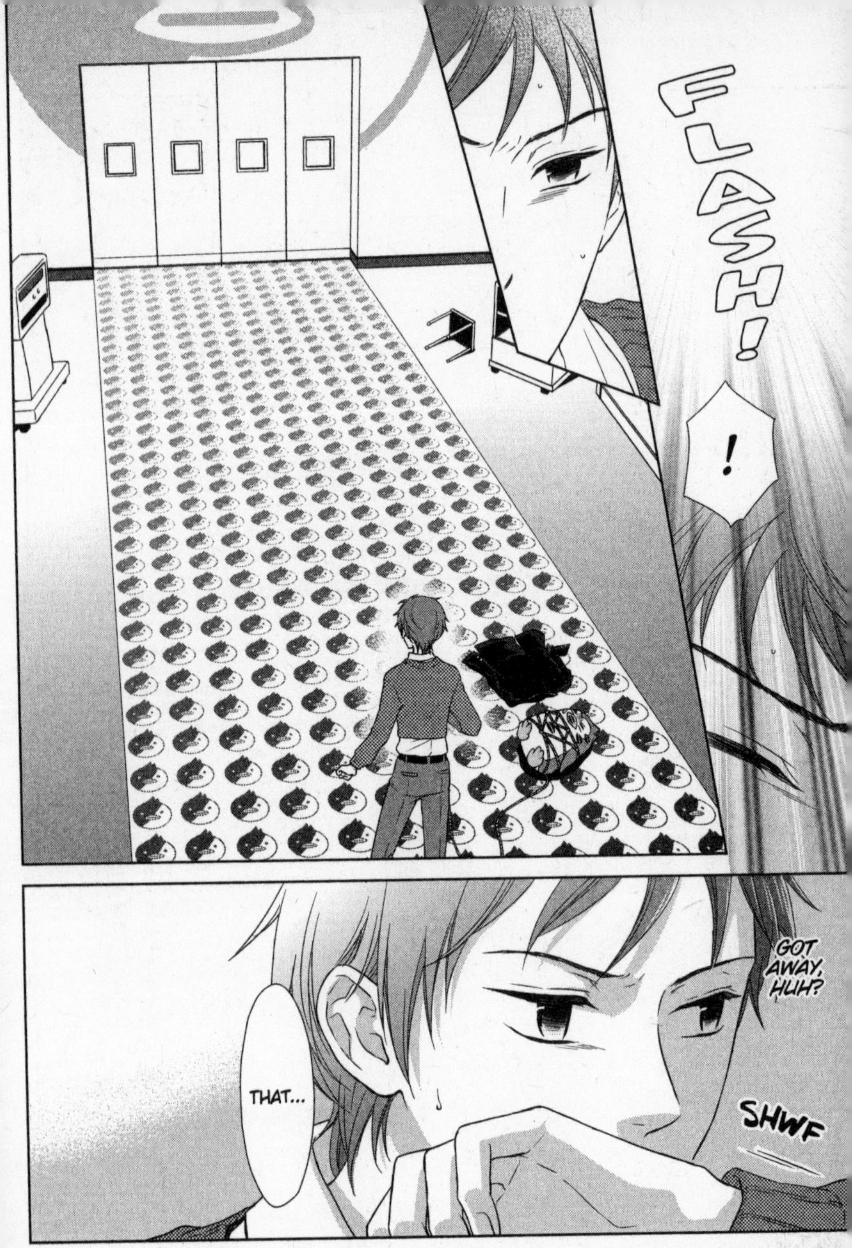
FLASH!
!
GOT AWAY, HUH?
SHWF
THAT...

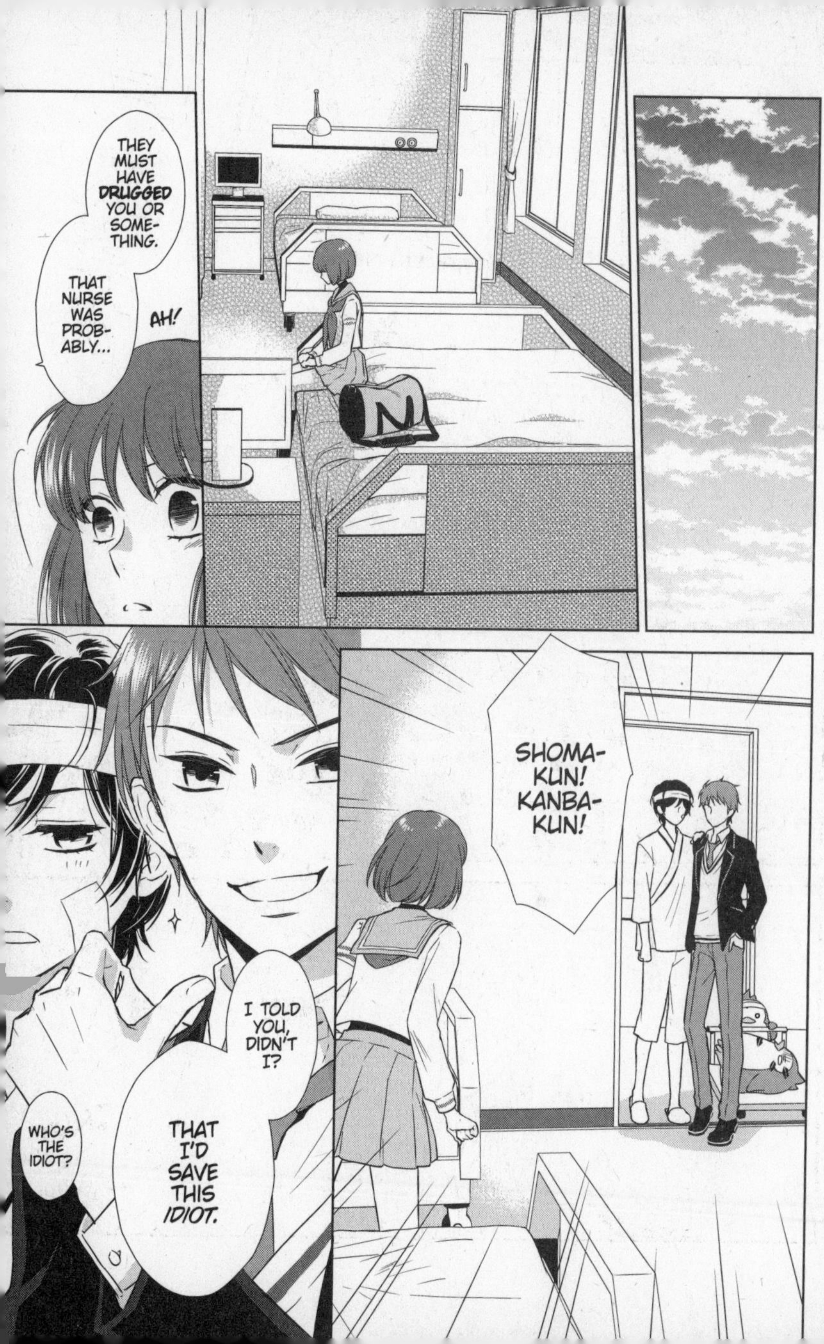
THEY MUST HAVE **DRUGGED** YOU OR SOMETHING.
THAT NURSE WAS PROBABLY...
AH!
SHOMA-KUN! KANBA-KUN!
I TOLD YOU, DIDN'T I?
THAT I'D SAVE THIS *IDIOT*.
WHO'S THE IDIOT?

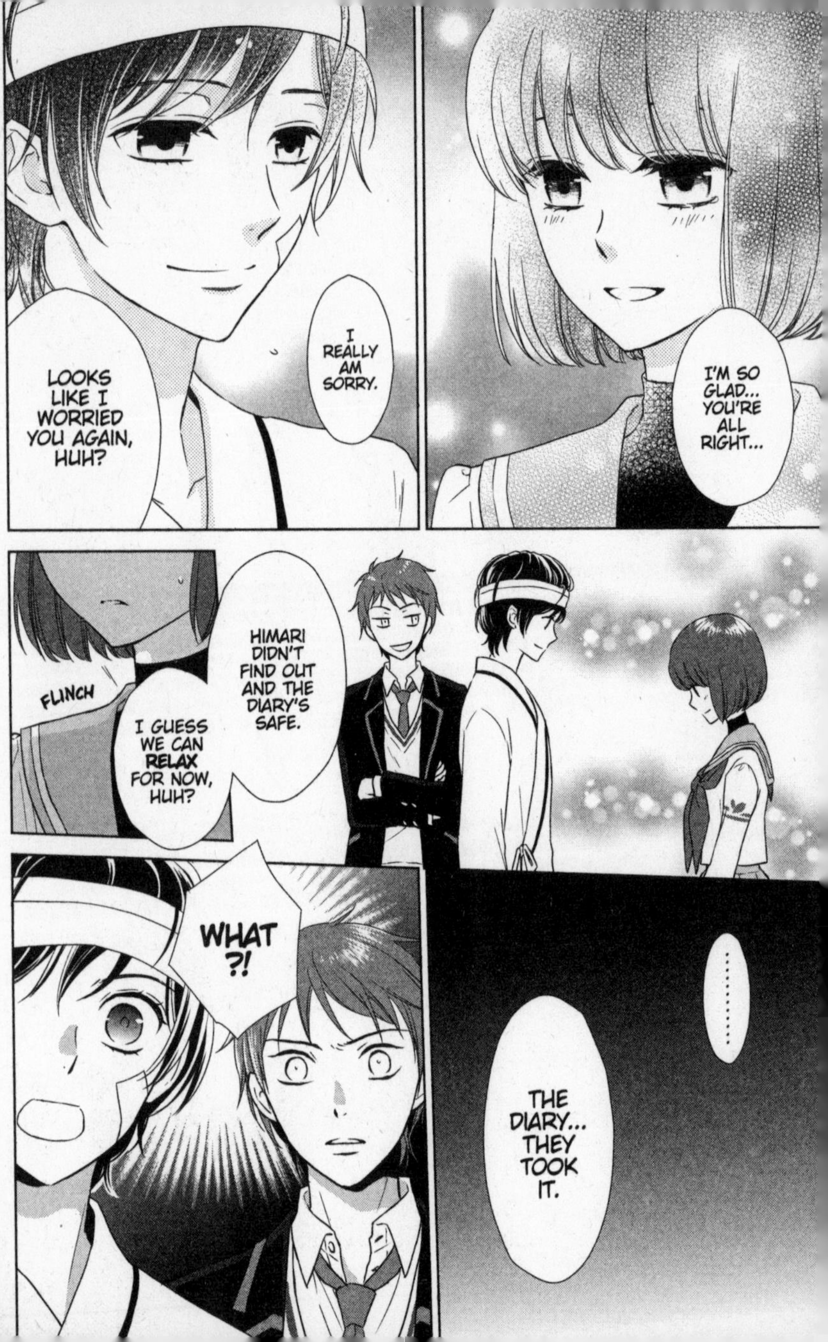
I'M SO GLAD... YOU'RE ALL RIGHT...
I REALLY AM SORRY.
LOOKS LIKE I WORRIED YOU AGAIN, HUH?
HIMARI DIDN'T FIND OUT AND THE DIARY'S SAFE.
I GUESS WE CAN RELAX FOR NOW, HUH?
FLINCH
......
THE DIARY... THEY TOOK IT.
WHAT ?!

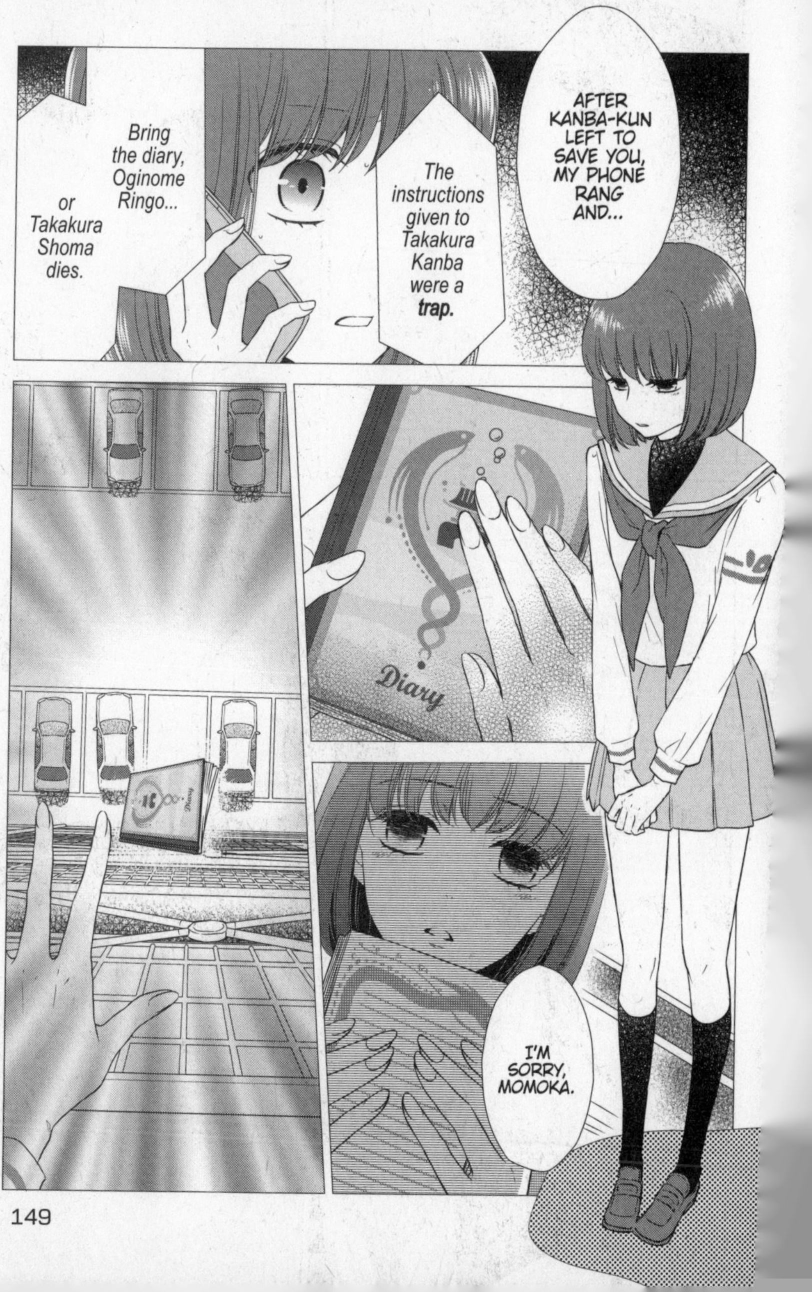
AFTER KANBA-KUN LEFT TO SAVE YOU, MY PHONE RANG AND...
The instructions given to Takakura Kanba were a **trap.**
Bring the diary, Oginome Ringo...
or Takakura Shoma dies.
Diary
I'M SORRY, MOMOKA.

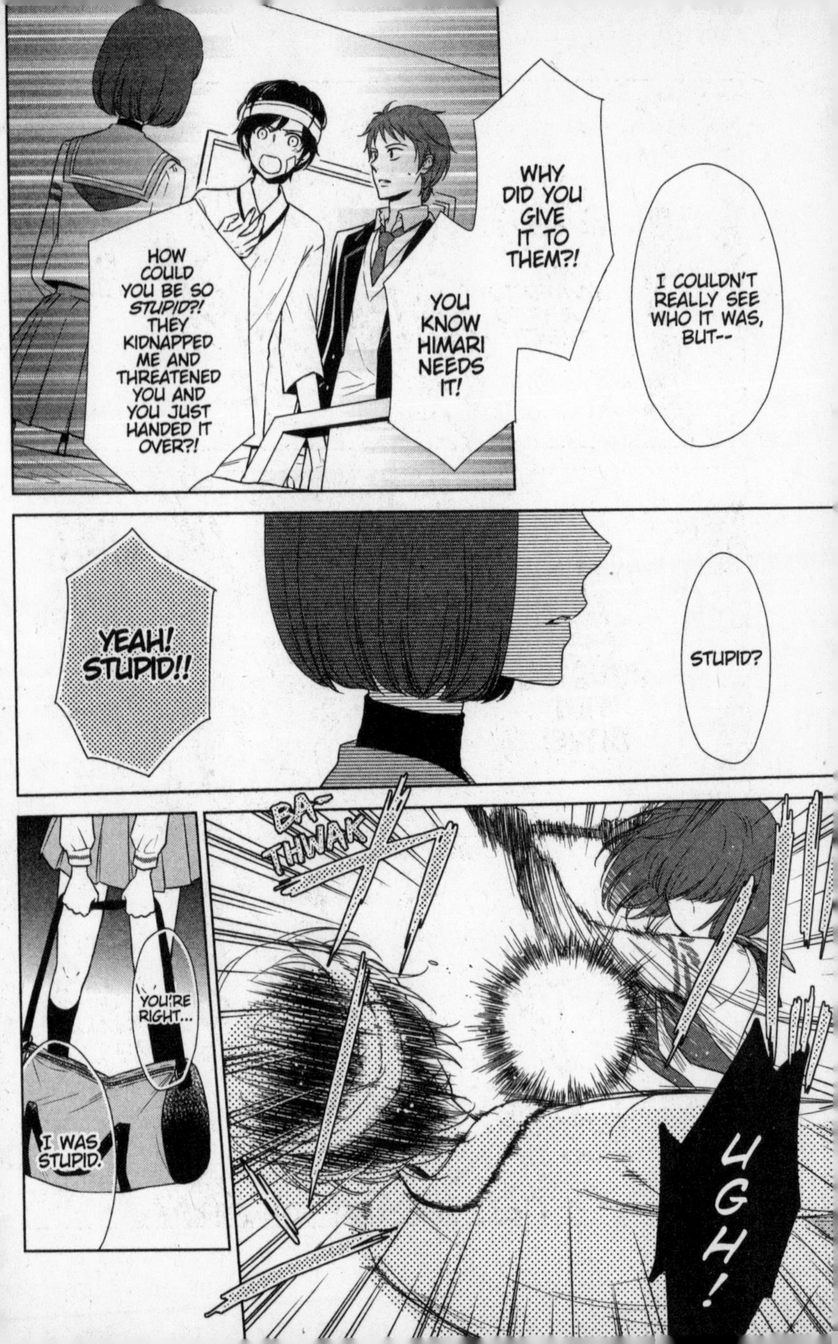

I COULDN'T REALLY SEE WHO IT WAS, BUT--
WHY DID YOU GIVE IT TO THEM?!
YOU KNOW HIMARI NEEDS IT!
HOW COULD YOU BE SO *STUPID?!* THEY KIDNAPPED ME AND THREATENED YOU AND YOU JUST HANDED IT OVER?!
STUPID?
YEAH! STUPID!!
BA-THWAK
UGH!
YOU'RE RIGHT...
I WAS STUPID.

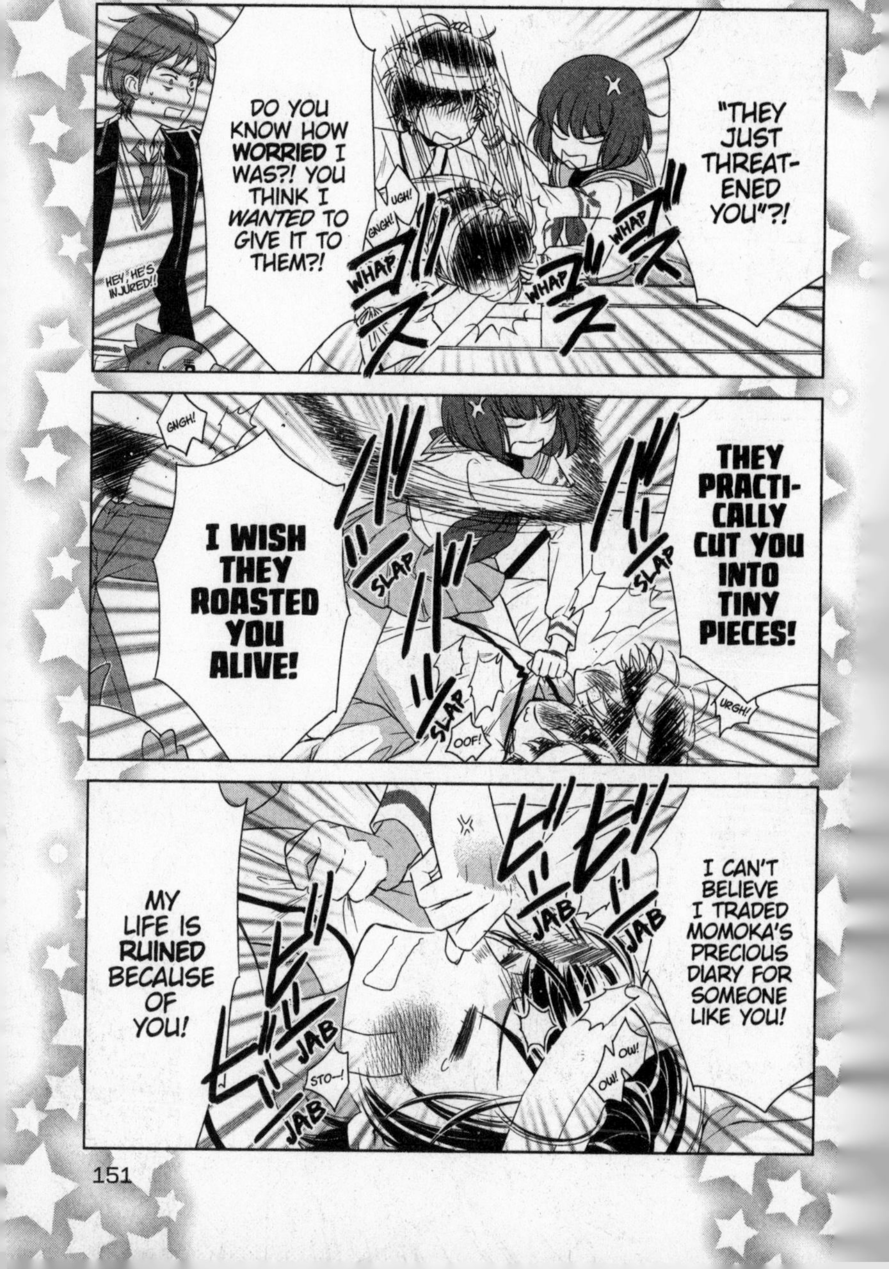
"THEY JUST THREAT-ENED YOU"?!
WHAP
WHAP
UGH!
DO YOU KNOW HOW WORRIED I WAS?! YOU THINK I WANTED TO GIVE IT TO THEM?!
GNGH!
WHAP
HEY, HE'S INJURED!!
THEY PRACTI-CALLY CUT YOU INTO TINY PIECES!
SLAP
URGH!
I WISH THEY ROASTED YOU ALIVE!
SLAP
SLAP
OOF!
GNGH!
I CAN'T BELIEVE I TRADED MOMOKA'S PRECIOUS DIARY FOR SOMEONE LIKE YOU!
JAB
JAB
OW!
OW!
MY LIFE IS RUINED BECAUSE OF YOU!
JAB
STO—!
JAB

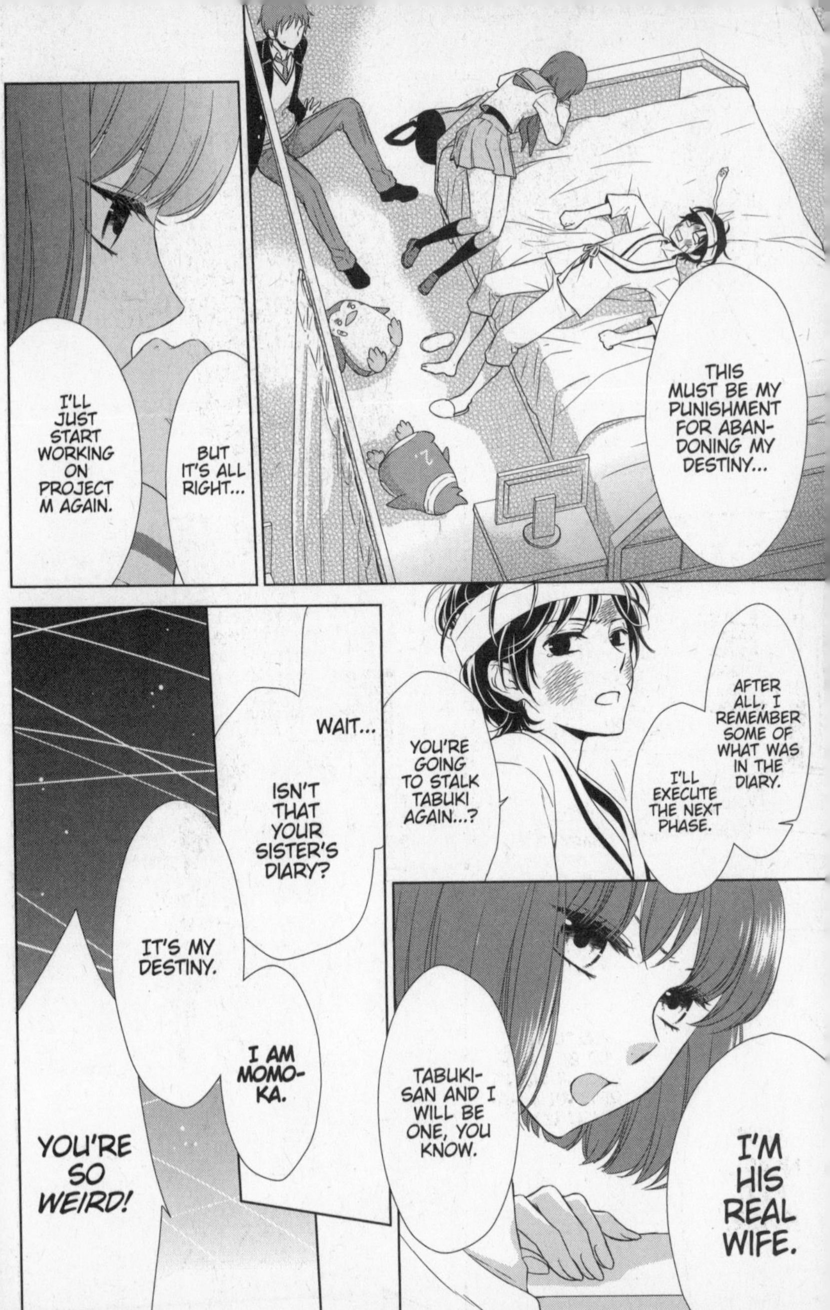

THIS MUST BE MY PUNISHMENT FOR ABAN-DONING MY DESTINY...
BUT IT'S ALL RIGHT...
I'LL JUST START WORKING ON PROJECT M AGAIN.
AFTER ALL, I REMEMBER SOME OF WHAT WAS IN THE DIARY.
I'LL EXECUTE THE NEXT PHASE.
YOU'RE GOING TO STALK TABUKI AGAIN...?
I'M HIS REAL WIFE.
TABUKI-SAN AND I WILL BE ONE, YOU KNOW.
WAIT...
ISN'T THAT YOUR SISTER'S DIARY?
IT'S MY DESTINY.
I AM MOMO-KA.
YOU'RE SO WEIRD!

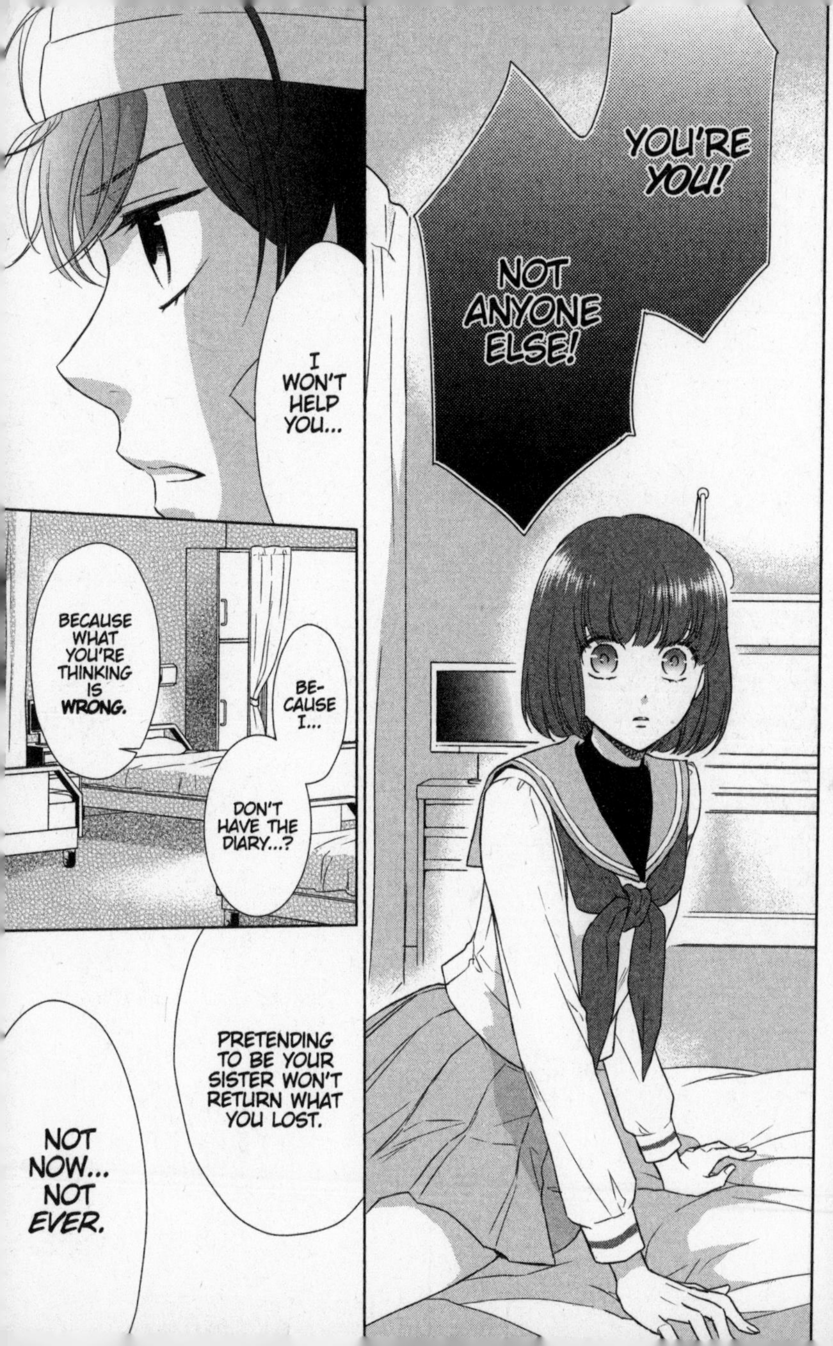
YOU'RE YOU!
NOT ANYONE ELSE!
I WON'T HELP YOU...
BE-CAUSE I...
DON'T HAVE THE DIARY...?
BECAUSE WHAT YOU'RE THINKING IS **WRONG.**
PRETENDING TO BE YOUR SISTER WON'T RETURN WHAT YOU LOST.
NOT NOW... NOT *EVER.*

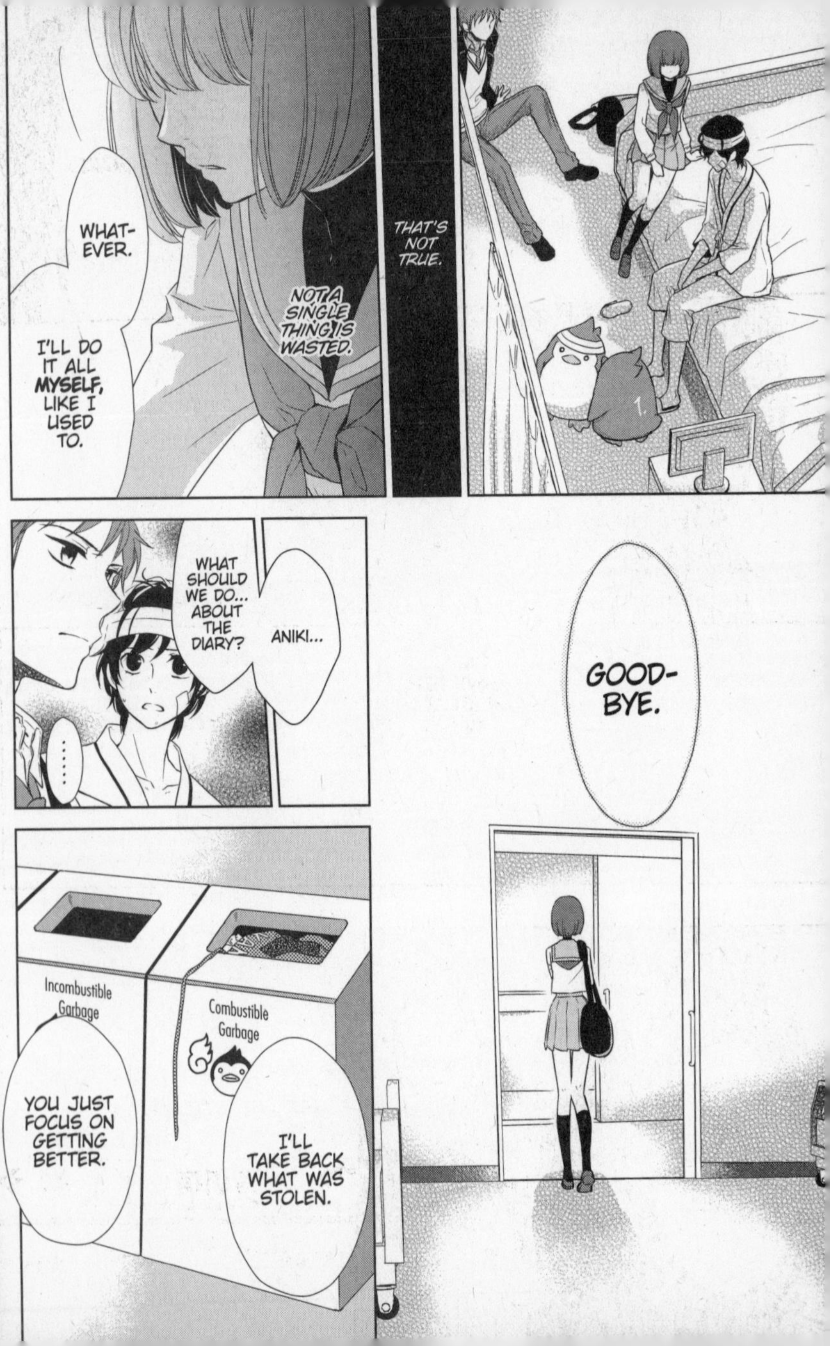
THAT'S NOT TRUE.
NOT A SINGLE THING IS WASTED.
WHAT-EVER.
I'LL DO IT ALL **MYSELF,** LIKE I USED TO.
GOOD-BYE.
ANIKI...
WHAT SHOULD WE DO... ABOUT THE DIARY?
......
Combustible Garbage
Incombustible Garbage
I'LL TAKE BACK WHAT WAS STOLEN.
YOU JUST FOCUS ON GETTING BETTER.

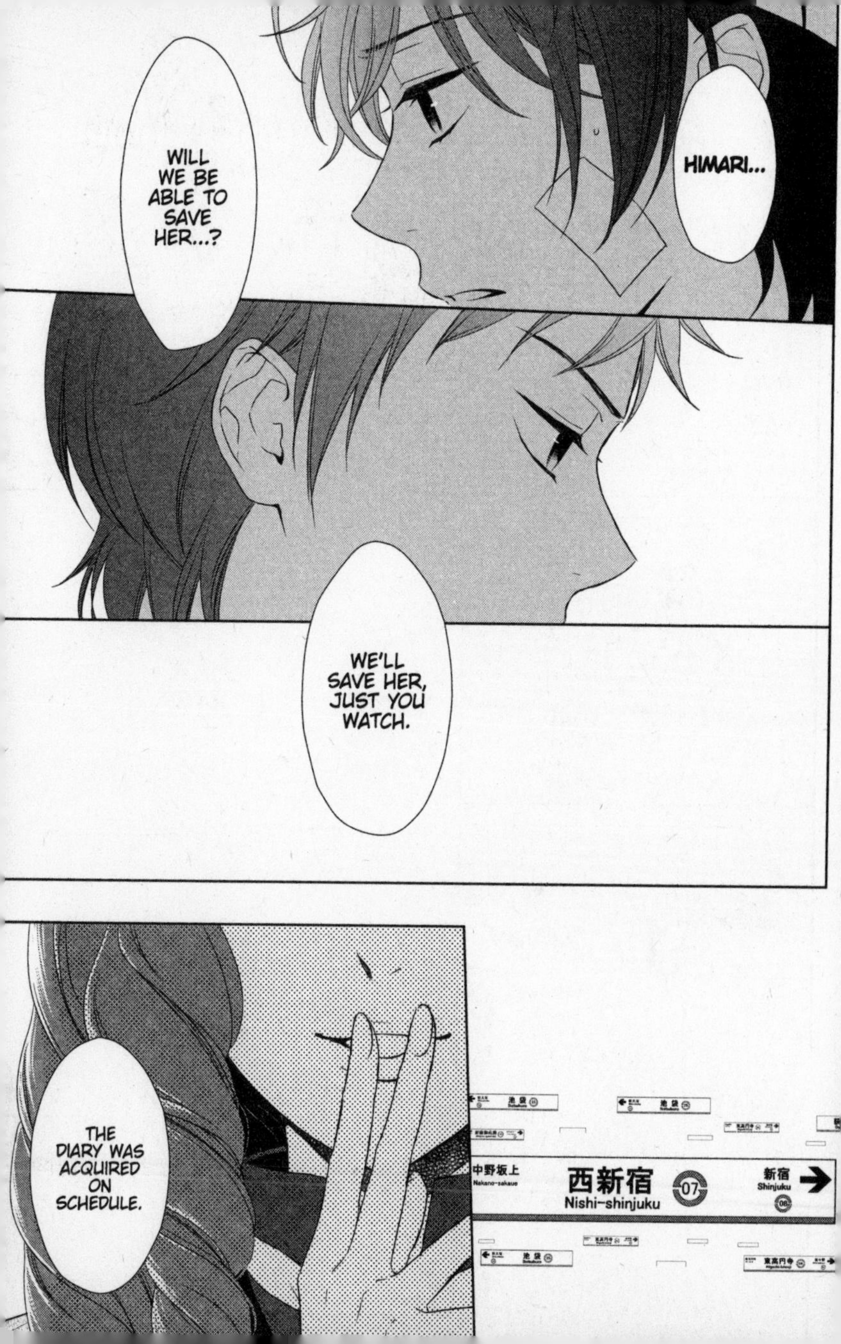
HIMARI...
WILL WE BE ABLE TO SAVE HER...?
WE'LL SAVE HER, JUST YOU WATCH.
新宿 Shinjuku 08
西新宿 07 Nishi-shinjuku
中野坂上 Nakano-sakaue
THE DIARY WAS ACQUIRED ON SCHEDULE.

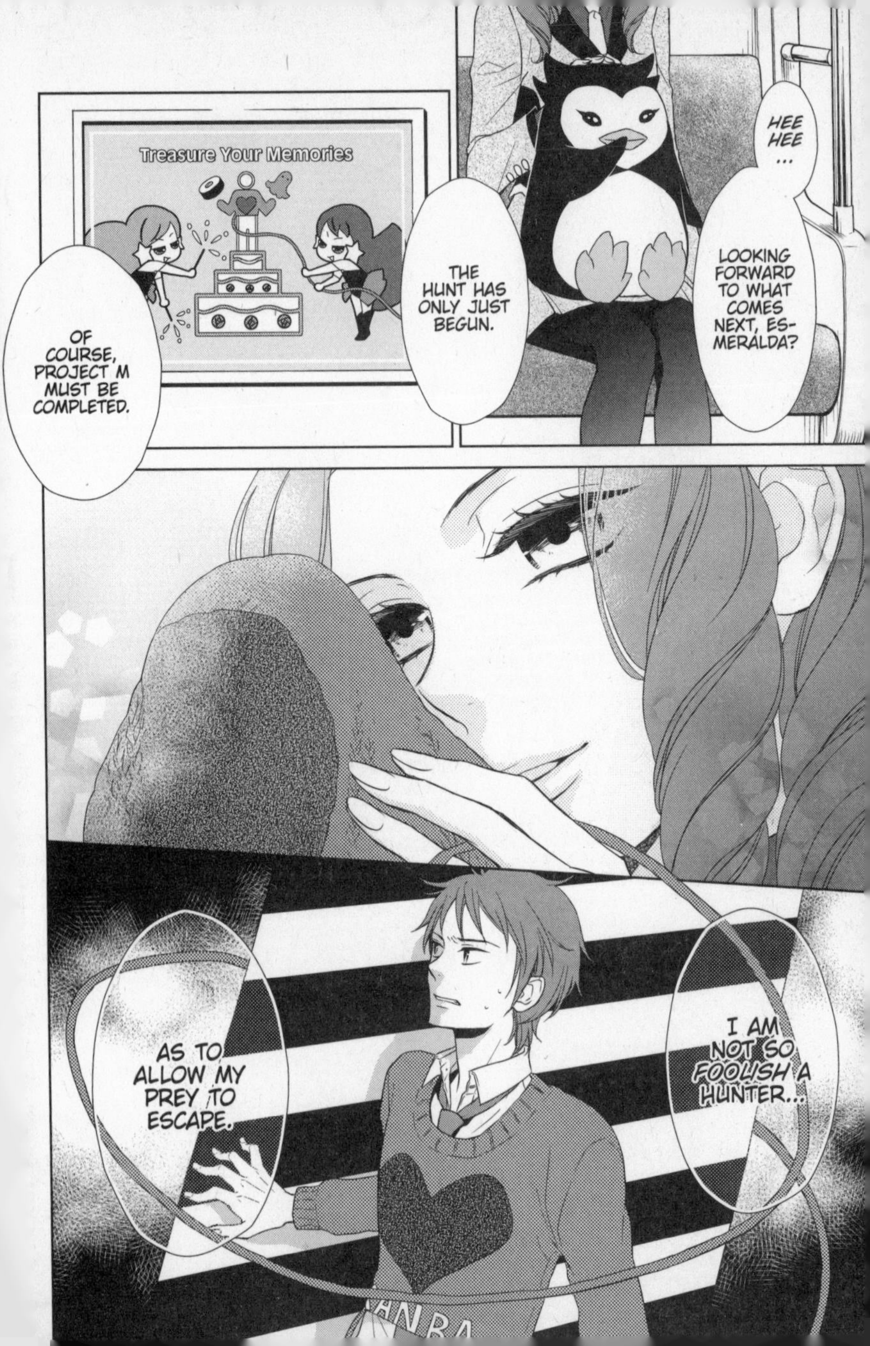
HEE HEE ...
LOOKING FORWARD TO WHAT COMES NEXT, ES-MERALDA?
THE HUNT HAS ONLY JUST BEGUN.
Treasure Your Memories
OF COURSE, PROJECT M MUST BE COMPLETED.
I AM NOT SO FOOLISH A HUNTER...
AS TO ALLOW MY PREY TO ESCAPE.

E N D

NEXT →
STATION
PENGUINDRUM

volume
#**3**

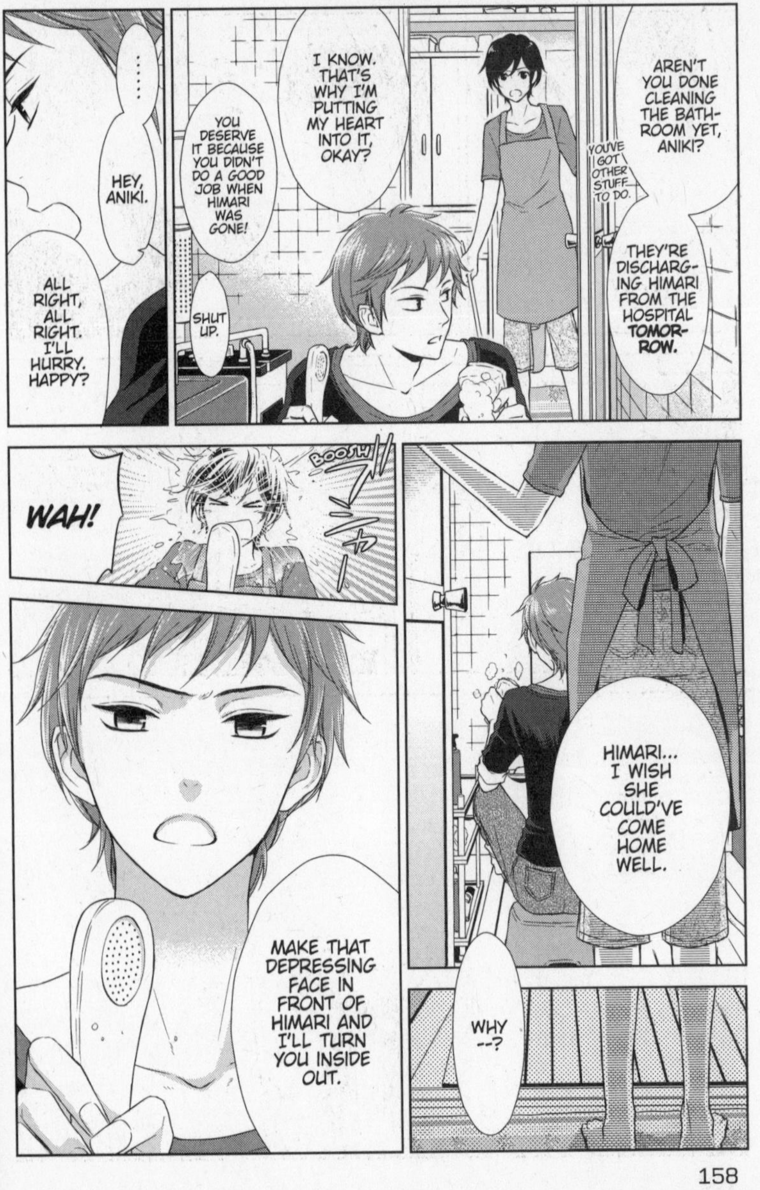
AREN'T YOU DONE CLEANING THE BATH-ROOM YET, ANIKI?
YOU'VE GOT OTHER STUFF TO DO.
THEY'RE DISCHARG-ING HIMARI FROM THE HOSPITAL **TOMOR-ROW.**
I KNOW. THAT'S WHY I'M PUTTING MY HEART INTO IT, OKAY?
YOU DESERVE IT BECAUSE YOU DIDN'T DO A GOOD JOB WHEN HIMARI WAS GONE!
SHUT UP.
......
HEY, ANIKI.
ALL RIGHT, ALL RIGHT. I'LL HURRY. HAPPY?
HIMARI... I WISH SHE COULD'VE COME HOME WELL.
WHY --?
WAH!
BOOSH
MAKE THAT DEPRESSING FACE IN FRONT OF HIMARI AND I'LL TURN YOU INSIDE OUT.

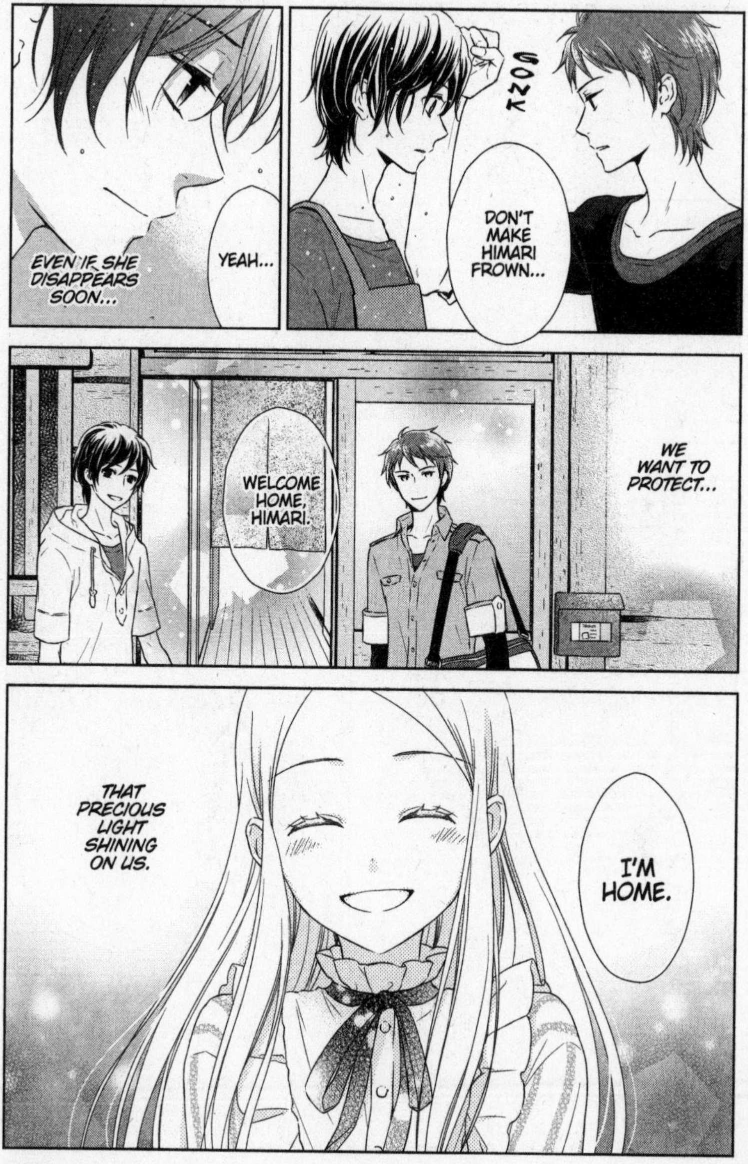
SONK
DON'T MAKE HIMARI FROWN...
YEAH...
EVEN IF SHE DISAPPEARS SOON...
WE WANT TO PROTECT...
WELCOME HOME, HIMARI.
I'M HOME.
THAT PRECIOUS LIGHT SHINING ON US.

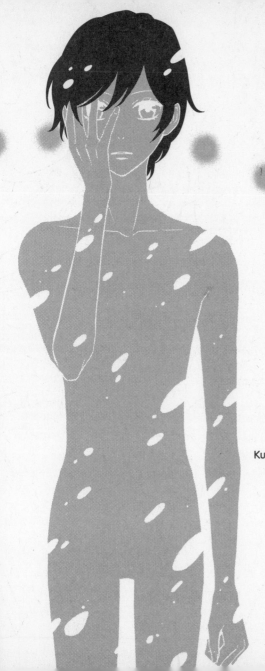

I like that the
Takakura siblings
get along so well.

Thank you to
Kunihiko Ikuhara (the director),
Lily Hoshino (the mangaka),
Fujimoto-san (my editor),
Rimu-san,
Wataru Osakabe-san,
and everyone else involved.
Thanks also to Akiba
Touko-san, my family,
and my readers...

I'd love to see you on
the next train. Thank you.

December 2014.

Isuzu Shibata